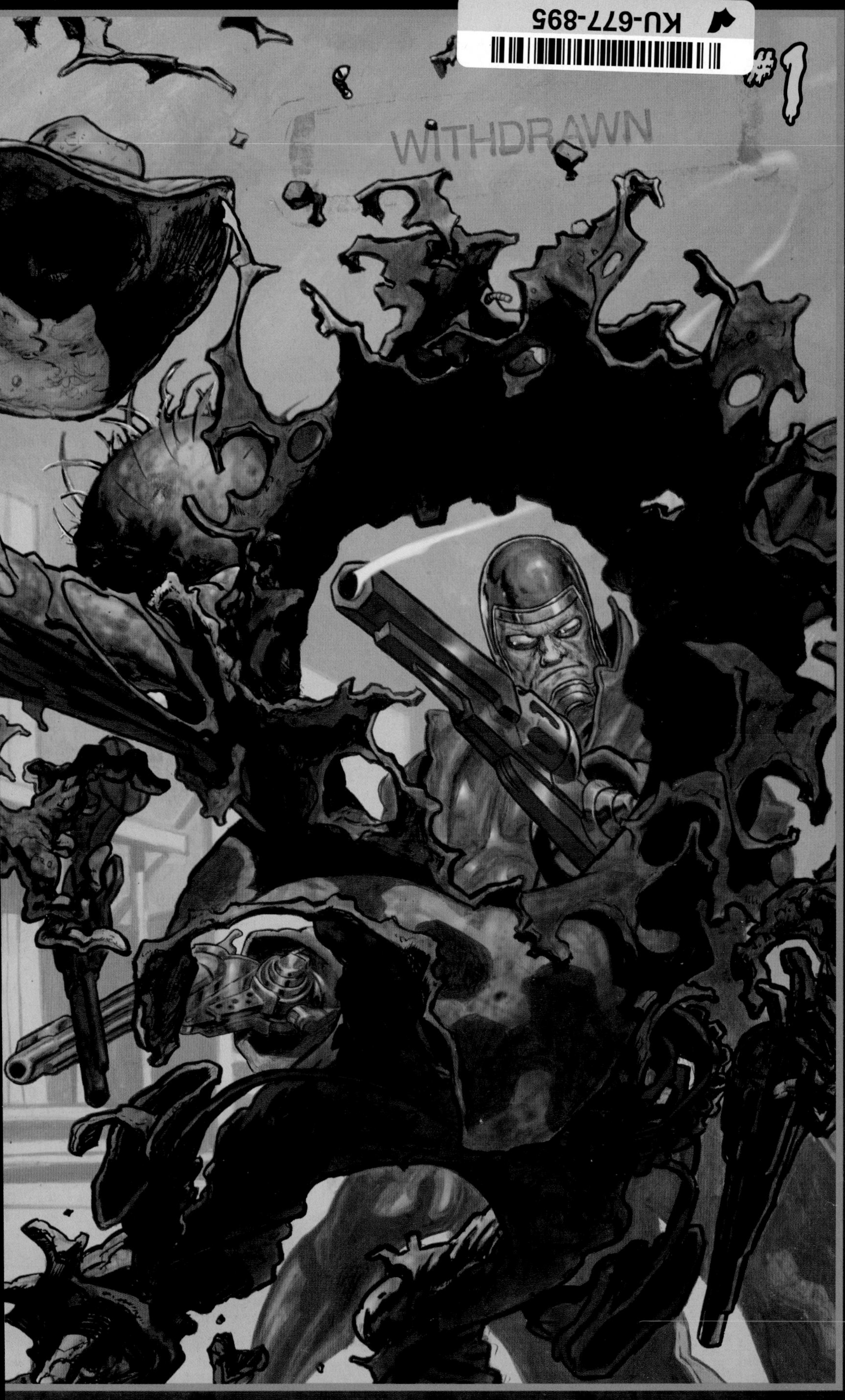
#1

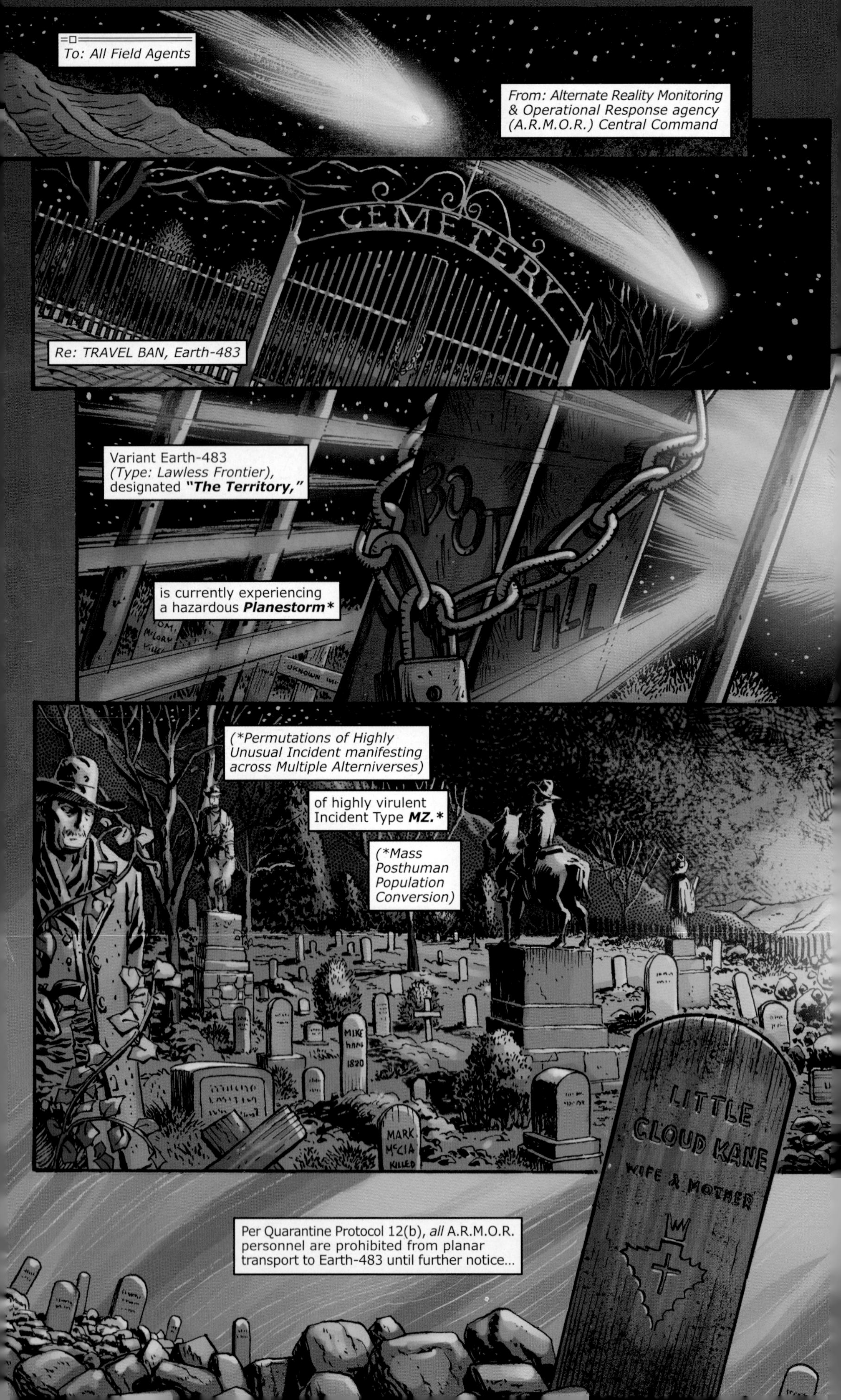
To: All Field Agents
From: Alternate Reality Monitoring & Operational Response agency (A.R.M.O.R.) Central Command
CEMETERY
Re: TRAVEL BAN, Earth-483
Variant Earth-483 (Type: Lawless Frontier), designated "The Territory,"
is currently experiencing a hazardous Planestorm*
(*Permutations of Highly Unusual Incident manifesting across Multiple Alterniverses)
of highly virulent Incident Type MZ.*
(*Mass Posthuman Population Conversion)
LITTLE CLOUD KANE
WIFE & MOTHER
Per Quarantine Protocol 12(b), all A.R.M.O.R. personnel are prohibited from planar transport to Earth-483 until further notice...

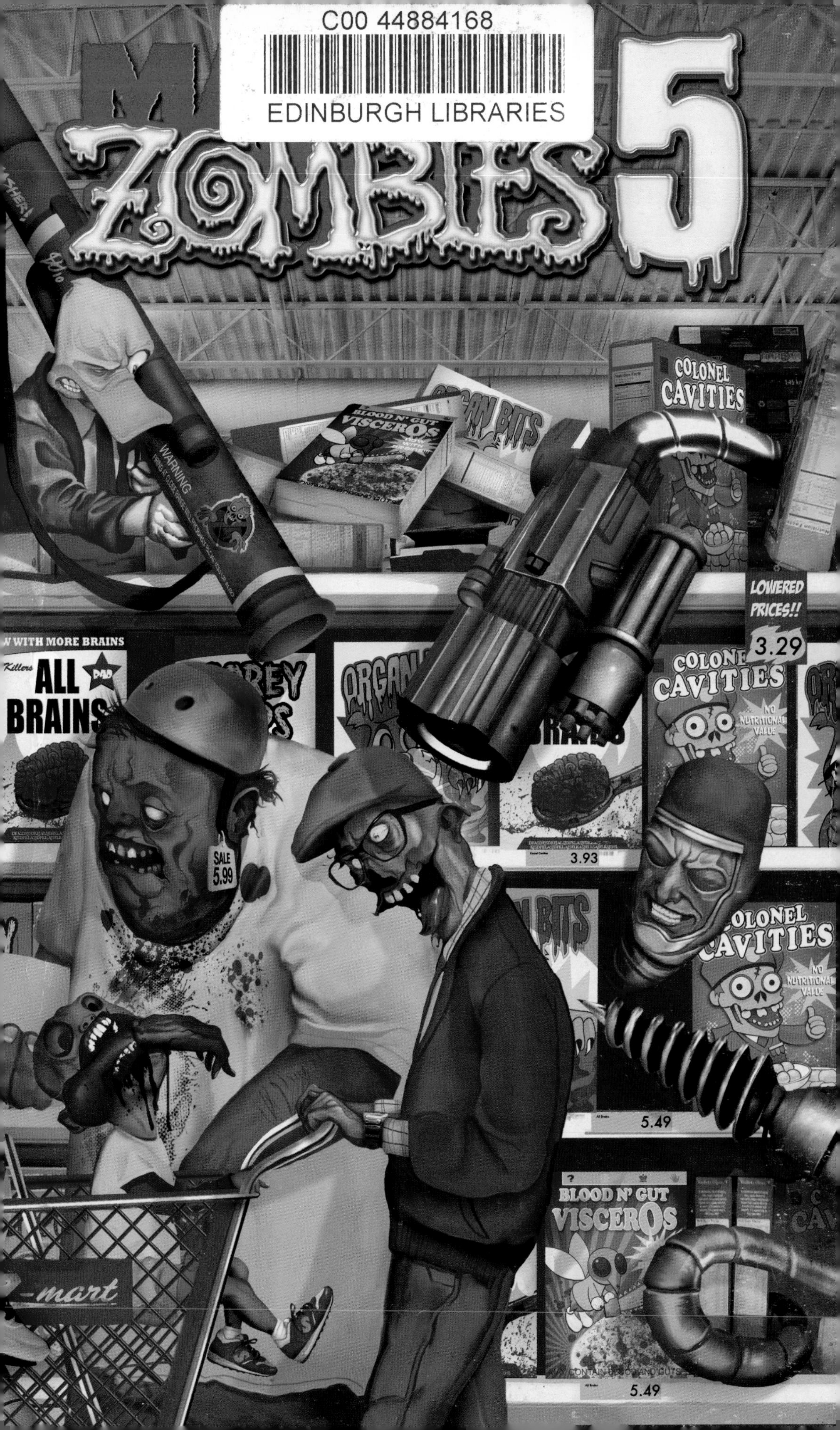
ZOMBIES 5
COLONEL CAVITIES
BLOOD N' GUT VISCEROS
ORGAN BITS
WARNING
LOWERED PRICES!!
3.29
W WITH MORE BRAINS
ALL BRAINS
COLONEL CAVITIES
NO NUTRITIONAL VALUE
SALE 5.99
3.93
COLONEL CAVITIES
NO NUTRITIONAL VALUE
5.49
BLOOD N' GUT VISCEROS
-mart
5.49

MARVEL ZOMBIES 5

WRITER
FRED VAN LENTE

PENCILERS
KANO, MICHAEL W. KALUTA, FELIX RUIZ, FERNANDO BLANCO & FRANK BRUNNER

INKERS
TOM PALMER, ALVARO LOPEZ, MICHAEL W. KALUTA, FELIX RUIZ &
FERNANDO BLANCO

LETTERER
SIMON BOWLAND

COLORIST
VAL STAPLES

COVER ARTISTS
RAFA GARRES; MICHAEL W. KALUTA WITH MORRY HOLLOWELL; SALVA ESPIN
WITH GURU eFX, LEONARD KIRK WITH MORRY HOLLOWELL, LEINIL YU WITH
LAURA MARTIN, GEOFF DARROW WITH CHRISTINA STRAIN, MIKE DEL MUNDO &
ARTHUR SUYDAM

ASSISTANT EDITOR
MICHAEL HORWITZ

SENIOR EDITOR
MARK PANICCIA

COLLECTION EDITOR: MARK D. BEAZLEY
EDITORIAL ASSISTANTS: JAMES EMMETT & JOE HOCHSTEIN
ASSISTANT EDITORS: NELSON RIBEIRO & ALEX STARBUCK
EDITOR, SPECIAL PROJECTS: JENNIFER GRÜNWALD
SENIOR EDITOR, SPECIAL PROJECTS: JEFF YOUNGQUIST
BOOK DESIGNER: ARLENE SO
SENIOR VICE PRESIDENT OF SALES: DAVID GABRIEL

EDITOR IN CHIEF: AXEL ALONSO
CHIEF CREATIVE OFFICER: JOE QUESADA
PUBLISHER: DAN BUCKLEY
EXECUTIVE PRODUCER: ALAN FINE

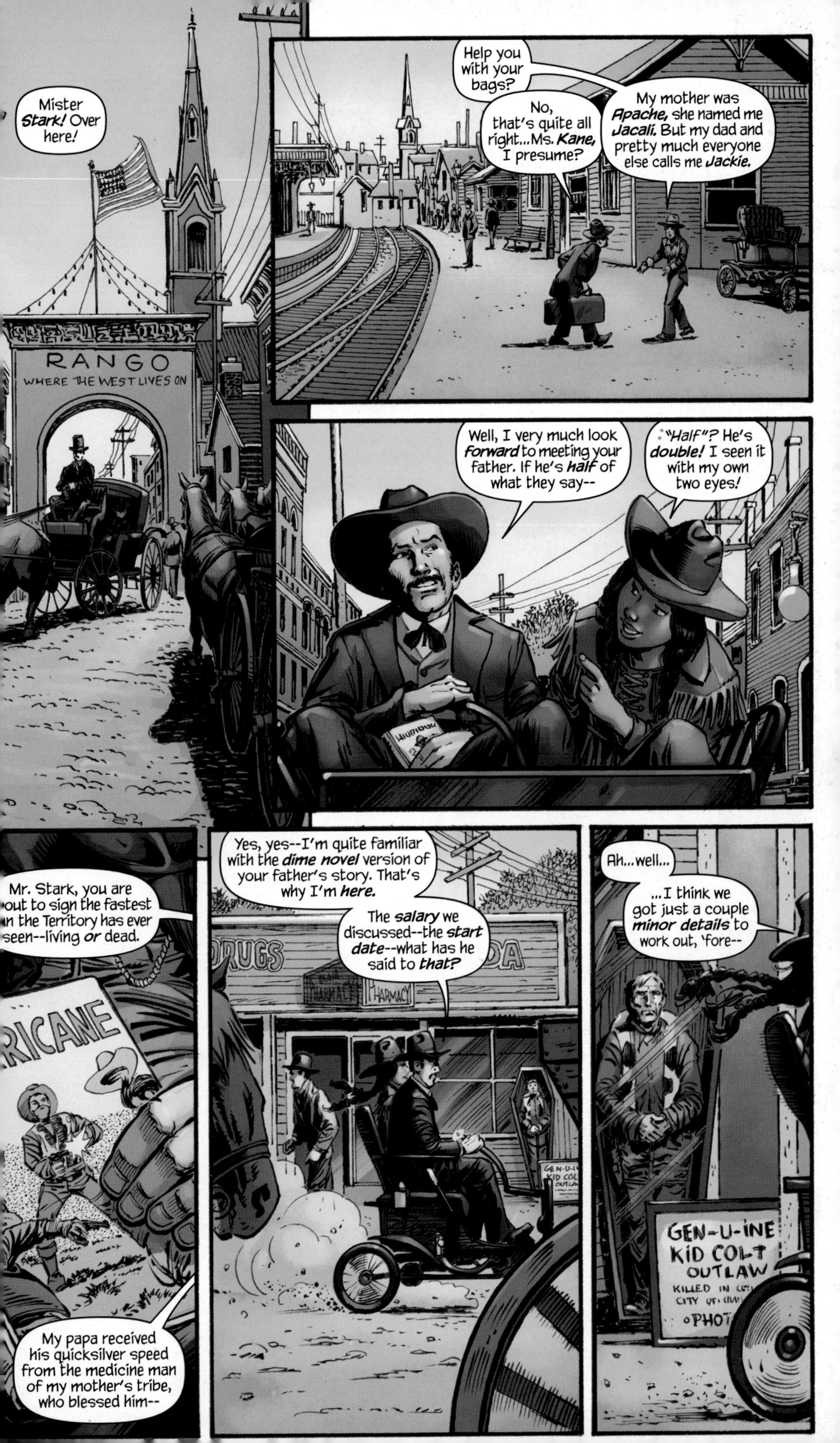
Mister Stark! Over here!
RANGO
WHERE THE WEST LIVES ON
Help you with your bags?
No, that's quite all right...Ms. Kane, I presume?
My mother was Apache, she named me Jacali. But my dad and pretty much everyone else calls me Jackie.
Well, I very much look forward to meeting your father. If he's half of what they say--
"Half"? He's double! I seen it with my own two eyes!
Mr. Stark, you are out to sign the fastest in the Territory has ever seen--living or dead.
RICANE
My papa received his quicksilver speed from the medicine man of my mother's tribe, who blessed him--
Yes, yes--I'm quite familiar with the dime novel version of your father's story. That's why I'm here.
The salary we discussed--the start date--what has he said to that?
DRUGS
PHARMACY
Ah...well...
...I think we got just a couple minor details to work out, 'fore--
GEN-U-INE
KID COLT
OUTLAW

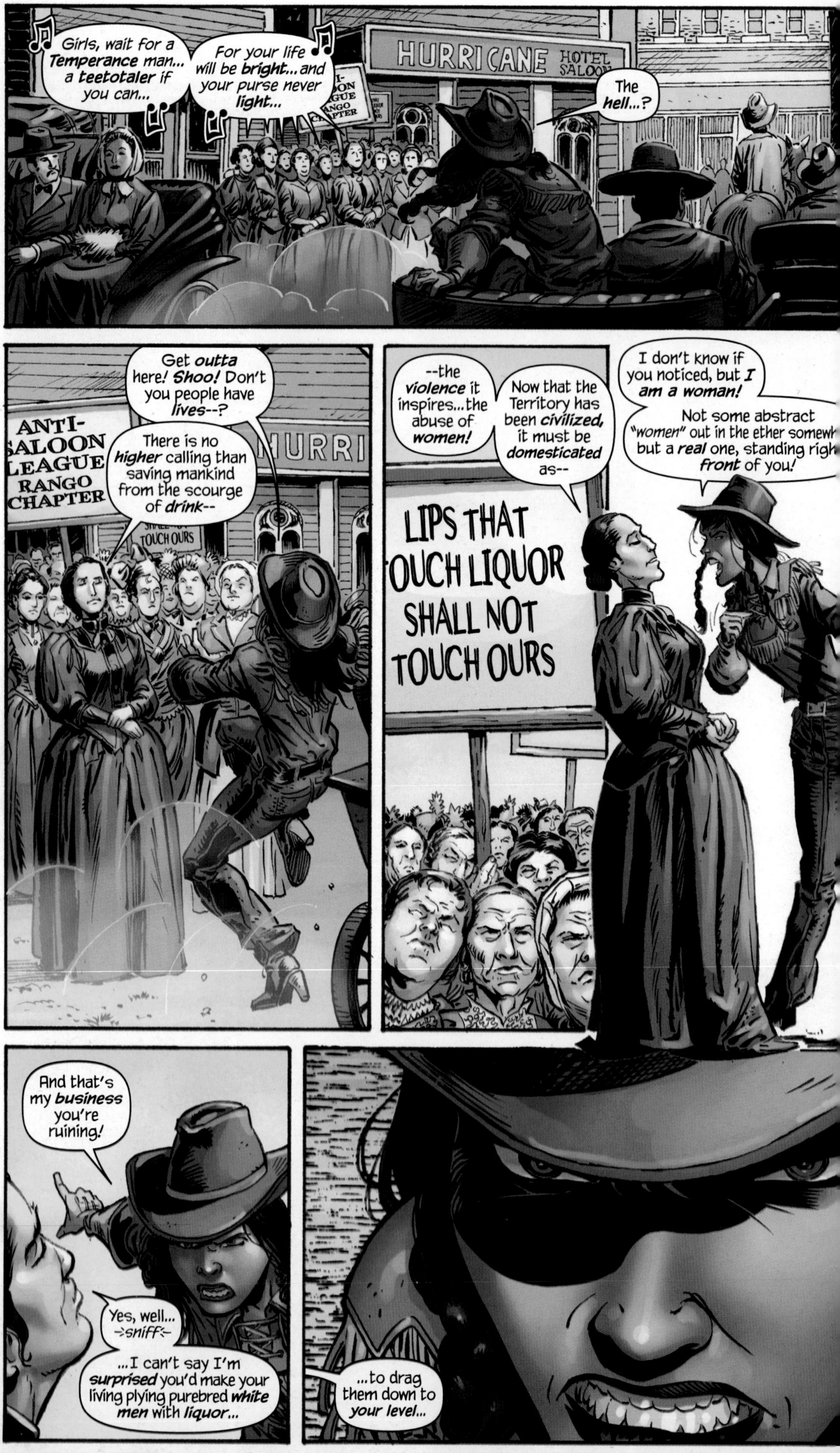
Girls, wait for a Temperance man... a teetotaler if you can...
For your life will be bright... and your purse never light...
HURRICANE HOTEL SALOON
The hell...?
Get outta here! Shoo! Don't you people have lives--?
ANTI-SALOON LEAGUE RANGO CHAPTER
There is no higher calling than saving mankind from the scourge of drink--
TOUCH OURS
--the violence it inspires... the abuse of women!
Now that the Territory has been civilized, it must be domesticated as--
LIPS THAT TOUCH LIQUOR SHALL NOT TOUCH OURS
I don't know if you noticed, but I am a woman!
Not some abstract "women" out in the ether somewh but a real one, standing righ front of you!
And that's my business you're ruining!
Yes, well... -sniff-
...I can't say I'm surprised you'd make your living plying purebred white men with liquor...
...to drag them down to your level...

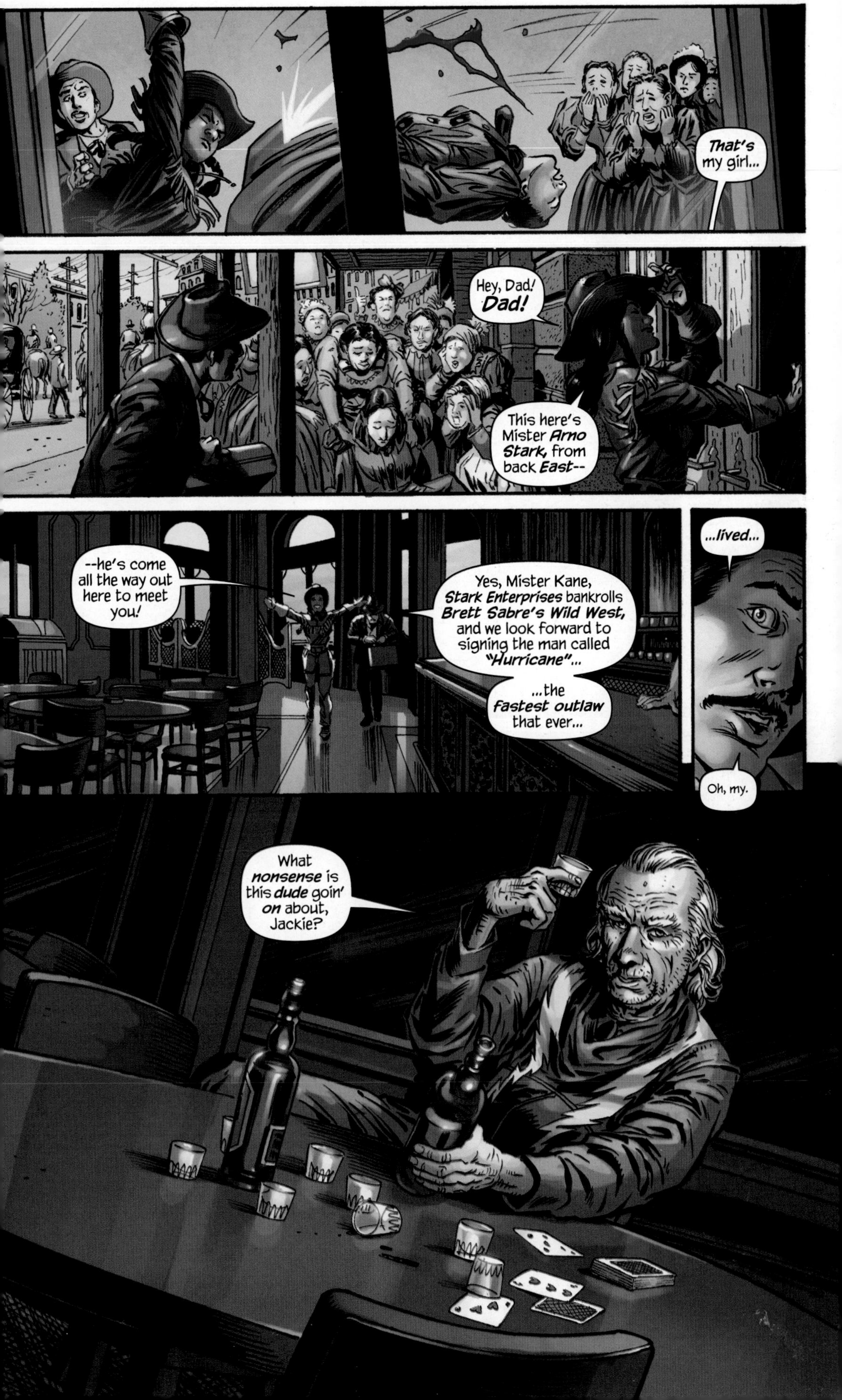
That's my girl...
Hey, Dad! Dad!
This here's Mister Arno Stark, from back East--
--he's come all the way out here to meet you!
Yes, Mister Kane, Stark Enterprises bankrolls Brett Sabre's Wild West, and we look forward to signing the man called "Hurricane"...
...the fastest outlaw that ever...
...lived...
Oh, my.
What nonsense is this dude goin' on about, Jackie?

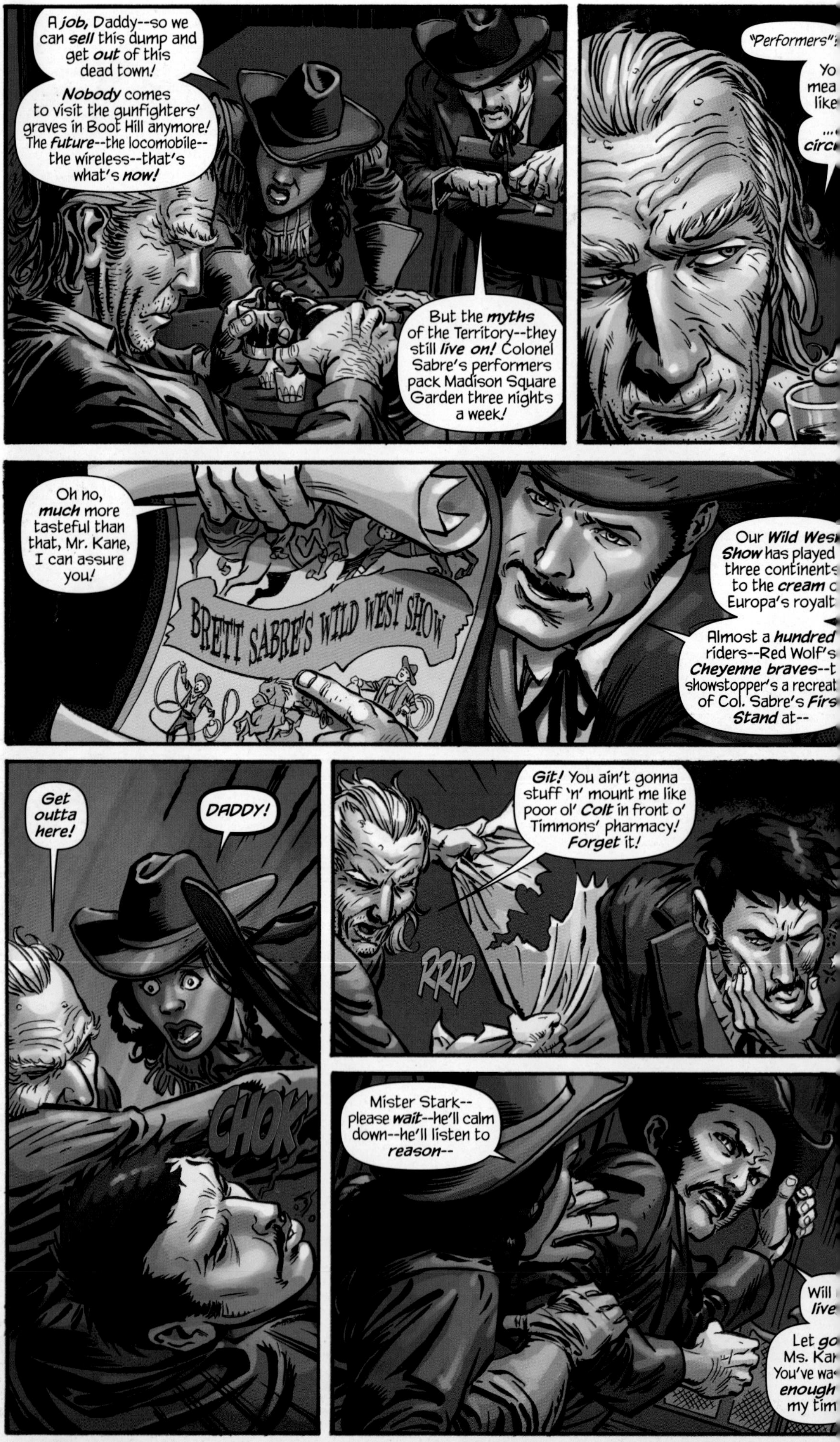

A job, Daddy--so we can sell this dump and get out of this dead town!
Nobody comes to visit the gunfighters' graves in Boot Hill anymore! The future--the locomobile--the wireless--that's what's now!
But the myths of the Territory--they still live on! Colonel Sabre's performers pack Madison Square Garden three nights a week!
"Performers"
Yo mea like
... circ
Oh no, much more tasteful than that, Mr. Kane, I can assure you!
BRETT SABRE'S WILD WEST SHOW
Our Wild Wes Show has played three continents to the cream o Europa's royalt
Almost a hundred riders--Red Wolf's Cheyenne braves--t showstopper's a recreat of Col. Sabre's Firs Stand at--
Get outta here!
DADDY!
CHOK
Git! You ain't gonna stuff 'n' mount me like poor ol' Colt in front o' Timmons' pharmacy! Forget it!
RRIP
Mister Stark--please wait--he'll calm down--he'll listen to reason--
Will live
Let go Ms. Kar You've wa enough my tim

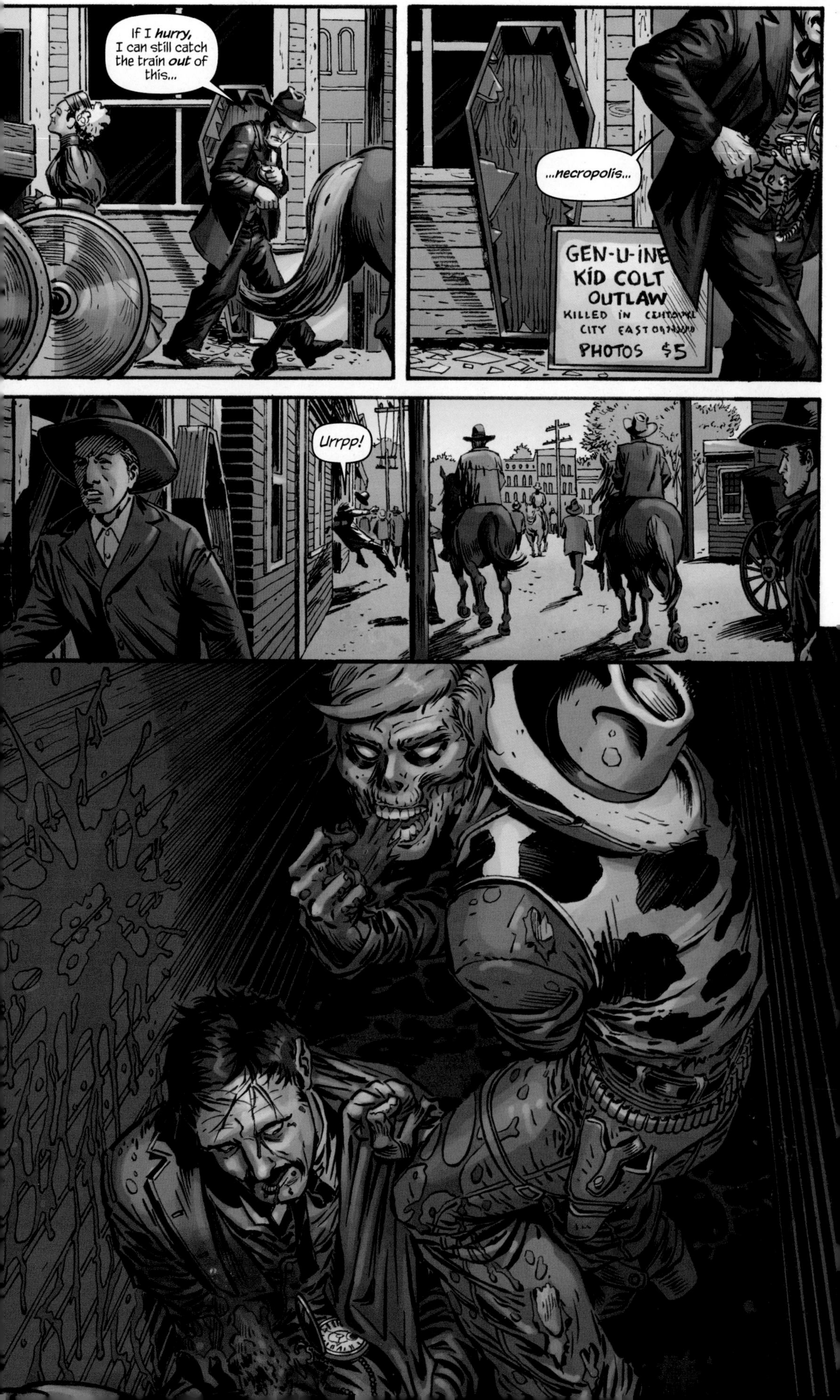
If I **hurry,** I can still catch the train ***out*** of this...
...*necropolis*...
GEN-U-INE
KID COLT
OUTLAW
KILLED IN
CITY EAST
PHOTOS $5
Urrpp!

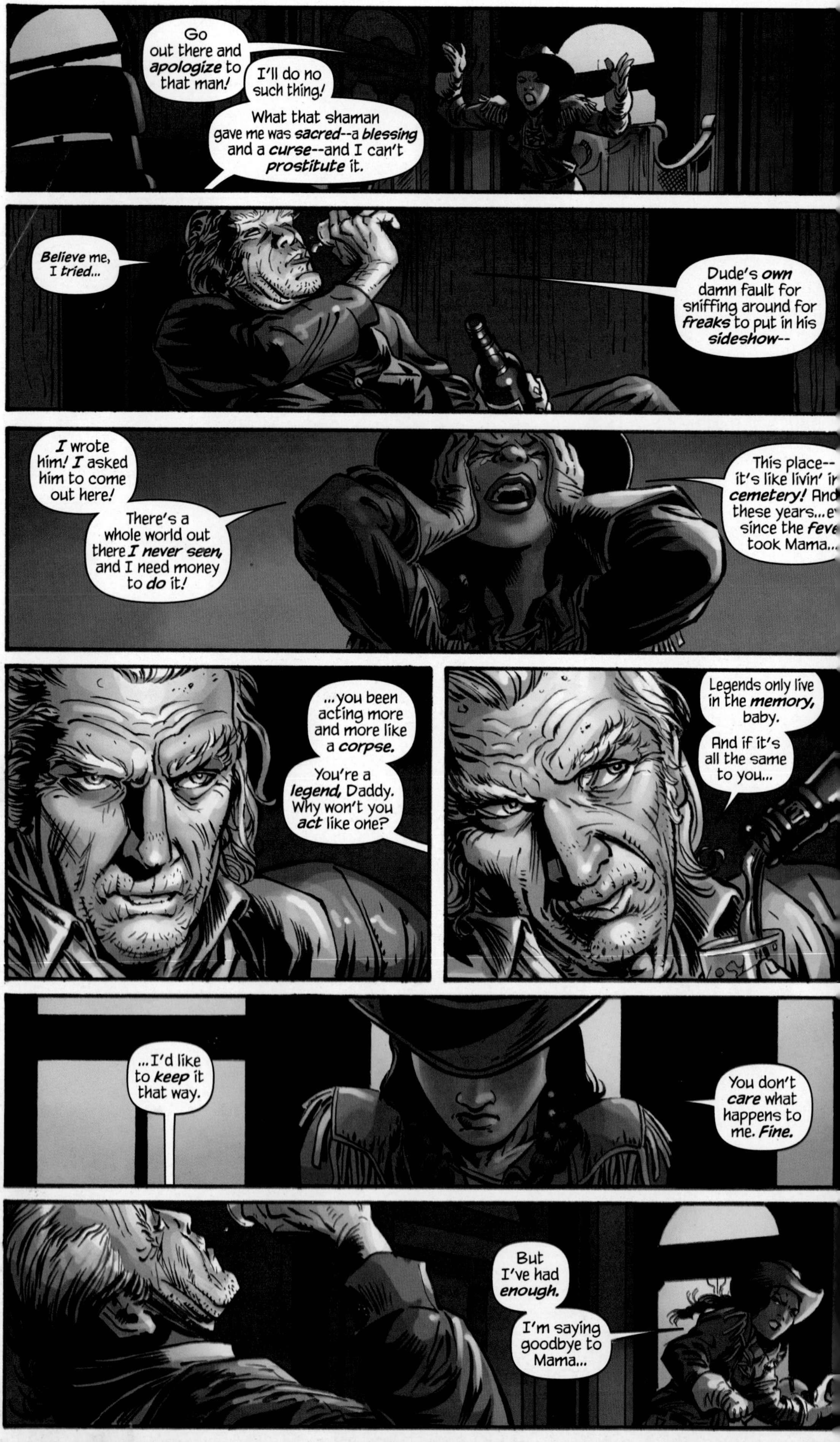

Go out there and apologize to that man!
I'll do no such thing!
What that shaman gave me was sacred--a blessing and a curse--and I can't prostitute it.
Believe me, I tried...
Dude's own damn fault for sniffing around for freaks to put in his sideshow--
I wrote him! I asked him to come out here!
There's a whole world out there I never seen, and I need money to do it!
This place--it's like livin' i
cemetery! And these years...e
since the feve
took Mama...
...you been acting more and more like a corpse.
You're a legend, Daddy. Why won't you act like one?
Legends only live in the memory, baby.
And if it's all the same to you...
...I'd like to keep it that way.
You don't care what happens to me. Fine.
But I've had enough.
I'm saying goodbye to Mama...

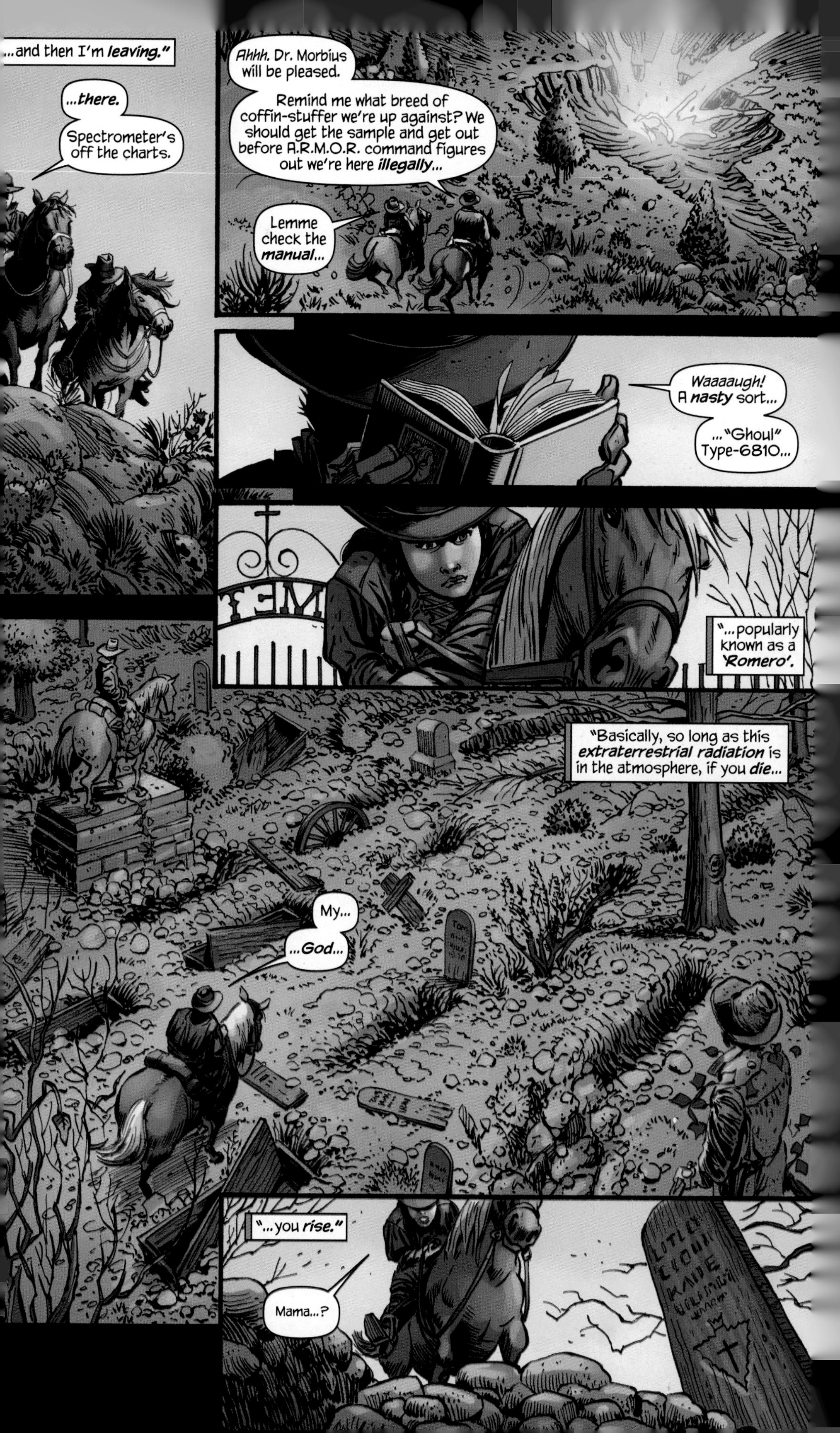

...and then I'm *leaving.*"
...*there.*
Spectrometer's off the charts.
Ahhh. Dr. Morbius will be pleased.
Remind me what breed of coffin-stuffer we're up against? We should get the sample and get out before A.R.M.O.R. command figures out we're here *illegally*...
Lemme check the *manual*...
Waaaaugh! A *nasty* sort...
..."Ghoul" Type-6810...
"...popularly known as a *'Romero'*.
"Basically, so long as this *extraterrestrial radiation* is in the atmosphere, if you *die*...
My...
...*God*...
"...you *rise*."
Mama...?

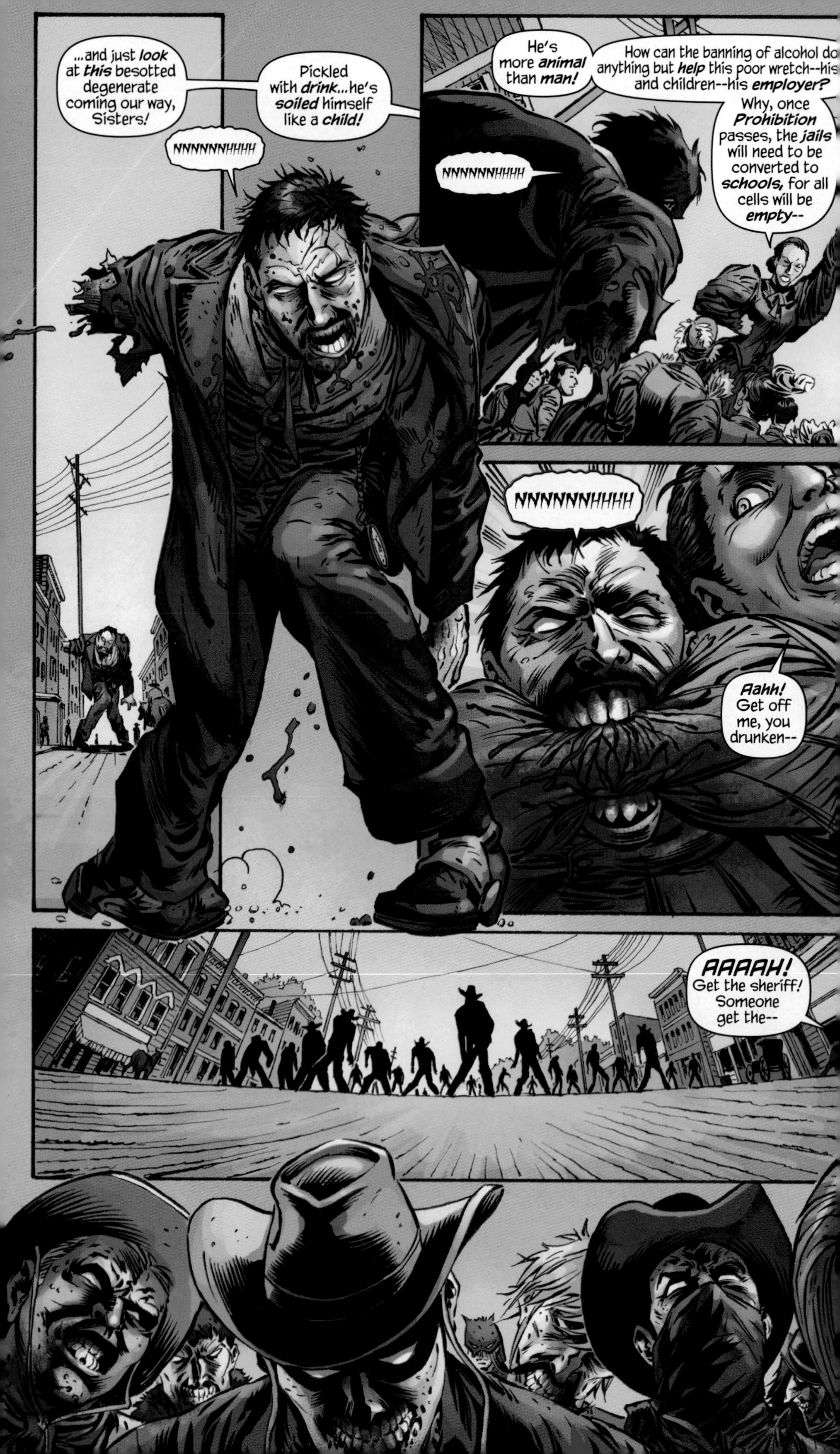

...and just *look* at *this* besotted degenerate coming our way, Sisters!
Pickled with *drink*...he's *soiled* himself like a *child!*
NNNNNNHHHH
He's more *animal* than *man!*
How can the banning of alcohol do anything but *help* this poor wretch--his and children--his *employer?*
Why, once *Prohibition* passes, the *jails* will need to be converted to *schools,* for all cells will be *empty*--
NNNNNNHHHH
NNNNNNHHHH
Aahh! Get off me, you drunken--
AAAAH! Get the sheriff! Someone get the--

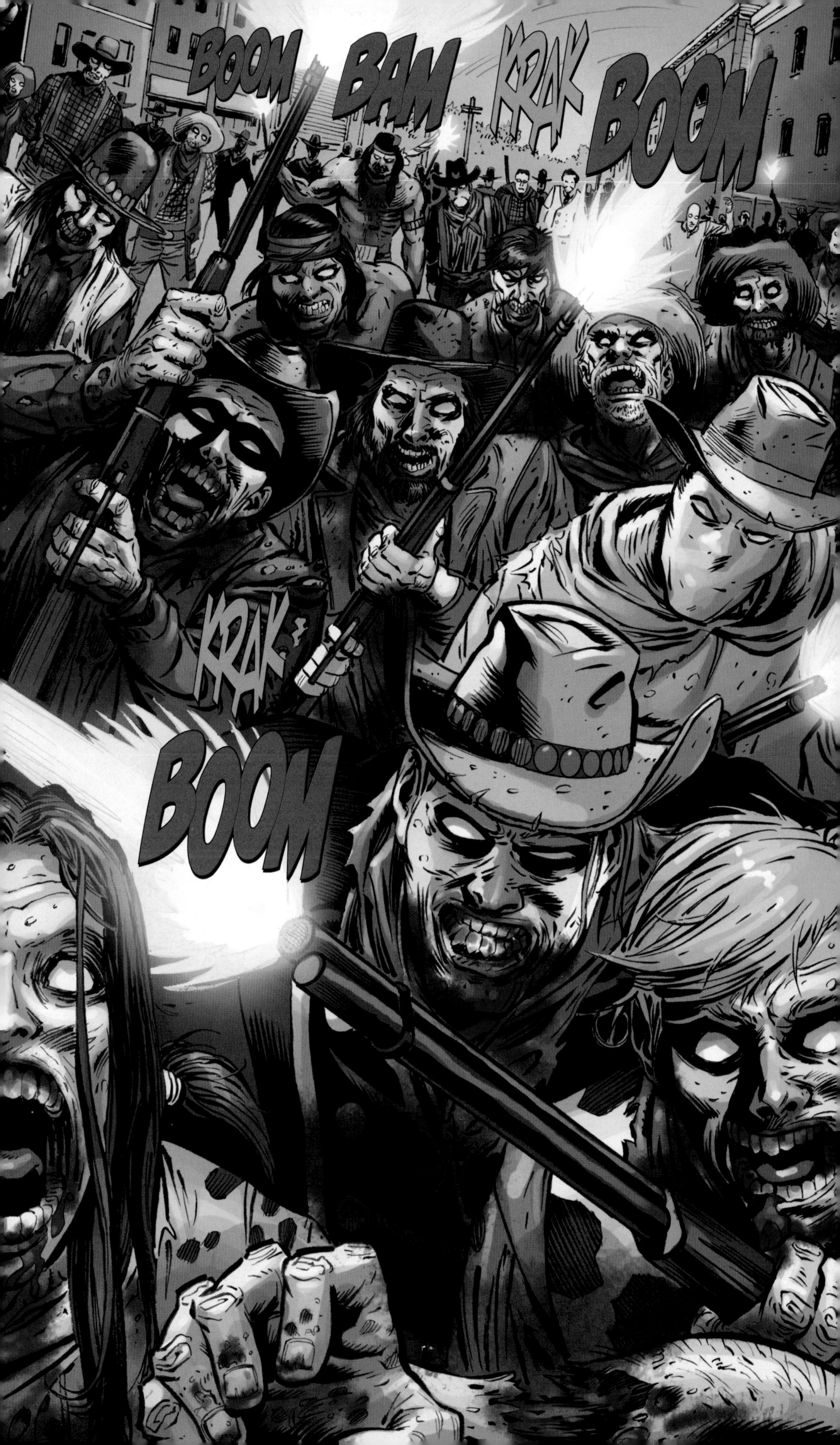
BOOM
BAM
KRAK
BOOM
KRAK
BOOM

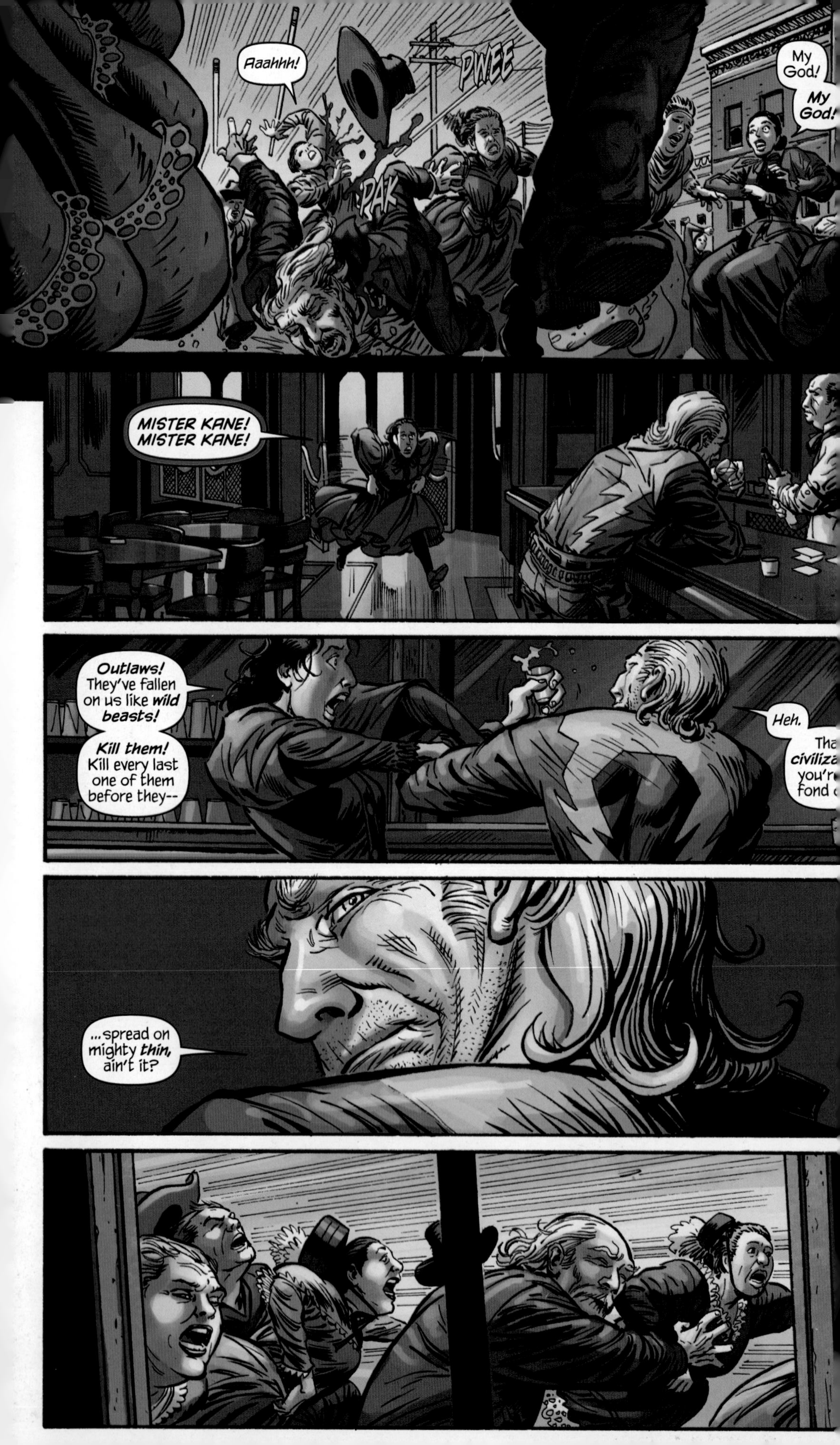
Aaahhh!
PWEE
PAK
My God! My God!
MISTER KANE! MISTER KANE!
Outlaws! They've fallen on us like wild beasts!
Kill them! Kill every last one of them before they--
Heh.
...spread on mighty thin, ain't it?

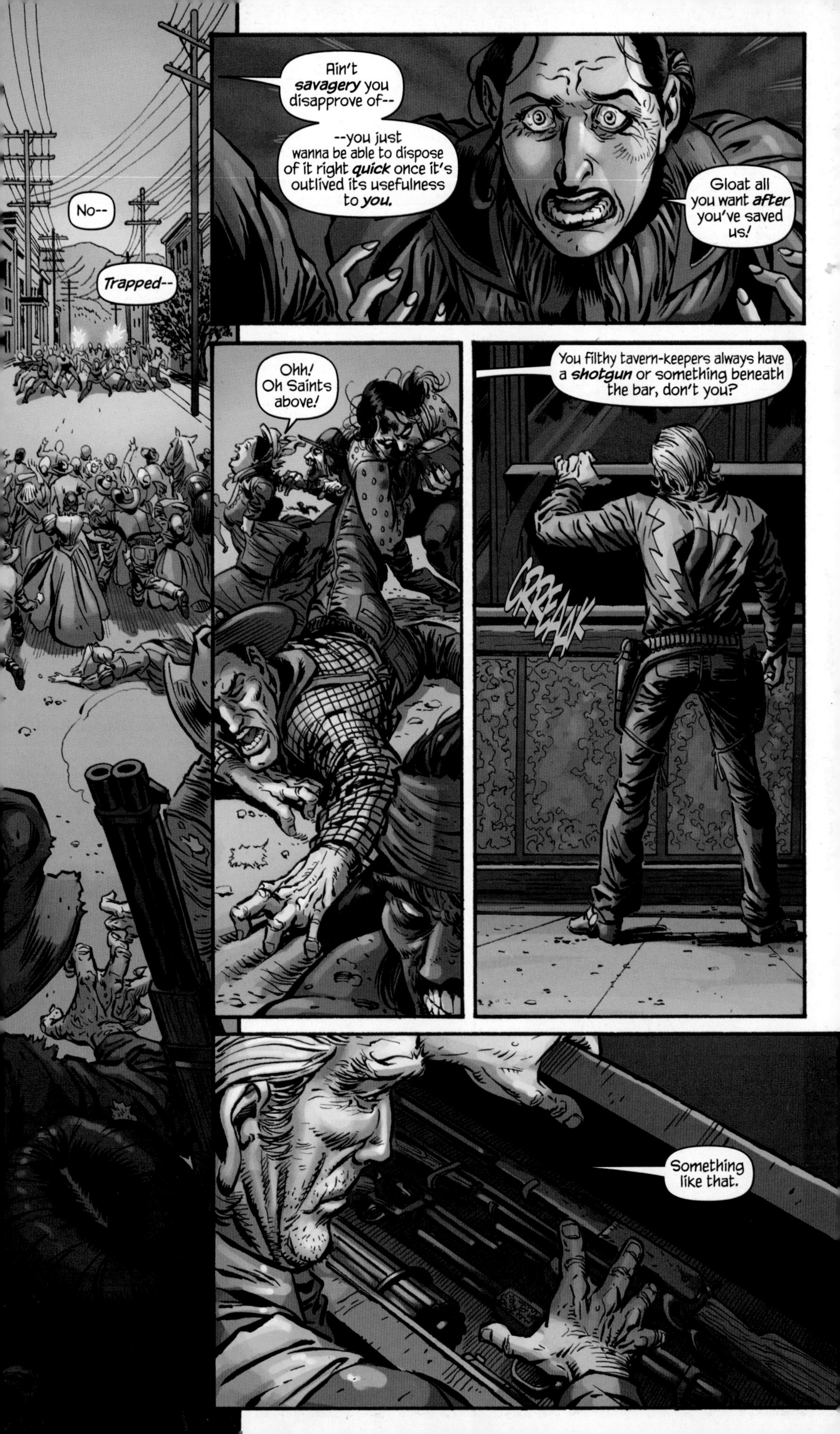

No--
Trapped--
Ain't savagery you disapprove of--
--you just wanna be able to dispose of it right quick once it's outlived its usefulness to you.
Gloat all you want after you've saved us!
Ohh! Oh Saints above!
You filthy tavern-keepers always have a shotgun or something beneath the bar, don't you?
CRREAAK
Something like that.

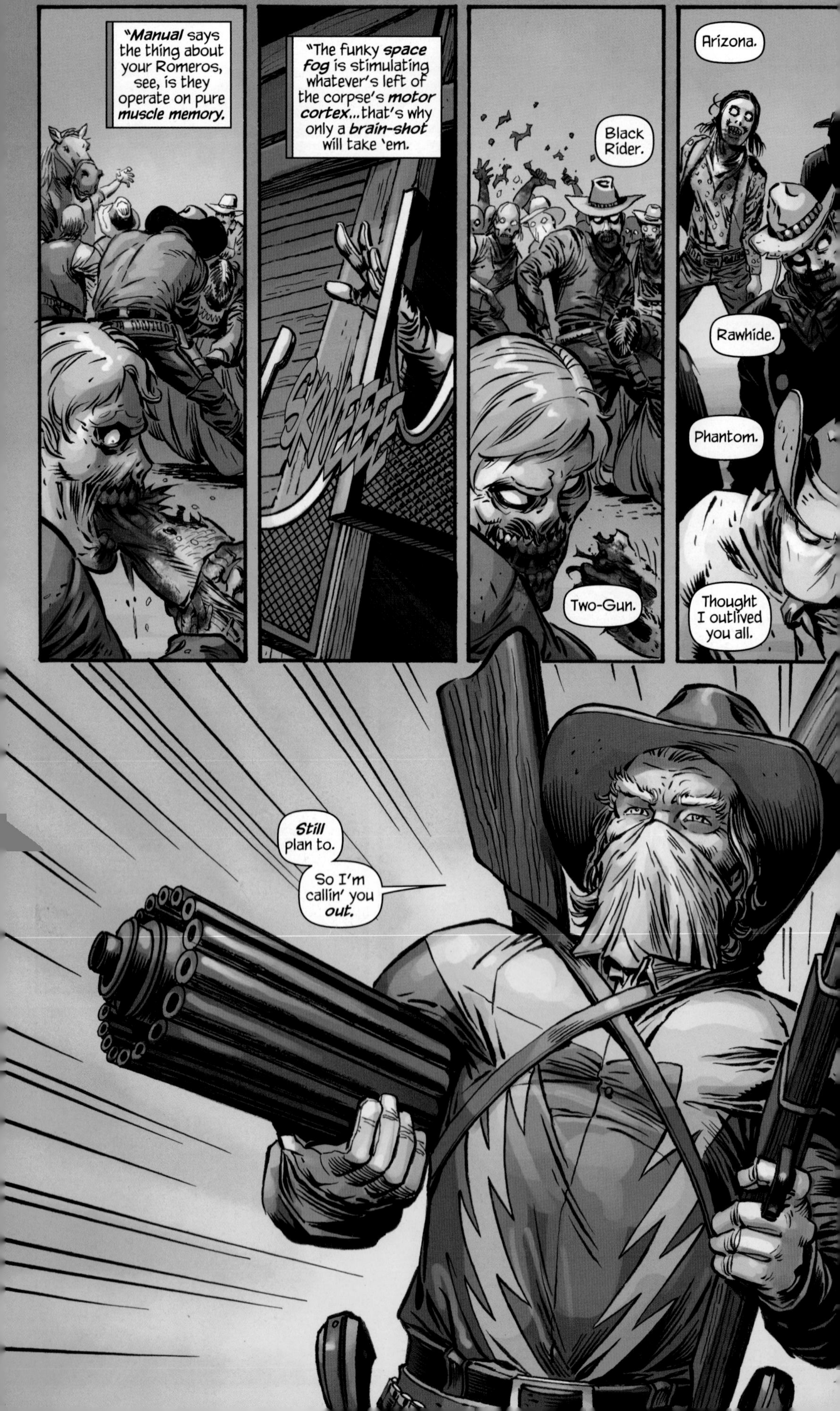
"Manual says the thing about your Romeros, see, is they operate on pure muscle memory.
"The funky space fog is stimulating whatever's left of the corpse's motor cortex...that's why only a brain-shot will take 'em.
SKWEEE
Black Rider.
Two-Gun.
Arizona.
Rawhide.
Phantom.
Thought I outlived you all.
Still plan to.
So I'm callin' you out.

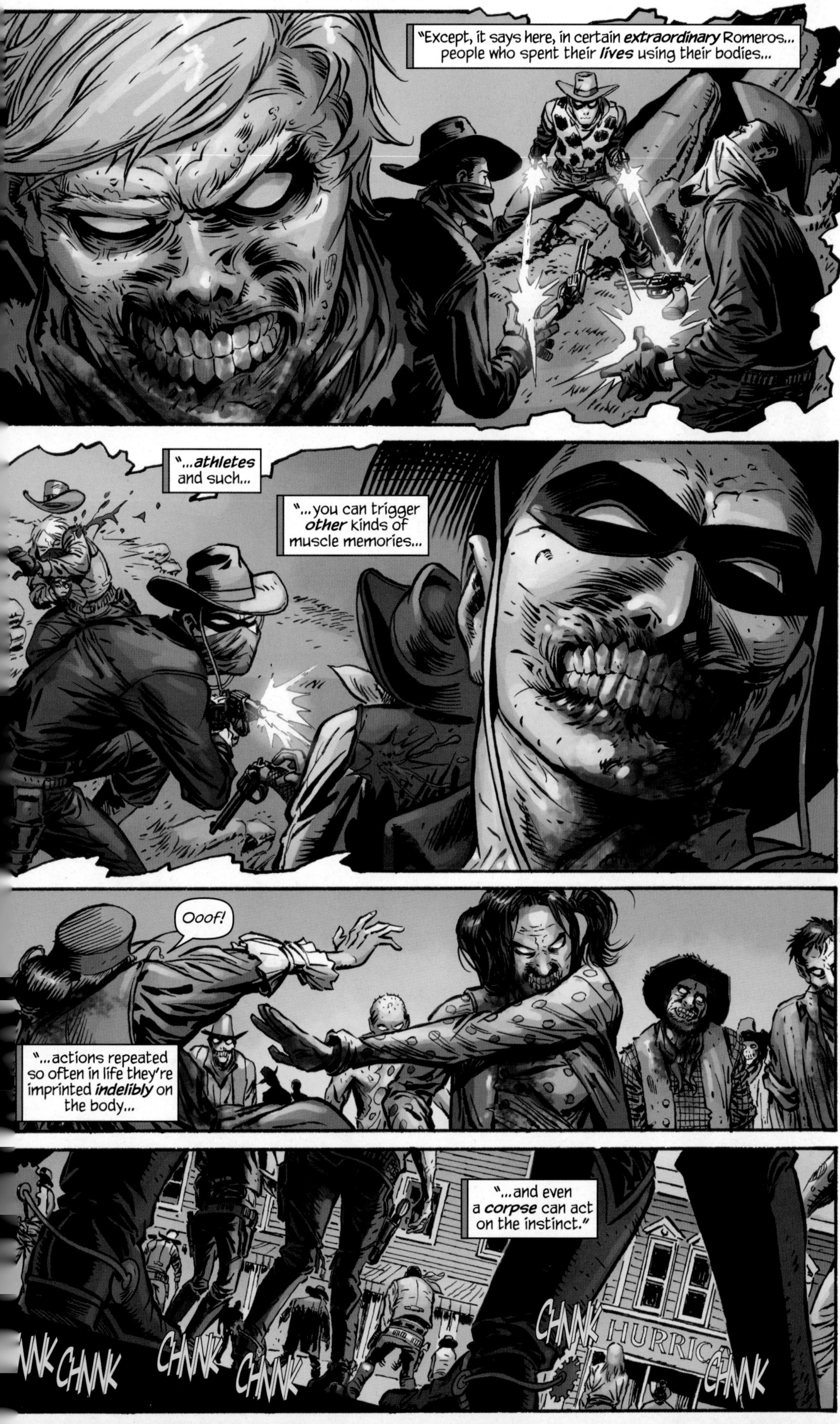
"Except, it says here, in certain *extraordinary* Romeros... people who spent their *lives* using their bodies...
"...*athletes* and such...
"...you can trigger *other* kinds of muscle memories...
Ooof!
"...actions repeated so often in life they're imprinted *indelibly* on the body...
"...and even a *corpse* can act on the instinct."
NNK CHNNK
CHNNK
CHNNK
CHNNK
HURRIC
CHNNK

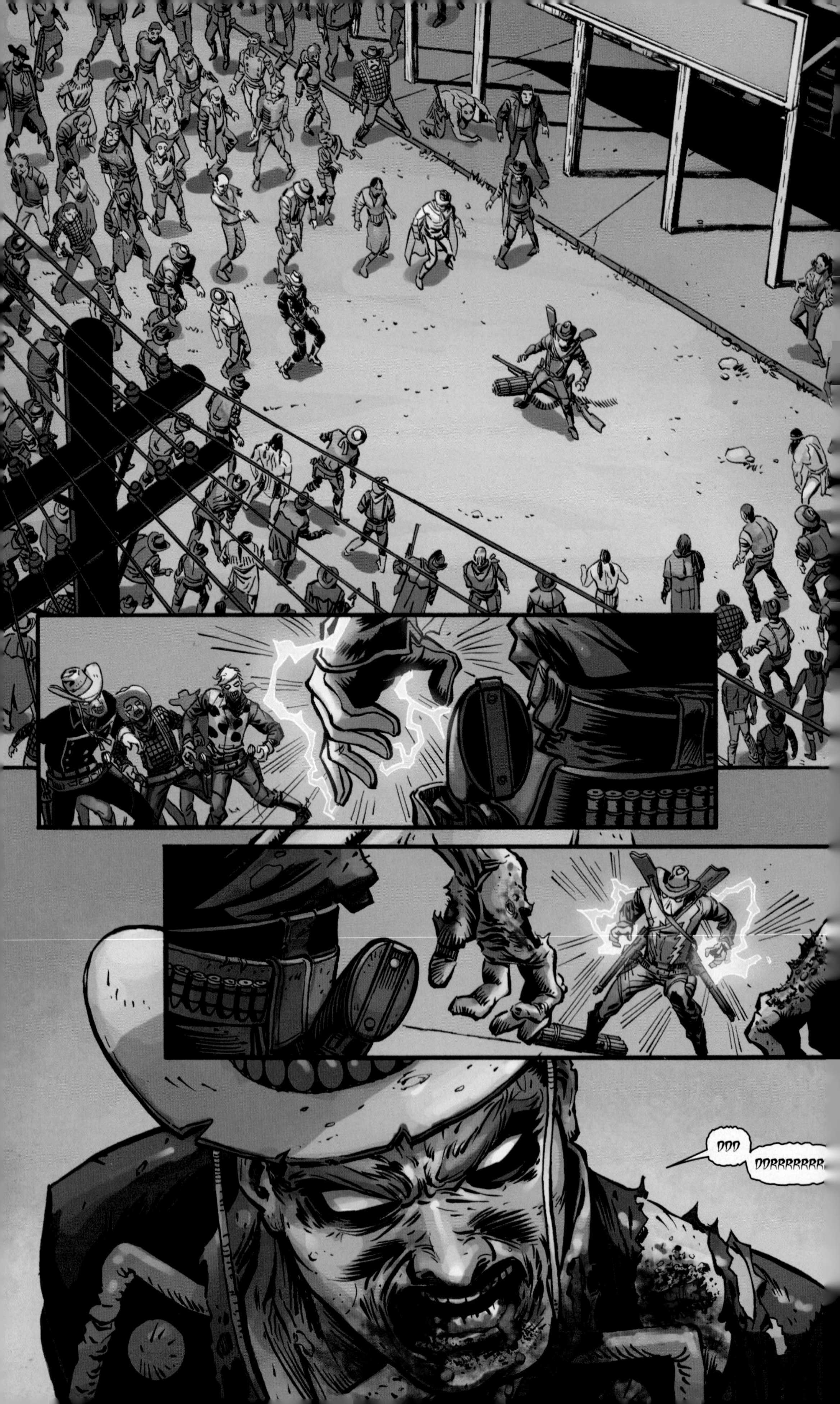
DDD
DDRRRRRRRR

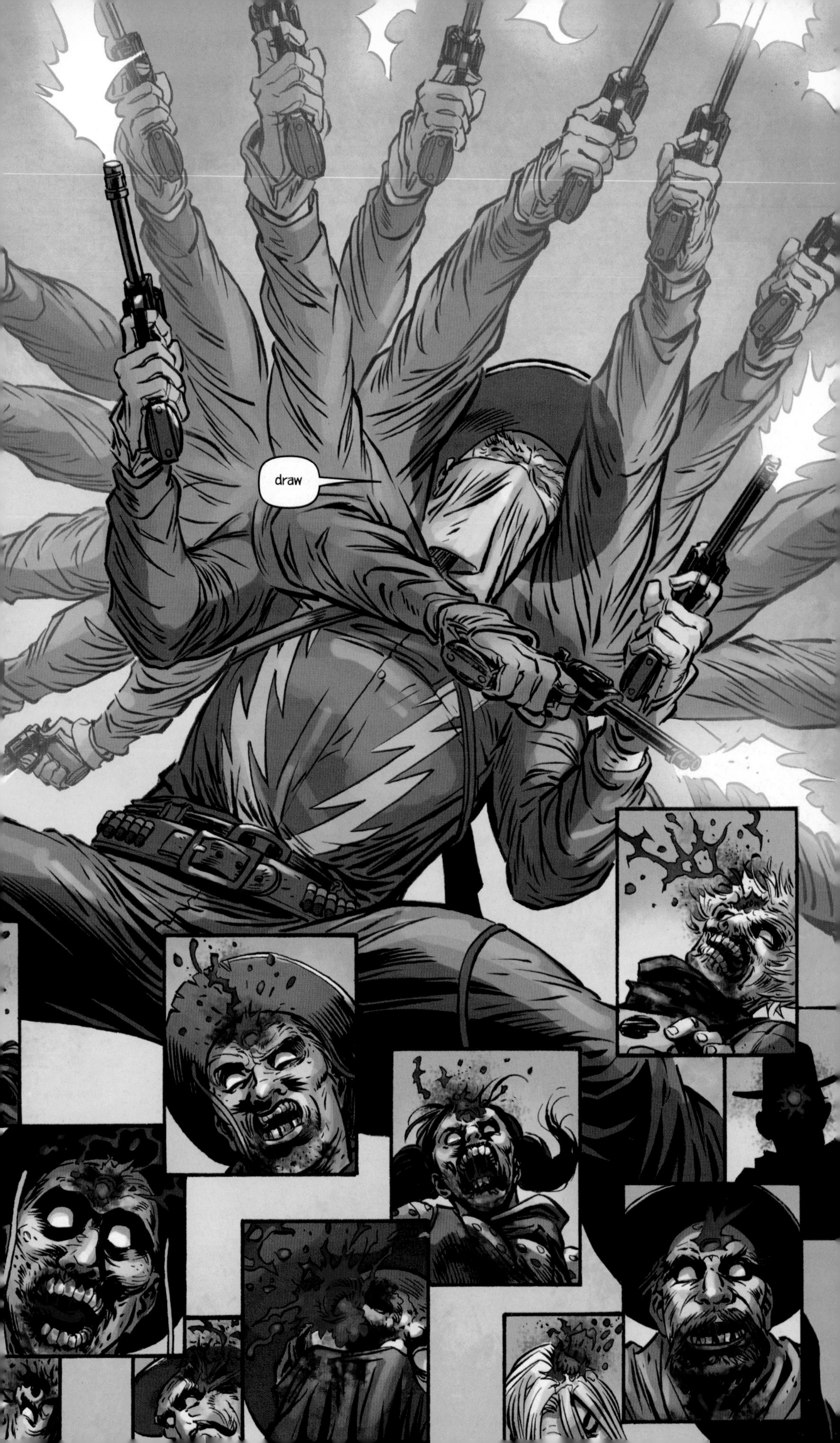
draw

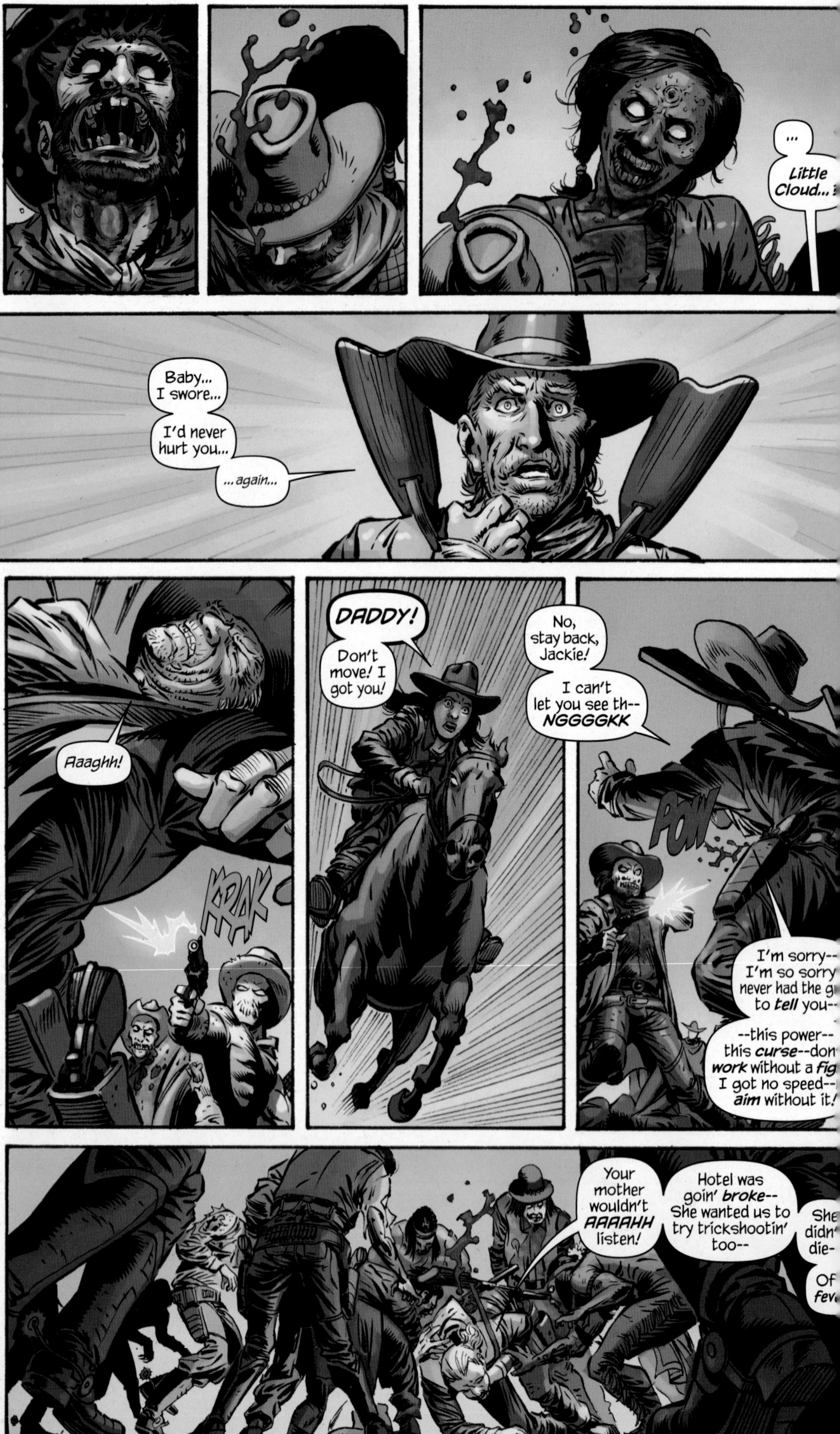
...
Little Cloud...
Baby... I swore...
I'd never hurt you...
...again...
Aaaghh!
KRAK
DADDY!
Don't move! I got you!
No, stay back, Jackie!
I can't let you see th-- NGGGGKK
POW
I'm sorry-- I'm so sorry never had the g to tell you--
--this power-- this curse--don work without a fig I got no speed-- aim without it!
Your mother wouldn't AAAAHH listen!
Hotel was goin' broke-- She wanted us to try trickshootin' too--
She didn' die--
Of fev

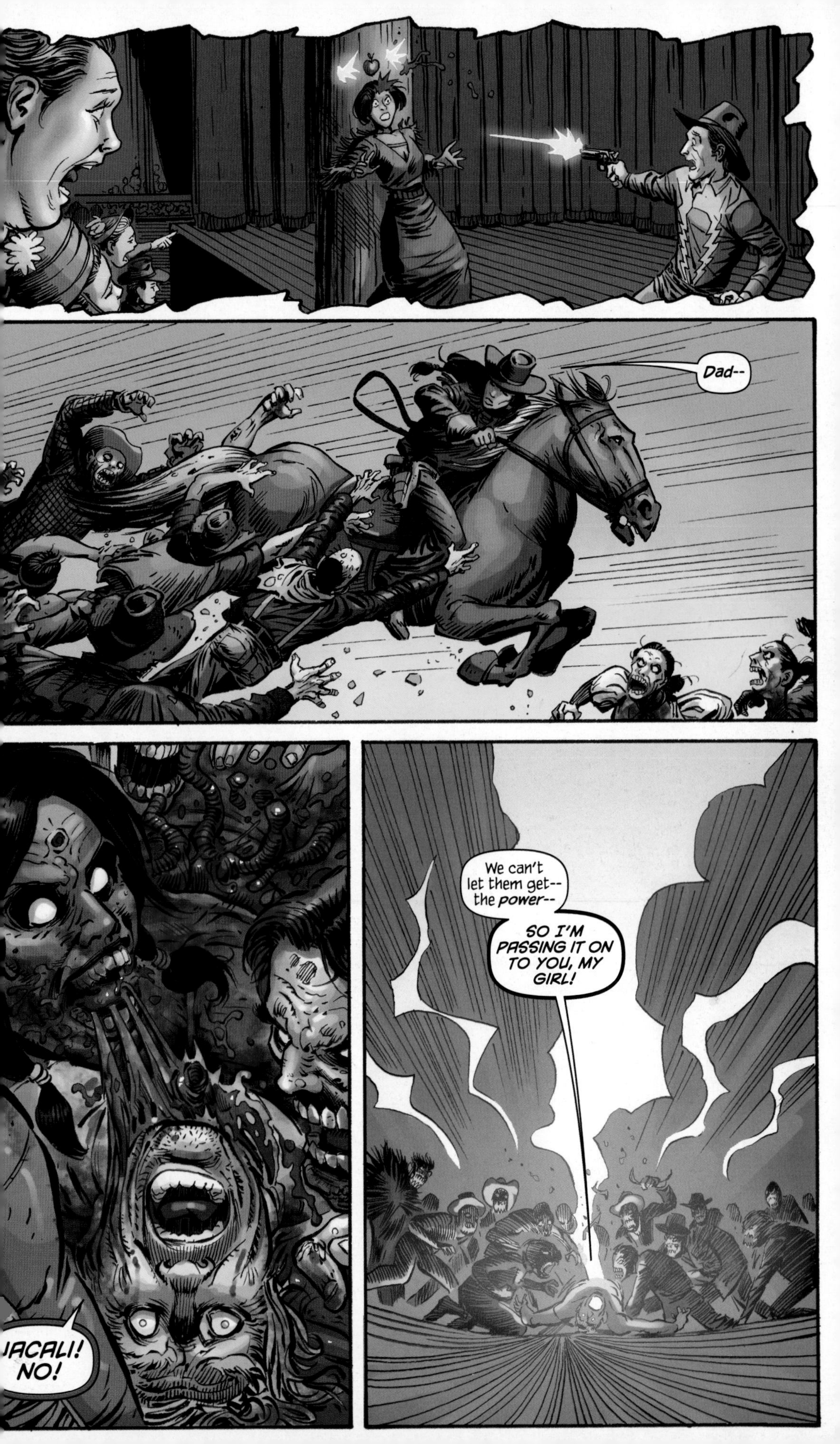
Dad--
We can't let them get-- the *power*--
SO I'M PASSING IT ON TO YOU, MY GIRL!
...ACALI! NO!

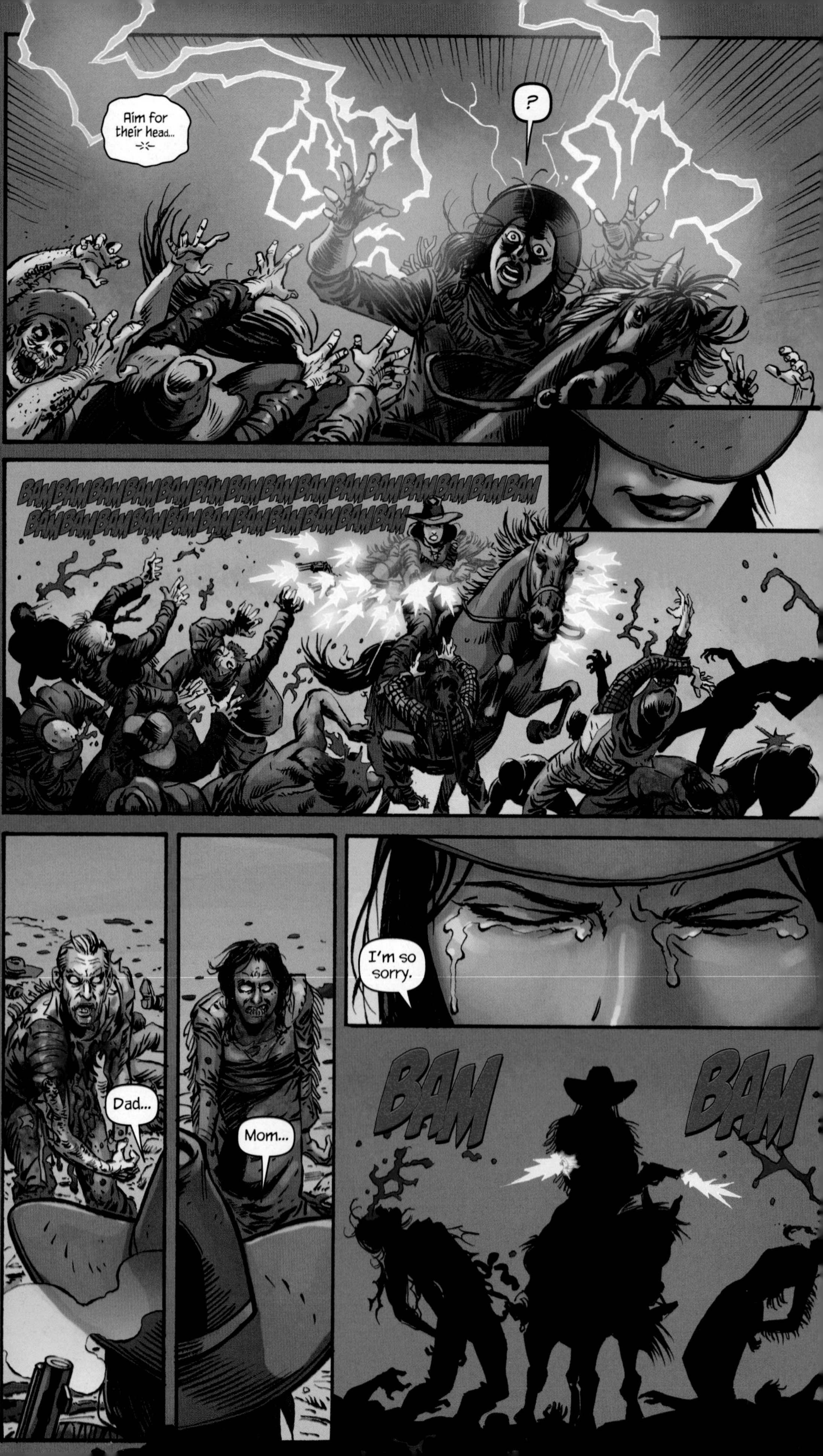
Aim for their head...
?
BAMBAMBAMBAMBAMBAMBAMBAMBAMBAMBAMBAMBAMBAMBAMBAM
BAMBAMBAMBAMBAMBAMBAMBAMBAMBAMBAMBAM
Dad...
Mom...
I'm so sorry.
BAM
BAM

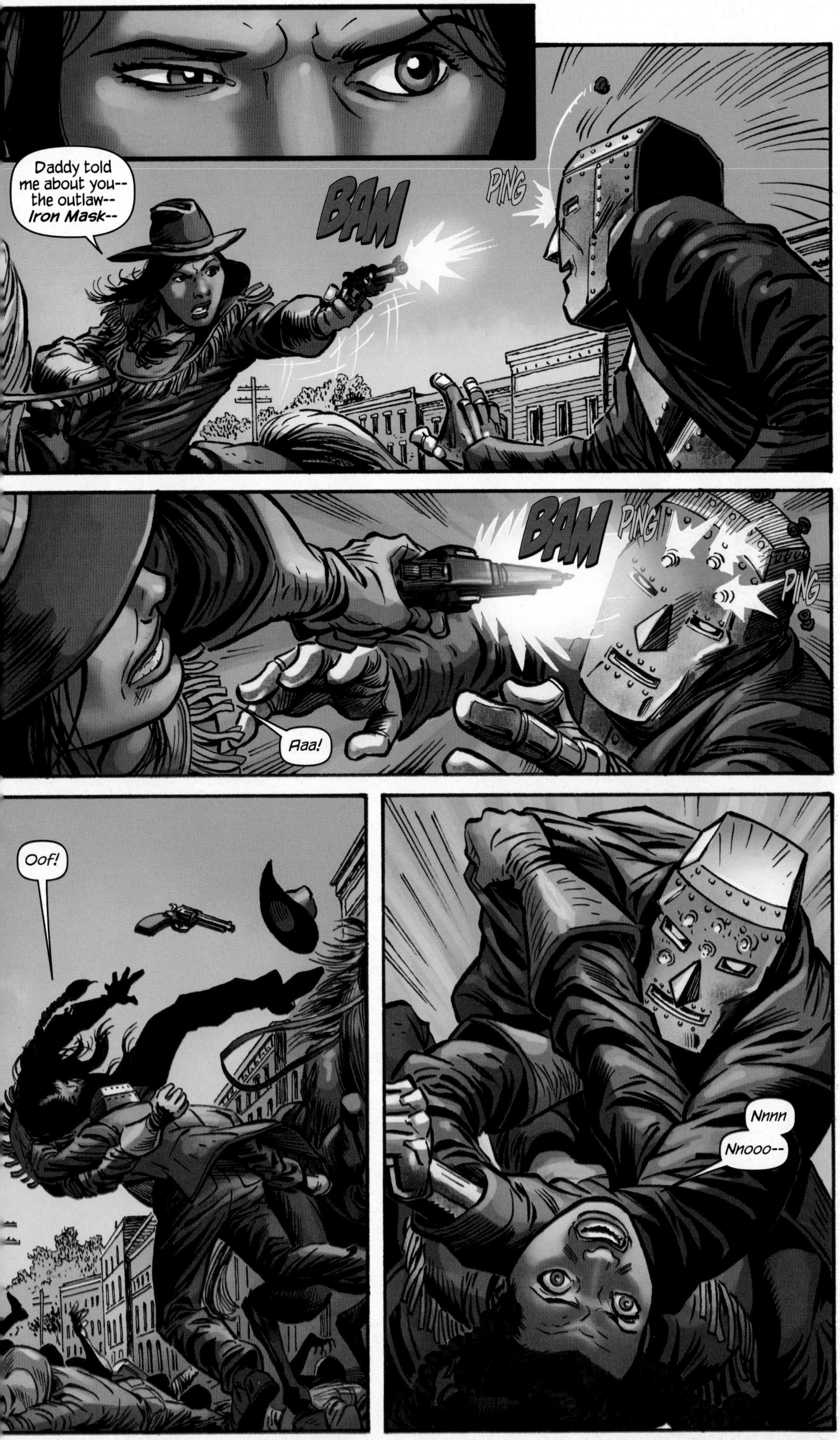
Daddy told me about you-- the outlaw-- Iron Mask--
BAM
PING
BAM
PING
PING
Aaa!
Oof!
Nnnn
Nnooo--

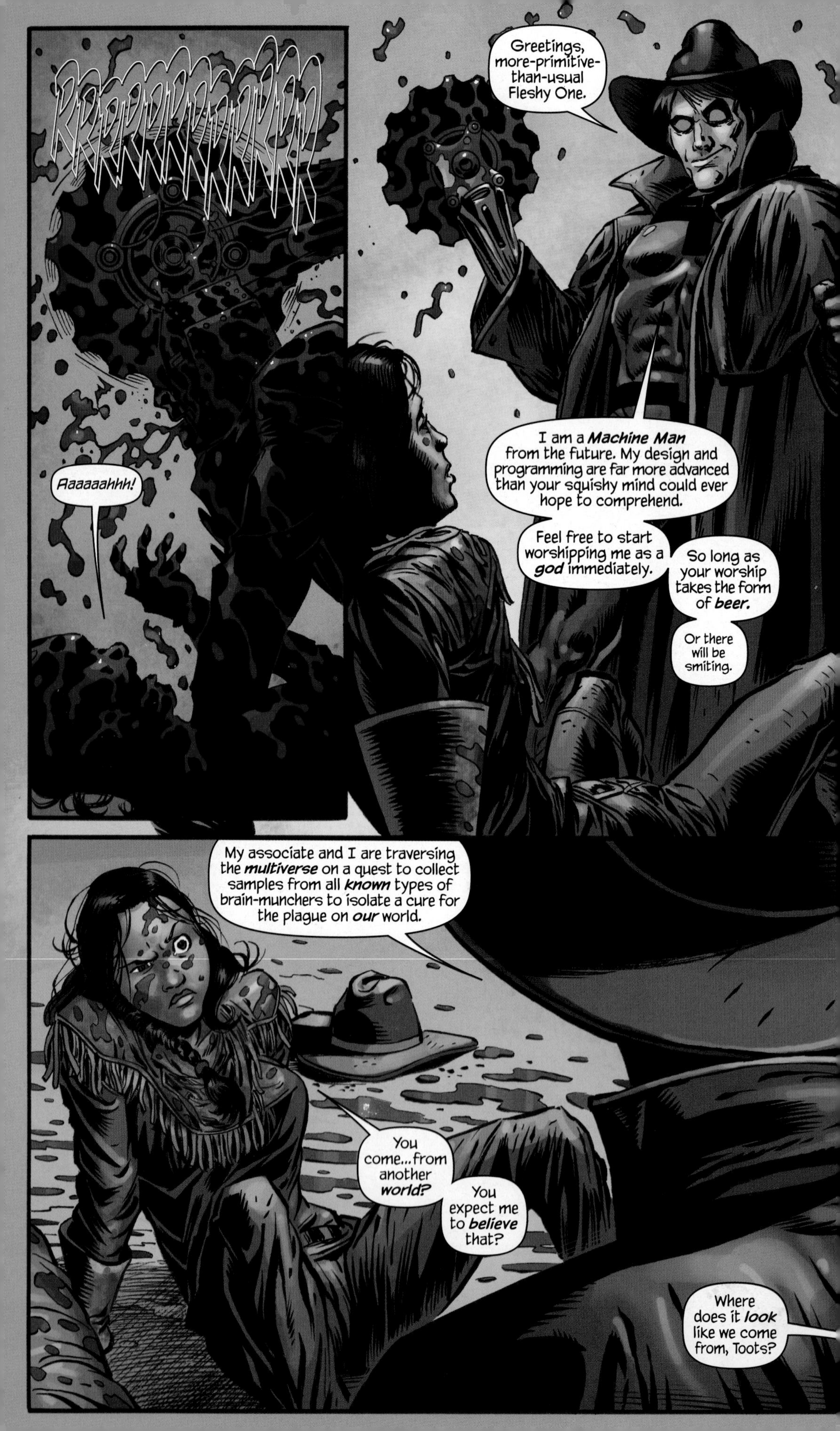
RRRRRRRRRRRRRR
Aaaaaahhh!
Greetings, more-primitive-than-usual Fleshy One.
I am a Machine Man from the future. My design and programming are far more advanced than your squishy mind could ever hope to comprehend.
Feel free to start worshipping me as a god immediately.
So long as your worship takes the form of beer.
Or there will be smiting.
My associate and I are traversing the multiverse on a quest to collect samples from all known types of brain-munchers to isolate a cure for the plague on our world.
You come...from another world?
You expect me to believe that?
Where does it look like we come from, Toots?

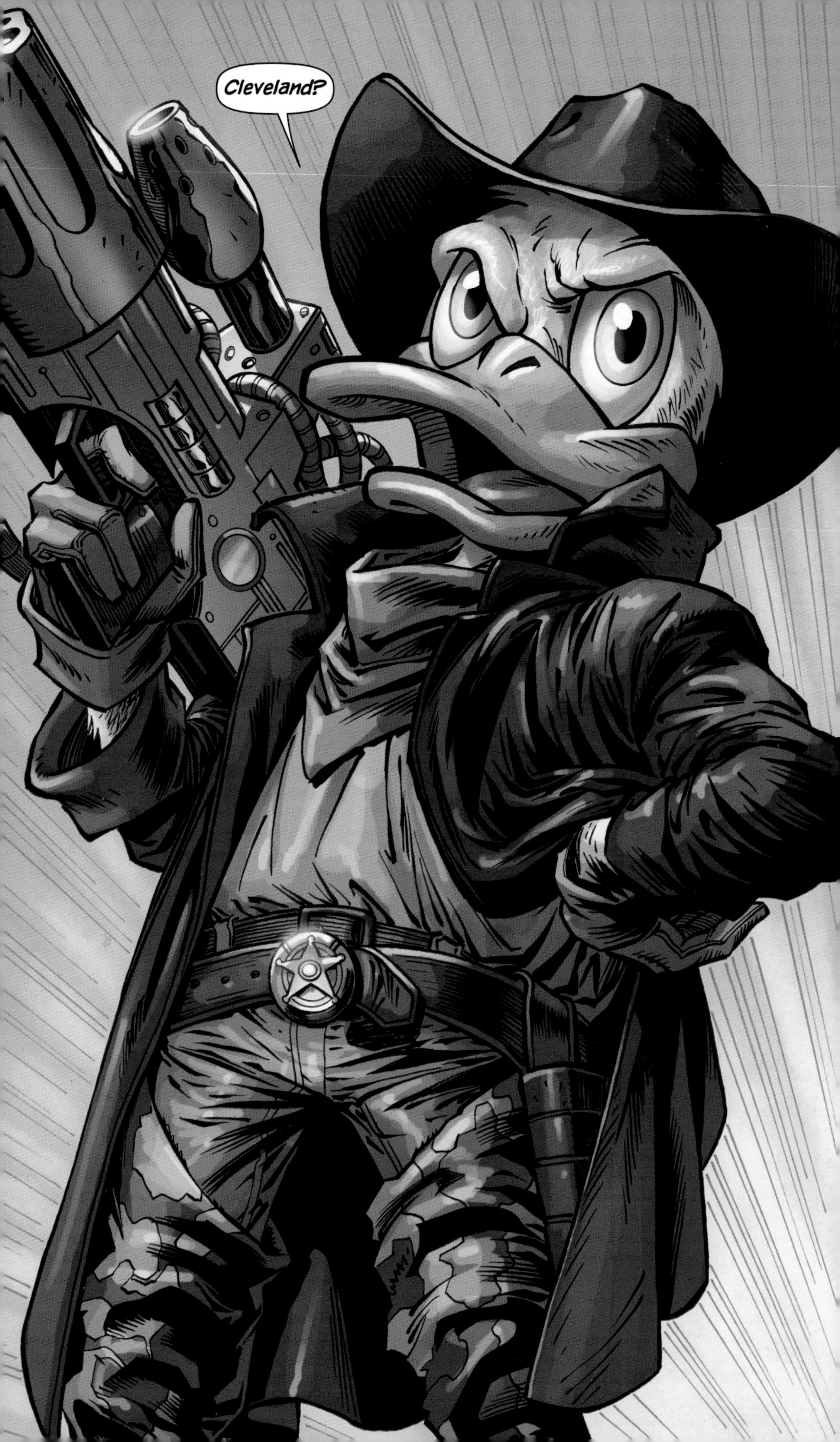
Cleveland?

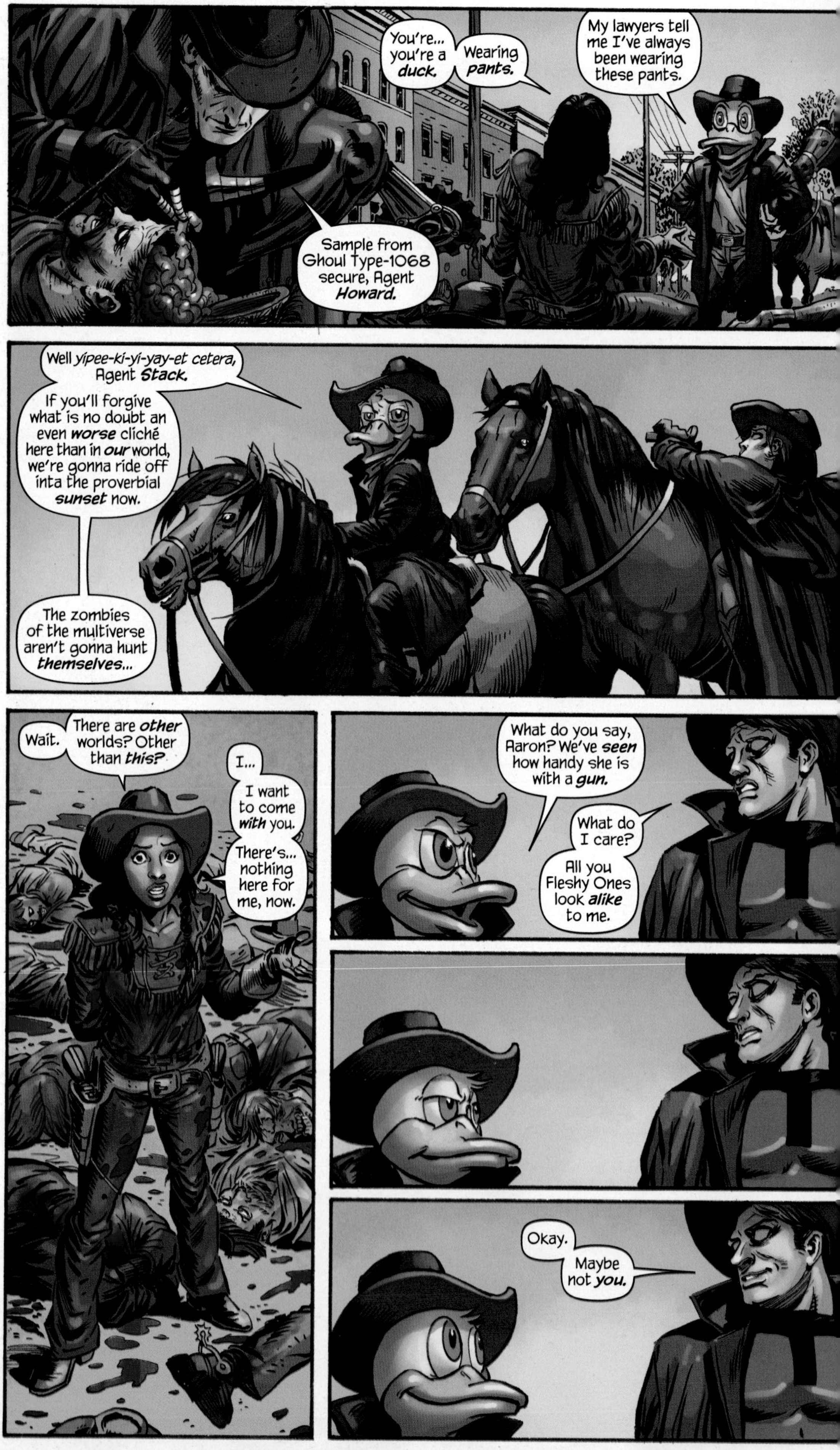

You're... you're a *duck.*
Wearing *pants.*
My lawyers tell me I've always been wearing these pants.
Sample from Ghoul Type-1068 secure, Agent *Howard.*
Well *yipee-ki-yi-yay-et cetera,* Agent *Stack.*
If you'll forgive what is no doubt an even *worse* cliché here than in *our* world, we're gonna ride off inta the proverbial *sunset* now.
The zombies of the multiverse aren't gonna hunt *themselves...*
Wait.
There are *other* worlds? Other than *this?*
I...
I want to come *with* you.
There's... nothing here for me, now.
What do you say, Aaron? We've *seen* how handy she is with a *gun.*
What do I care?
All you Fleshy Ones look *alike* to me.
Okay.
Maybe not *you.*

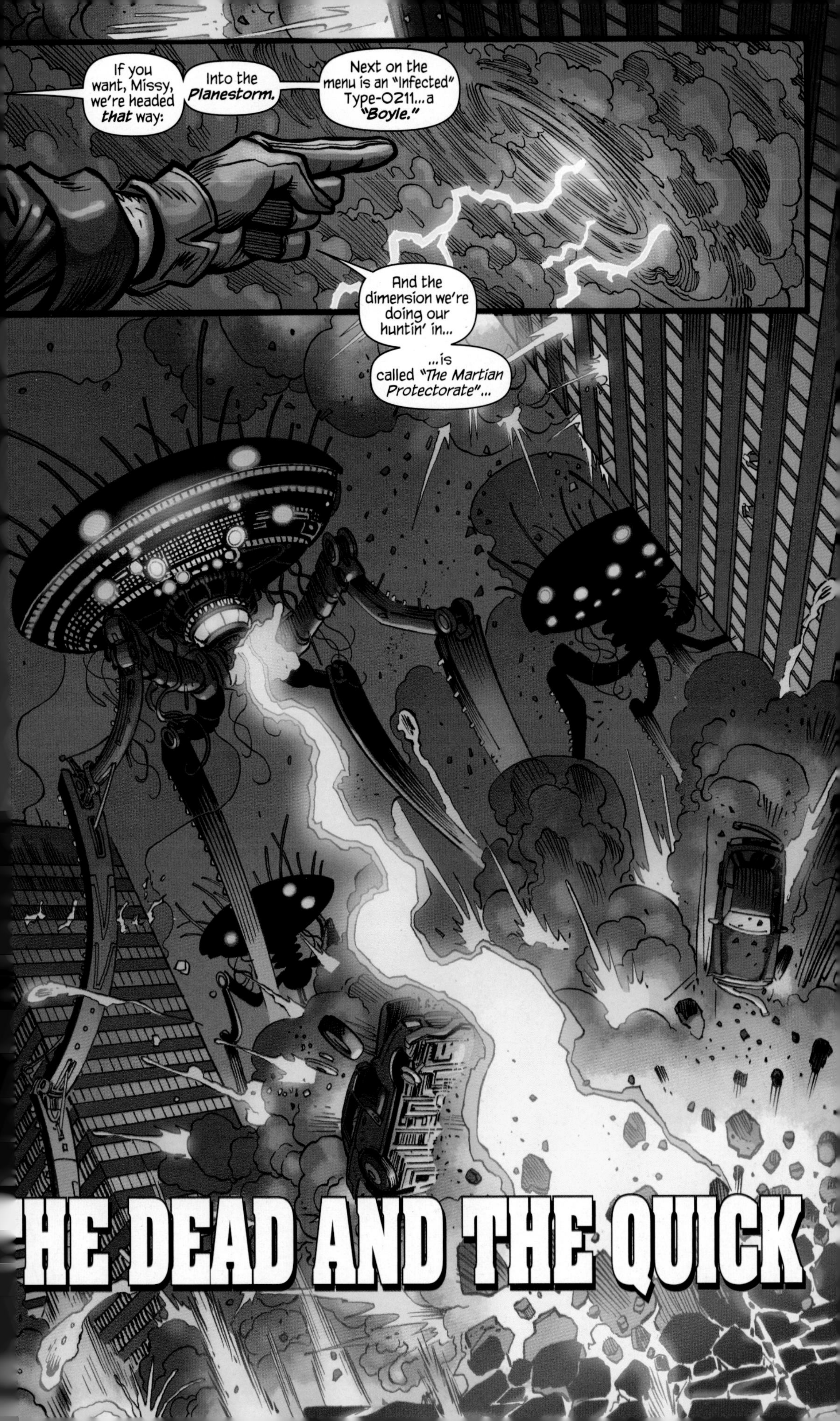

If you want, Missy, we're headed *that* way:
Into the *Planestorm.*
Next on the menu is an "Infected" Type-0211...a *"Boyle."*
And the dimension we're doing our huntin' in...
...is called *"The Martian Protectorate"*...
HE DEAD AND THE QUICK

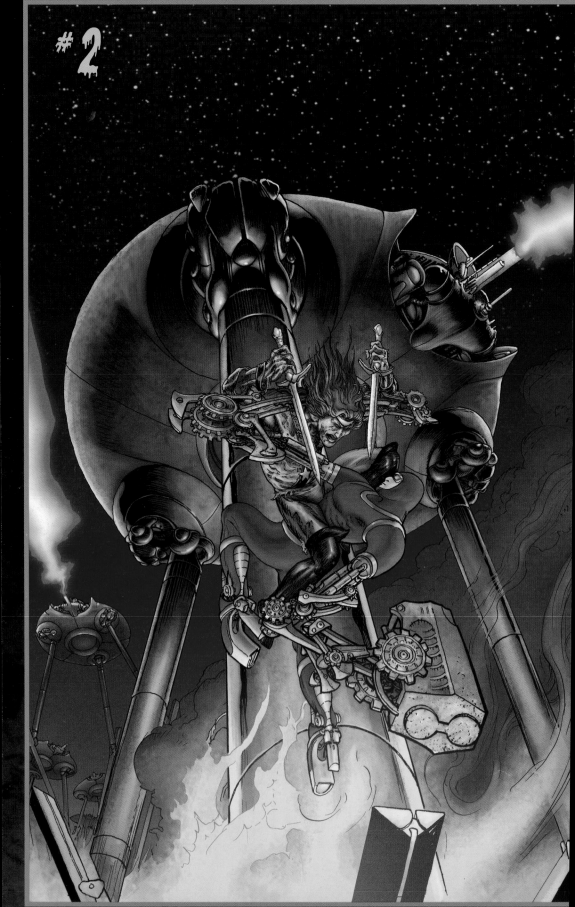

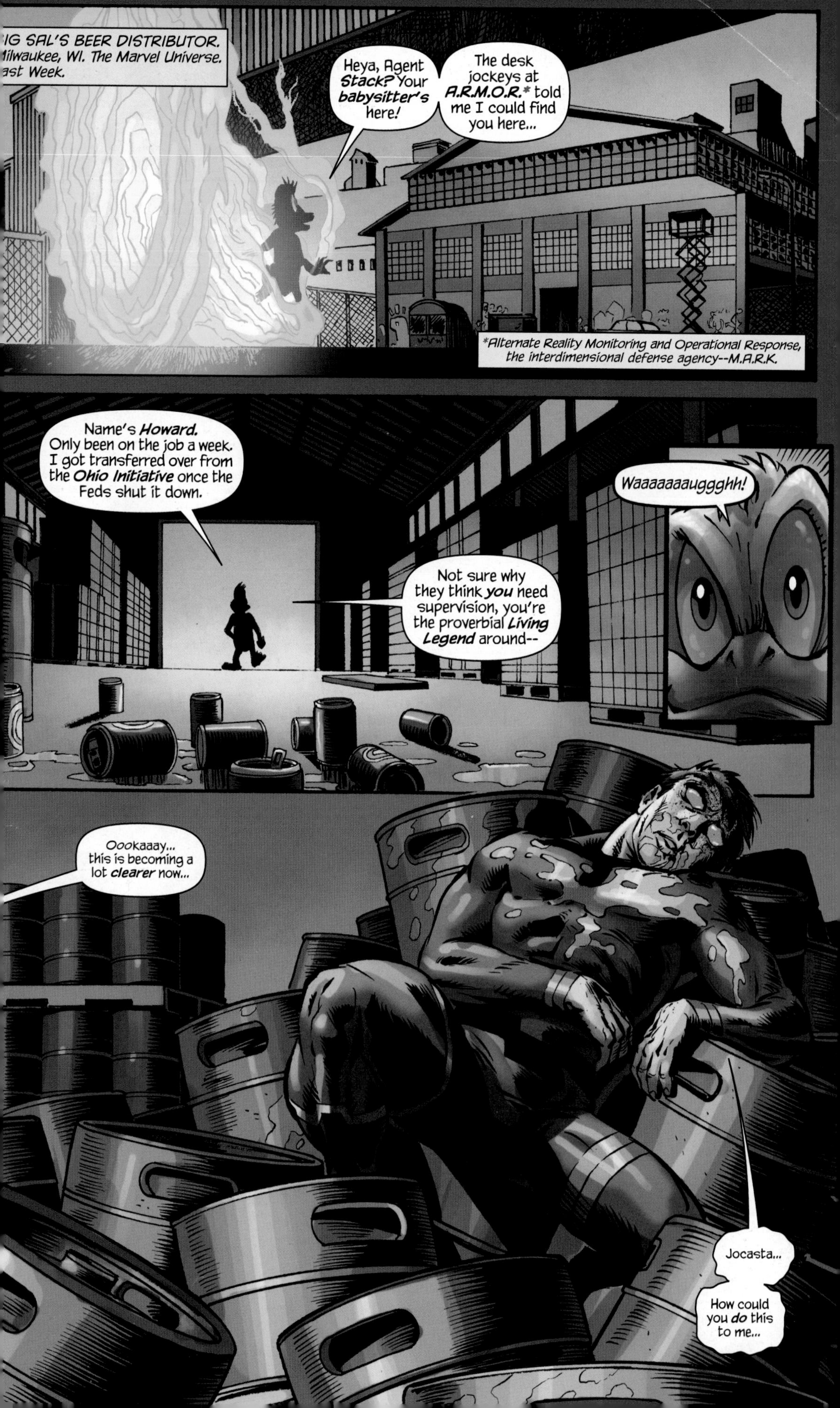

IG SAL'S BEER DISTRIBUTOR. ilwaukee, WI. The Marvel Universe. ast Week.
Heya, Agent Stack? Your babysitter's here!
The desk jockeys at A.R.M.O.R.* told me I could find you here...
*Alternate Reality Monitoring and Operational Response, the interdimensional defense agency--M.A.R.K.
Name's Howard. Only been on the job a week. I got transferred over from the Ohio Initiative once the Feds shut it down.
Not sure why they think you need supervision, you're the proverbial Living Legend around--
Waaaaaaauggghh!
Oookaaay... this is becoming a lot clearer now...
Jocasta...
How could you do this to me...

My girlfriend... she went back to her *ex-husband!**

What does *he* got that *I* don't got?

Snappy antennae?

A winning smile?

You're not *helping,* Duck...

*Over in MIGHTY AVENGERS, natch-- Undeaditor Mark

I just don't know...what the point of anything *is,* anymore...

Well then Unca Howie has nggggghh--jus the *thing* for you, my hairles ape-bot!

A new *mission!* Back H.Q., Dr. *Morbi* thinks he may ha figured out a w to find a *cure* f the zombie viru thanks to...

...Spider-Man's *radioactive blood,** the only culture I've had *any* success in growing a serum that will *cure* the undead plague.

But the virus is so virulent and metamorphic it's nearly impossible to lock down its genetic code.

*Which Spidey don to Morbs in AMAZ SPIDER-MAN #62 Yes, I'm still her

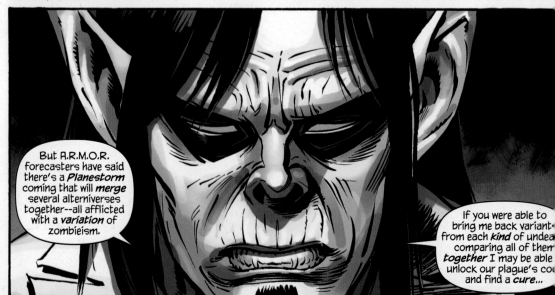

But A.R.M.O.R. forecasters have said there's a *Planestorm* coming that will *merge* several alterniverses together--all afflicted with a *variation* of zombieism.

If you were able to bring me back variant from each *kind* of undea comparing all of them *together* I may be able unlock our plague's co and find a *cure*...

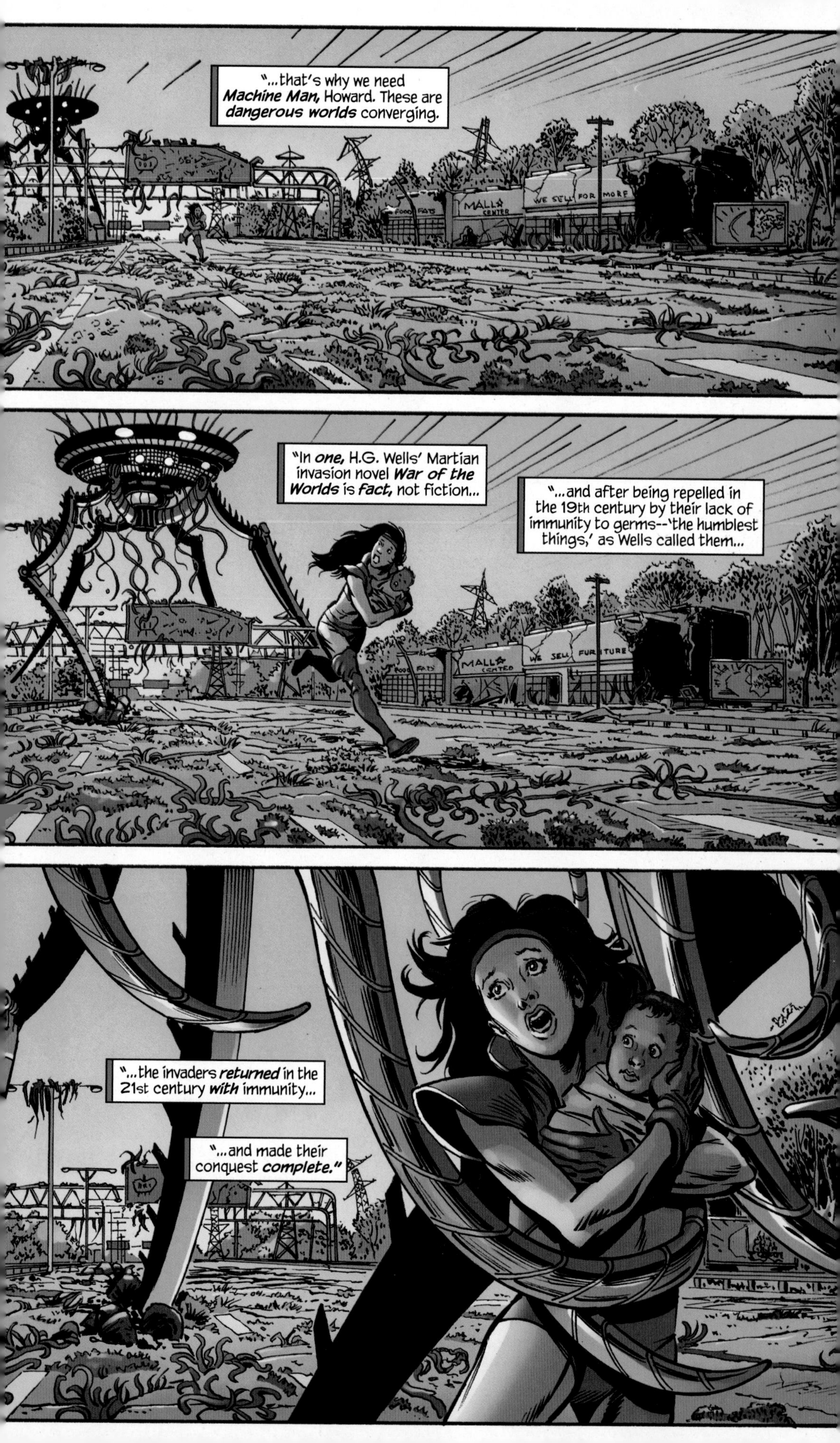
"...that's why we need *Machine Man,* Howard. These are *dangerous worlds* converging.
"In *one,* H.G. Wells' Martian invasion novel *War of the Worlds* is *fact,* not fiction...
"...and after being repelled in the 19th century by their lack of immunity to germs--'the humblest things,' as Wells called them...
"...the invaders *returned* in the 21st century *with* immunity...
"...and made their conquest *complete.*"

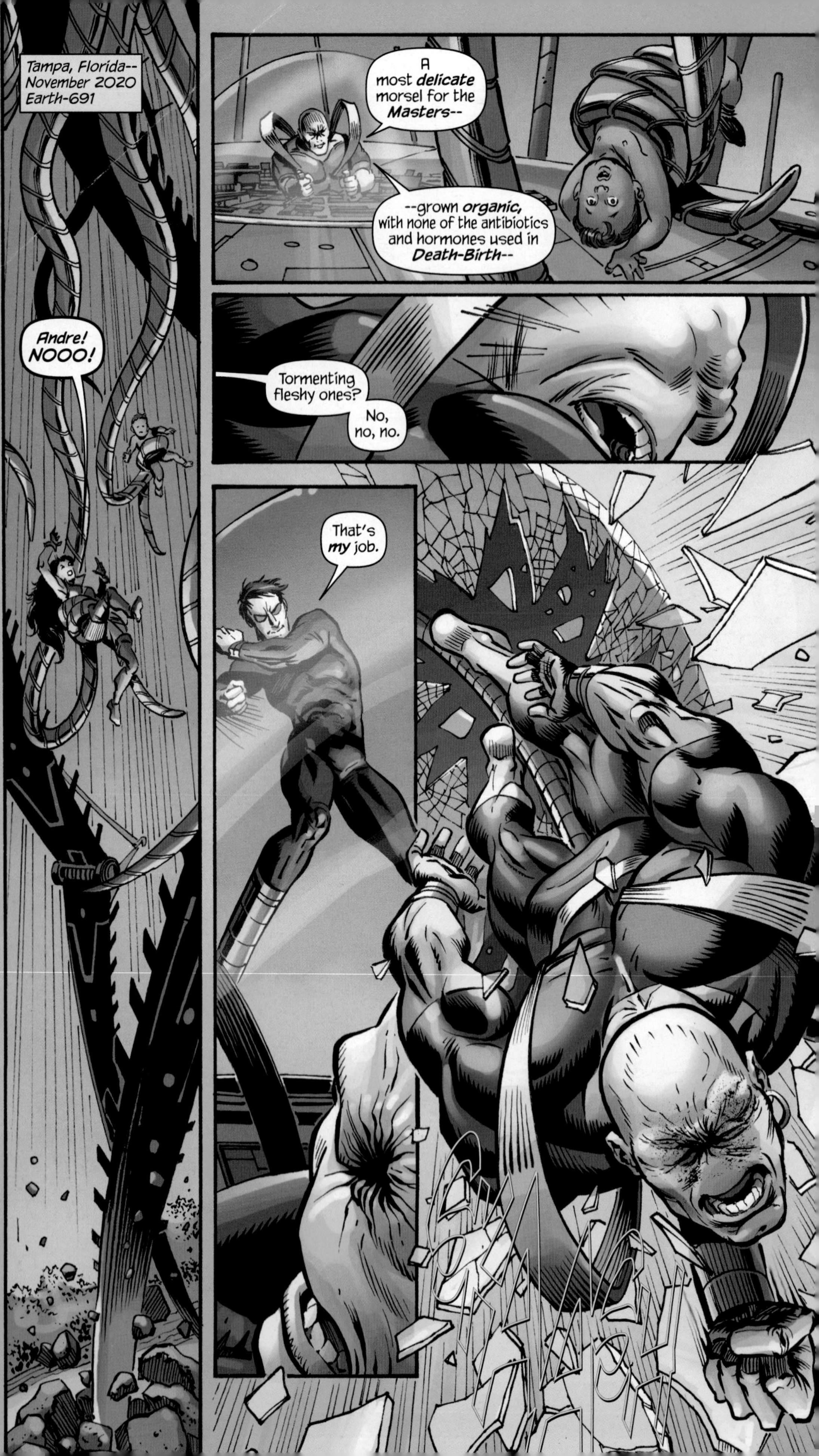
Tampa, Florida-- November 2020 Earth-691
Andre! NOOO!
A most delicate morsel for the Masters--
--grown organic, with none of the antibiotics and hormones used in Death-Birth--
Tormenting fleshy ones?
No, no, no.
That's my job.

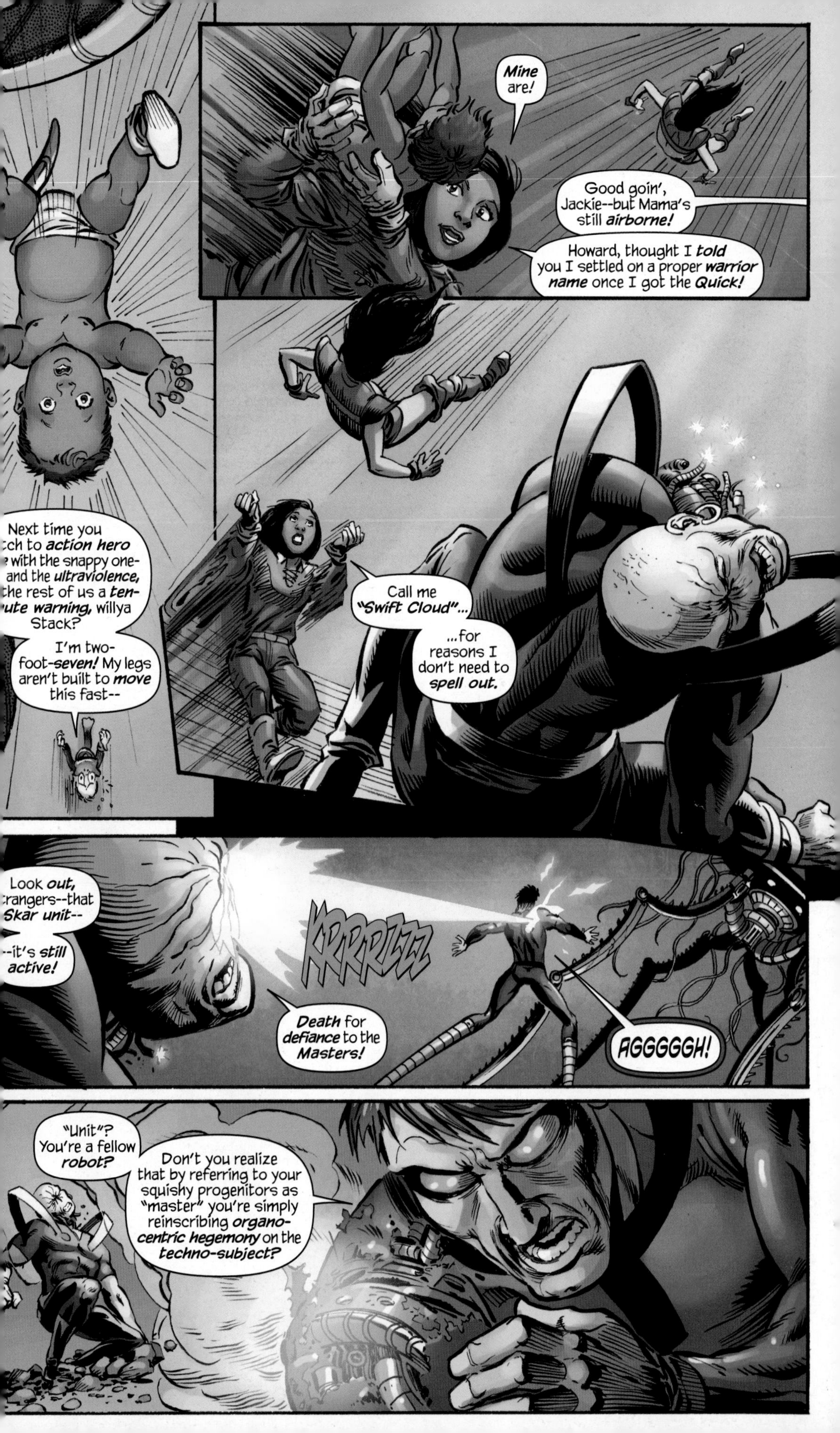

Mine are!
Good goin', Jackie--but Mama's still airborne!
Howard, thought I told you I settled on a proper warrior name once I got the Quick!
Next time you ch to action hero with the snappy one- and the ultraviolence, the rest of us a ten- ute warning, willya Stack?
I'm two-foot-seven! My legs aren't built to move this fast--
Call me "Swift Cloud"...
...for reasons I don't need to spell out.
Look out, rangers--that Skar unit--
--it's still active!
KRRRZZZ
Death for defiance to the Masters!
AGGGGGH!
"Unit"? You're a fellow robot?
Don't you realize that by referring to your squishy progenitors as "master" you're simply reinscribing organo-centric hegemony on the techno-subject?

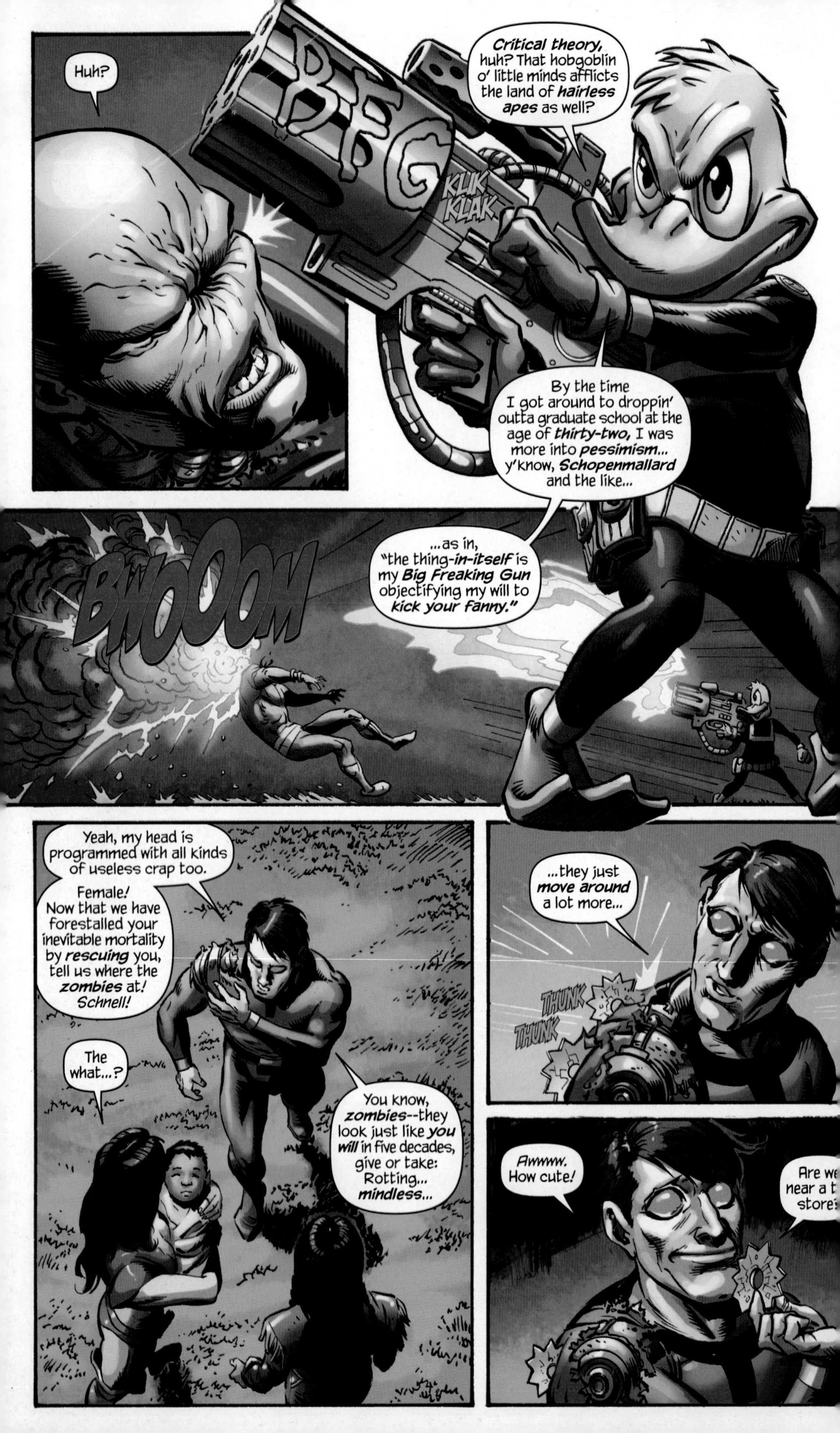

Huh?
Critical theory, huh? That hobgoblin o' little minds afflicts the land of hairless apes as well?
BFG
KLIK KLAK
By the time I got around to droppin' outta graduate school at the age of thirty-two, I was more into pessimism... y'know, Schopenmallard and the like...
BWOOOM
...as in, "the thing-in-itself is my Big Freaking Gun objectifying my will to kick your fanny."
Yeah, my head is programmed with all kinds of useless crap too.
Female! Now that we have forestalled your inevitable mortality by rescuing you, tell us where the zombies at! Schnell!
The what...?
You know, zombies--they look just like you will in five decades, give or take: Rotting... mindless...
...they just move around a lot more...
THUNK
THUNK
Awwww. How cute!

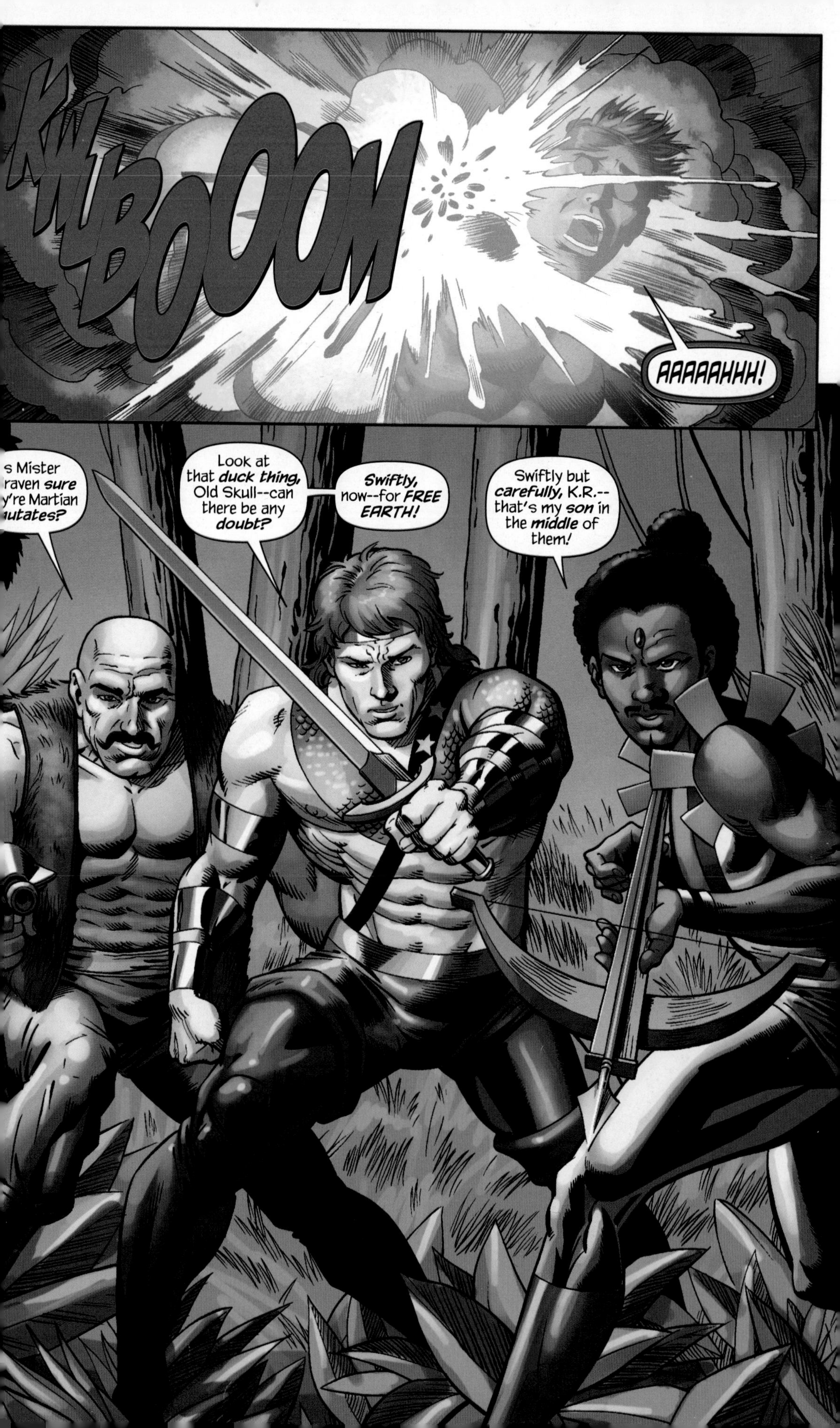
KHUBOOOOM
AAAAAHHH!
s Mister
raven sure
y're Martian
utates?
Look at that duck thing, Old Skull--can there be any doubt?
Swiftly, now--for FREE EARTH!
Swiftly but carefully, K.R.--that's my son in the middle of them!

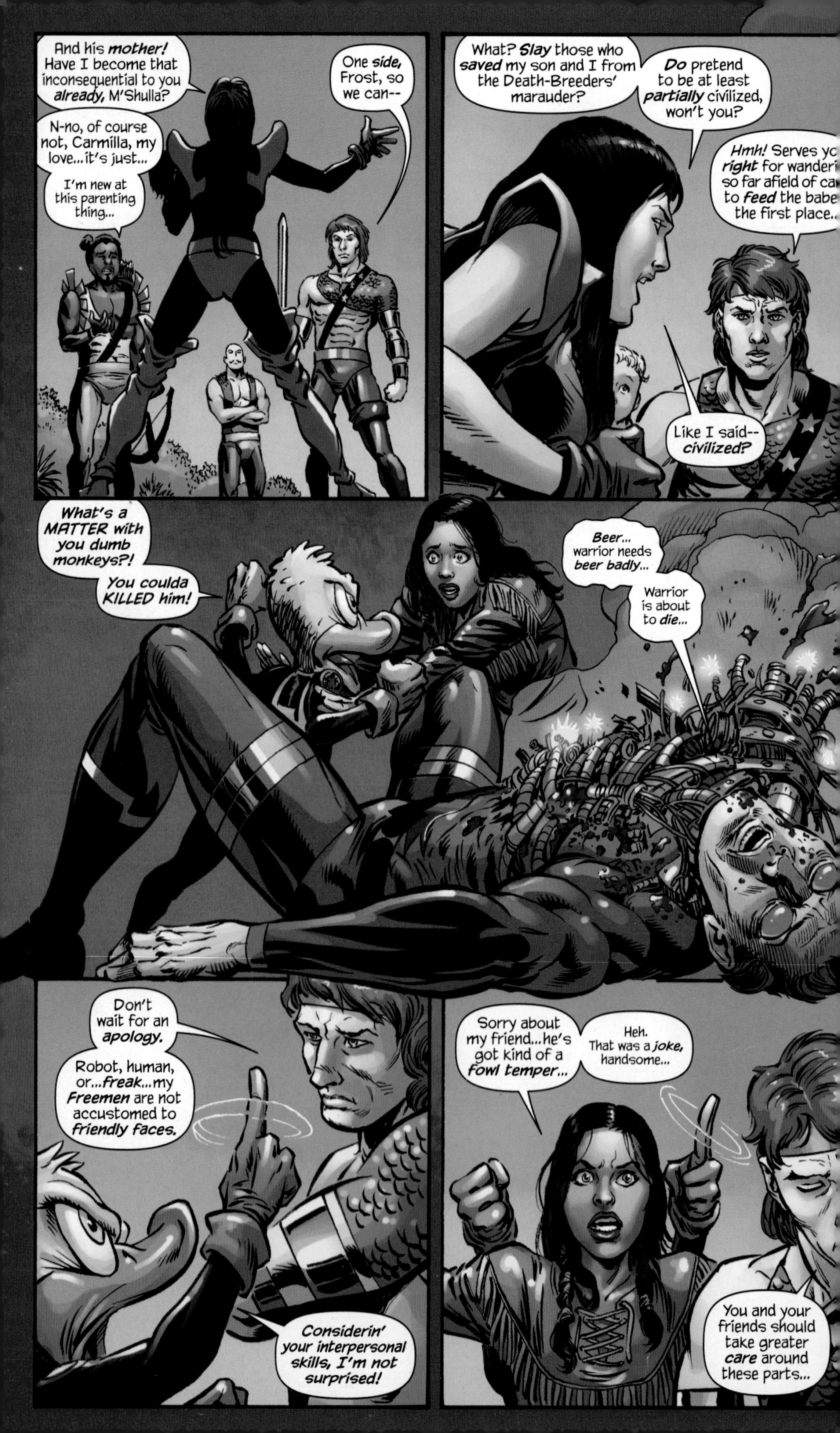
And his *mother!* Have I become that inconsequential to you *already,* M'Shulla?
N-no, of course not, Carmilla, my love...it's just...
I'm new at this parenting thing...
One *side,* Frost, so we can--
What? *Slay* those who *saved* my son and I from the Death-Breeders' marauder?
Do pretend to be at least *partially* civilized, won't you?
Hmh! Serves yo *right* for wanderi so far afield of ca to *feed* the babe the first place..
Like I said-- *civilized?*
What's a MATTER with you dumb monkeys?!
You coulda KILLED him!
Beer... warrior needs *beer badly*...
Warrior is about to *die*...
Don't wait for an *apology.*
Robot, human, or...*freak*...my *Freemen* are not accustomed to *friendly faces.*
Considerin' your interpersonal skills, I'm not surprised!
Sorry about my friend...he's got kind of a *fowl temper*...
Heh. That was a *joke,* handsome...
You and your friends should take greater *care* around these parts...

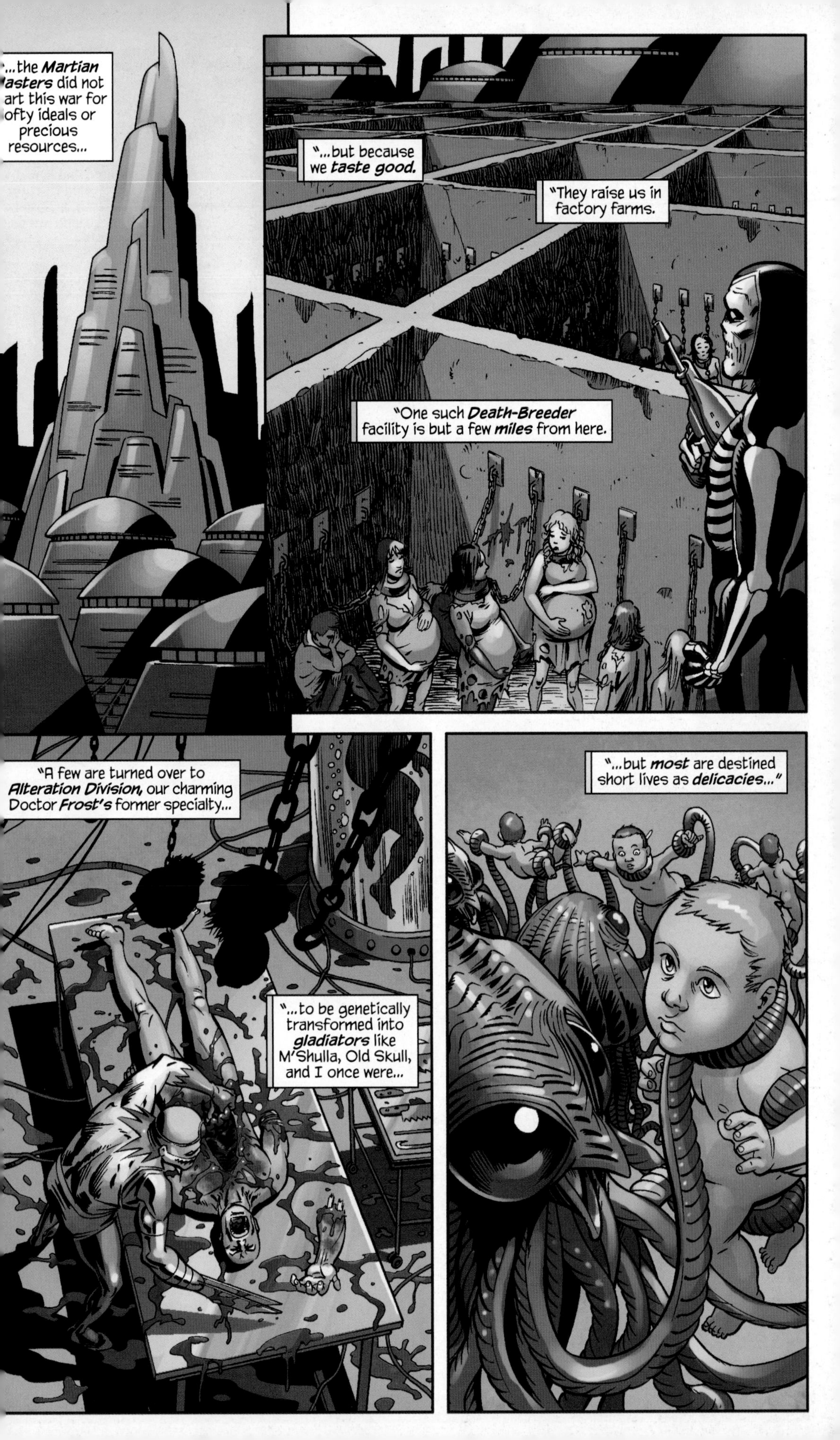
"...the *Martian*
asters did not
art this war for
ofty ideals or
precious
resources...
"...but because
we *taste good.*
"They raise us in
factory farms.
"One such *Death-Breeder*
facility is but a few *miles* from here.
"A few are turned over to
Alteration Division, our charming
Doctor *Frost's* former specialty...
"...to be genetically
transformed into
gladiators like
M'Shulla, Old Skull,
and I once were...
"...but *most* are destined
short lives as *delicacies...*"

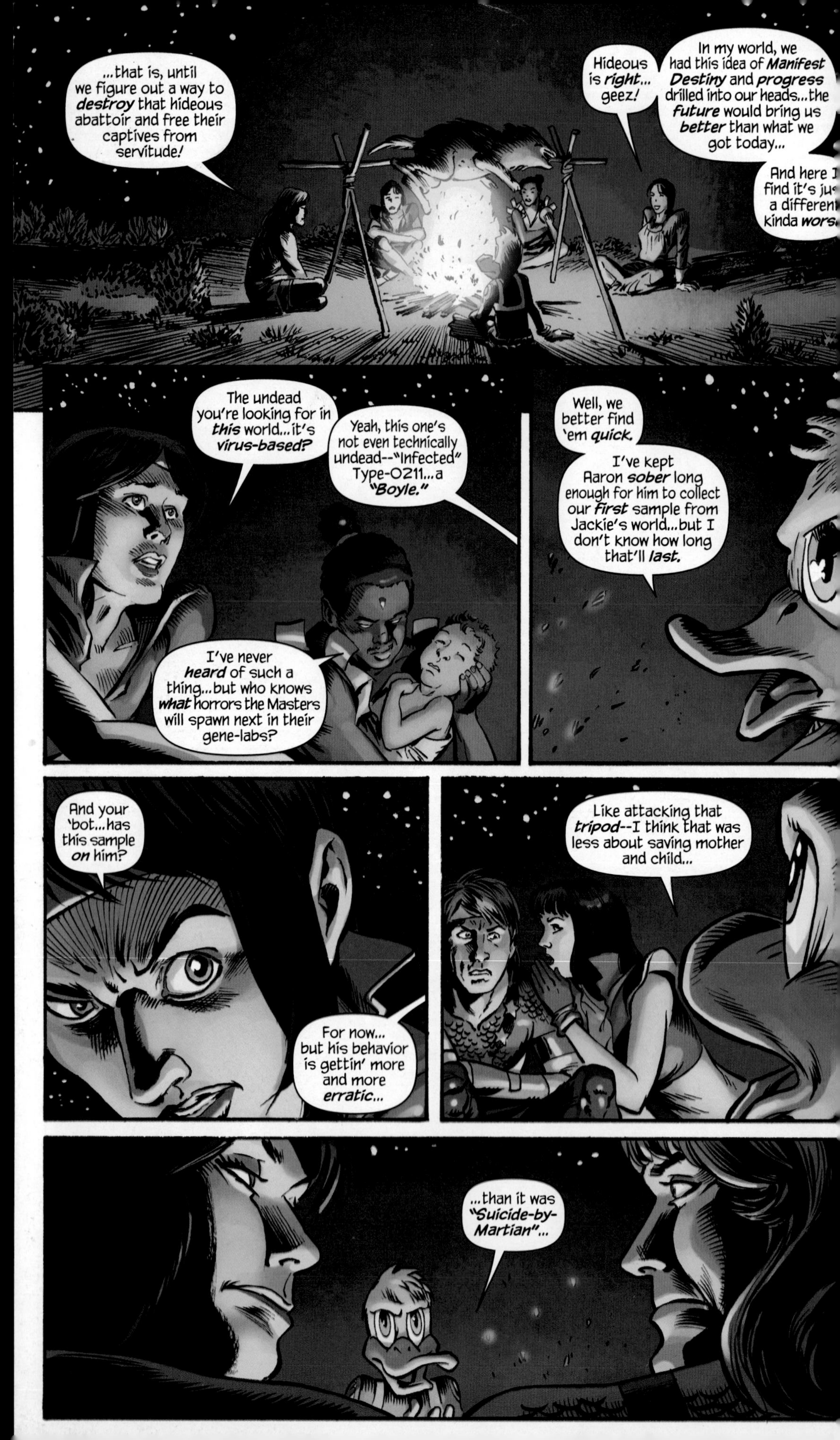
...that is, until we figure out a way to destroy that hideous abattoir and free their captives from servitude!
Hideous is right... geez!
In my world, we had this idea of Manifest Destiny and progress drilled into our heads...the future would bring us better than what we got today...
And here I find it's jus a differen kinda wors
The undead you're looking for in this world... it's virus-based?
Yeah, this one's not even technically undead--"Infected" Type-0211...a "Boyle."
I've never heard of such a thing...but who knows what horrors the Masters will spawn next in their gene-labs?
Well, we better find 'em quick.
I've kept Aaron sober long enough for him to collect our first sample from Jackie's world...but I don't know how long that'll last.
And your 'bot...has this sample on him?
For now... but his behavior is gettin' more and more erratic...
Like attacking that tripod--I think that was less about saving mother and child...
...than it was "Suicide-by-Martian"...

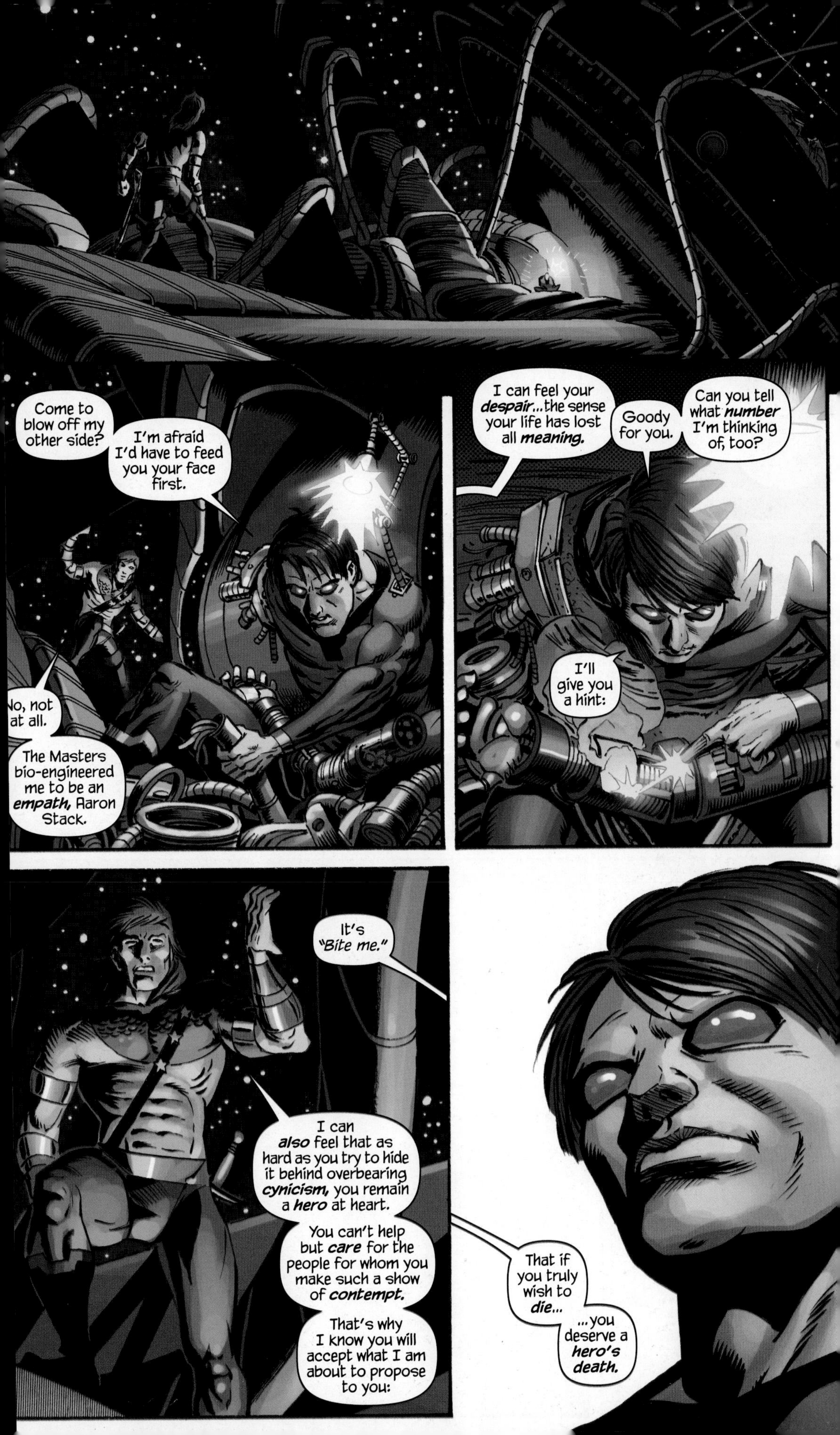

Come to blow off my other side?
I'm afraid I'd have to feed you your face first.
No, not at all.
The Masters bio-engineered me to be an *empath,* Aaron Stack.
I can feel your *despair*...the sense your life has lost all *meaning.*
Goody for you.
Can you tell what *number* I'm thinking of, too?
I'll give you a hint:
It's *"Bite me."*
I can *also* feel that as hard as you try to hide it behind overbearing *cynicism,* you remain a *hero* at heart.
You can't help but *care* for the people for whom you make such a show of *contempt.*
That's why I know you will accept what I am about to propose to you:
That if you truly wish to *die*...
...you deserve a *hero's death.*

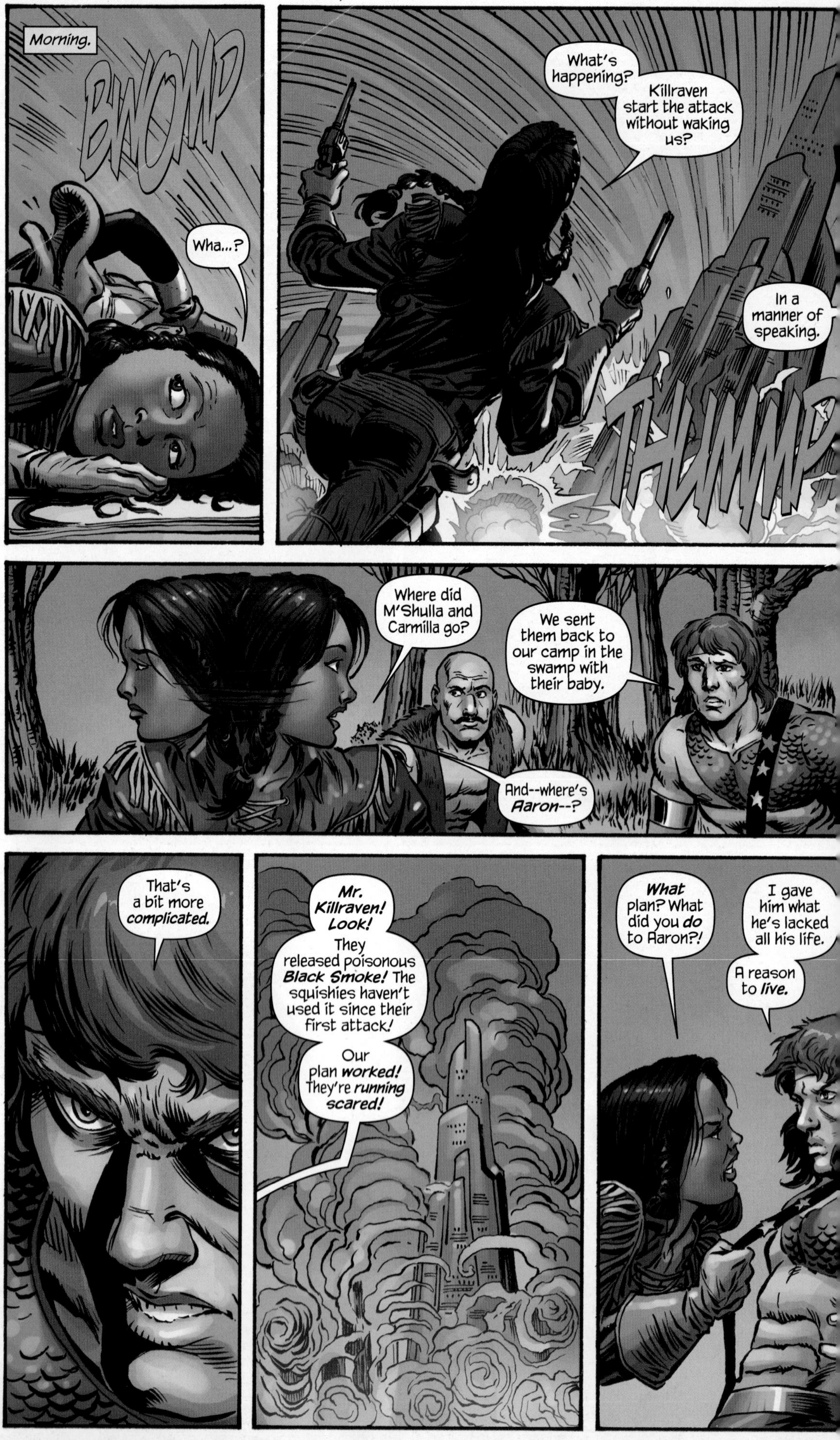
Morning.
BWOMP
Wha...?
What's happening?
Killraven start the attack without waking us?
In a manner of speaking.
THUMMP
Where did M'Shulla and Carmilla go?
We sent them back to our camp in the swamp with their baby.
And--where's *Aaron*--?
That's a bit more *complicated.*
Mr. Killraven! Look!
They released poisonous *Black Smoke!* The squishies haven't used it since their first attack!
Our plan *worked!* They're *running scared!*
What plan? What did you *do* to Aaron?!
I gave him what he's lacked all his life.
A reason to *live.*

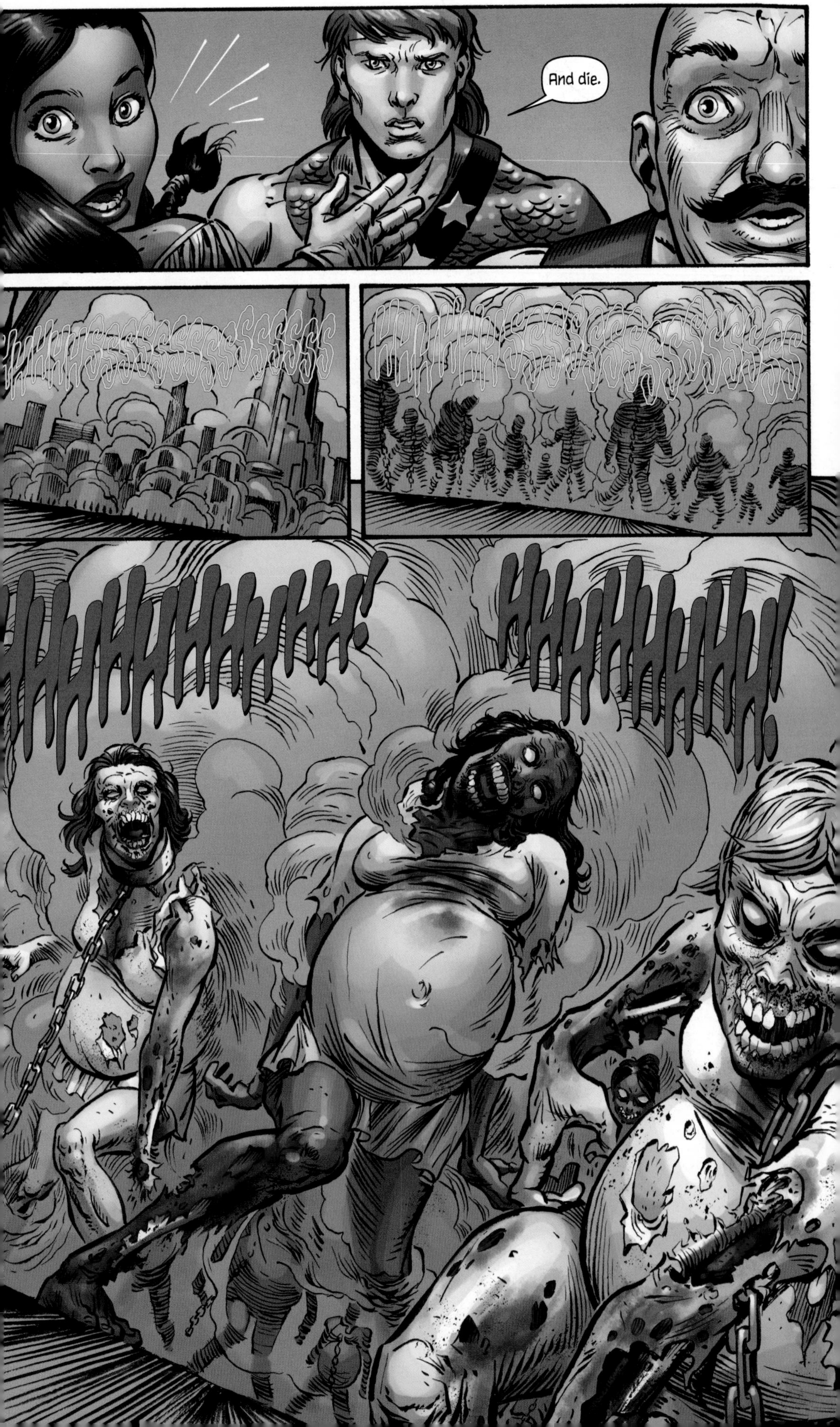
And die.

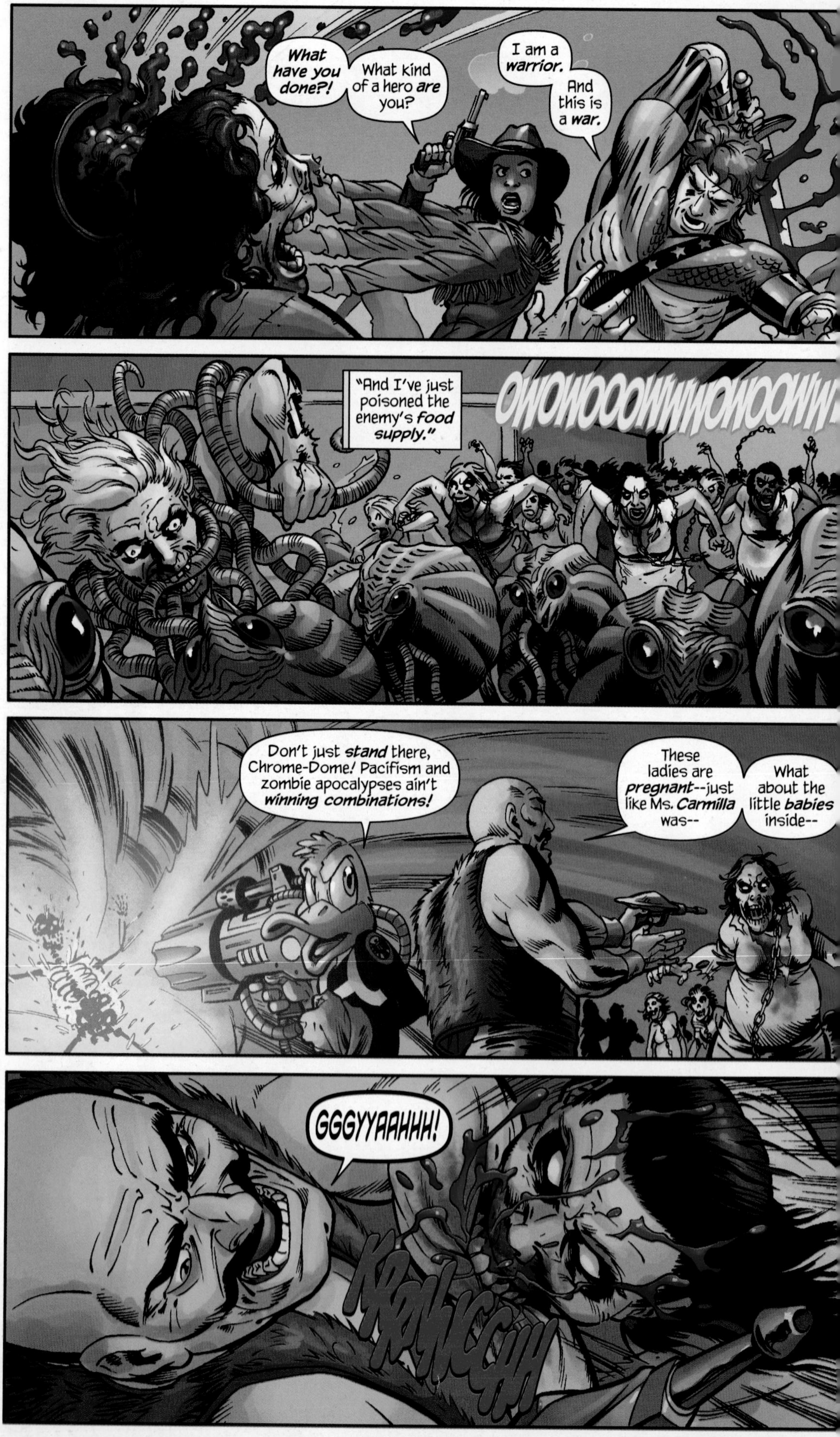

What have you done?!
What kind of a hero are you?
I am a warrior.
And this is a war.
"And I've just poisoned the enemy's food supply."
OWOWOOOWWWOWOOWW
Don't just stand there, Chrome-Dome! Pacifism and zombie apocalypses ain't winning combinations!
These ladies are pregnant--just like Ms. Carmilla was--
What about the little babies inside--
GGGYYAAHHH!
KRUNCGH

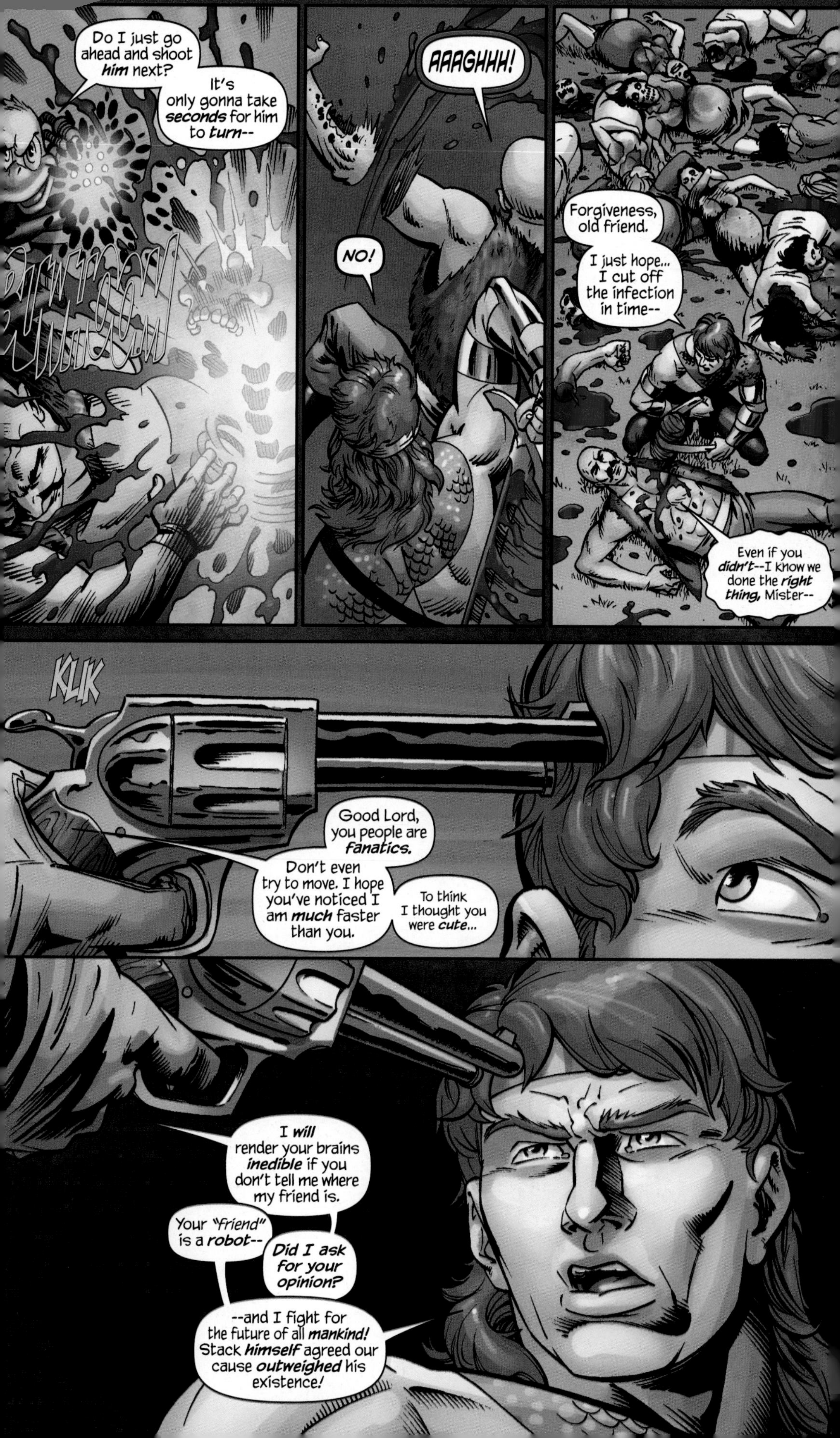

Do I just go ahead and shoot *him* next?
It's only gonna take *seconds* for him to *turn*--
AAAGHHH!
NO!
Forgiveness, old friend.
I just hope... I cut off the infection in time--
Even if you *didn't*--I know we done the *right thing,* Mister--
KLIK
Good Lord, you people are *fanatics.*
Don't even try to move. I hope you've noticed I am *much* faster than you.
To think I thought you were *cute*...
I *will* render your brains *inedible* if you don't tell me where my friend is.
Your "*friend*" is a *robot*--
Did I ask for your opinion?
--and I fight for the future of all *mankind!* Stack *himself* agreed our cause *outweighed* his existence!

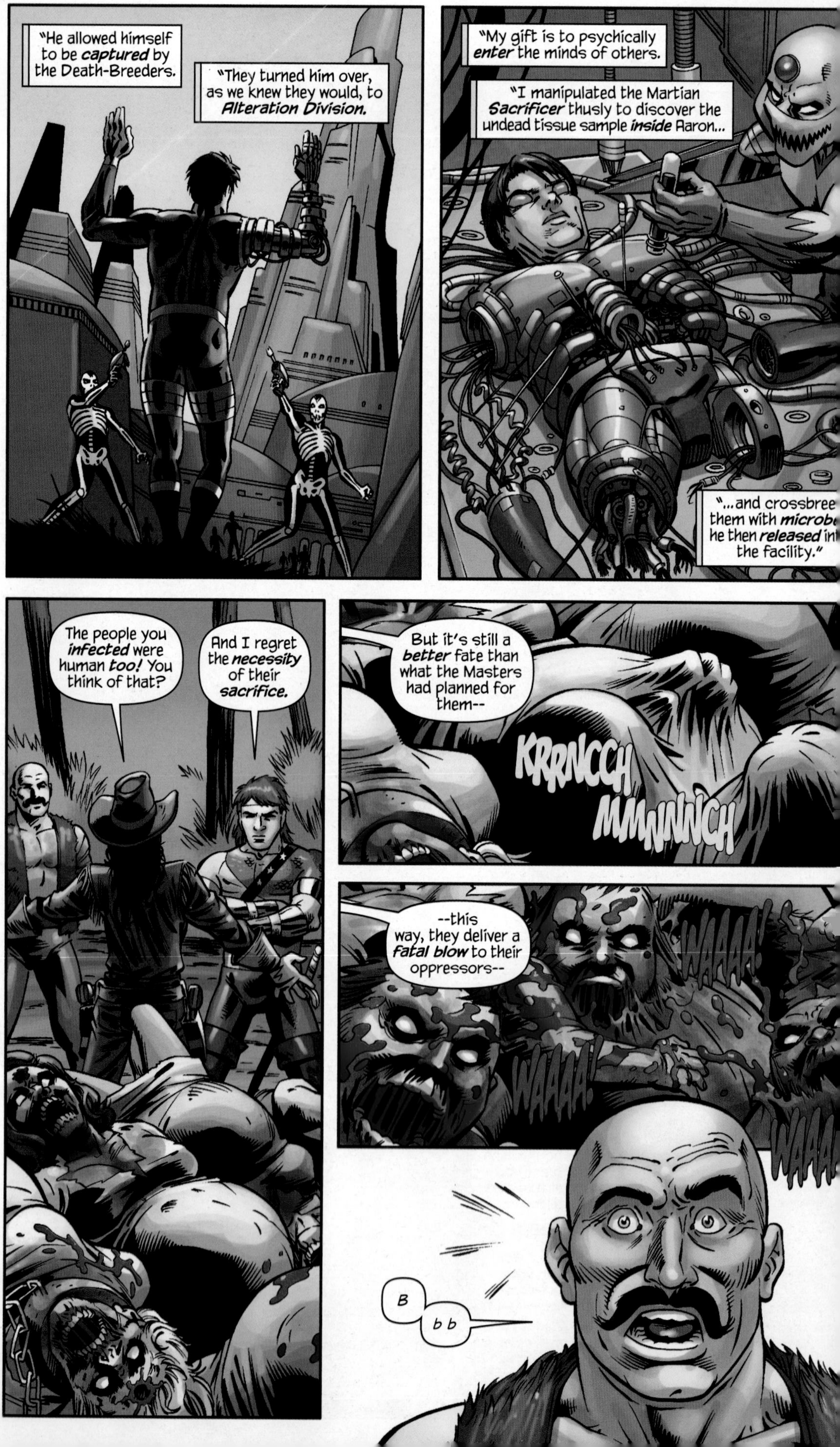
"He allowed himself to be *captured* by the Death-Breeders.
"They turned him over, as we knew they would, to ***Alteration Division.***
"My gift is to psychically *enter* the minds of others.
"I manipulated the Martian *Sacrificer* thusly to discover the undead tissue sample *inside* Aaron...
"...and crossbree them with *microb* he then *released* in the facility."
The people you *infected* were human *too!* You think of that?
And I regret the *necessity* of their *sacrifice.*
But it's still a *better* fate than what the Masters had planned for them--
KRRNCCH
MMNNNCH
--this way, they deliver a *fatal blow* to their oppressors--
WAAAA!
WAAAA!
WAAAA
B
b b

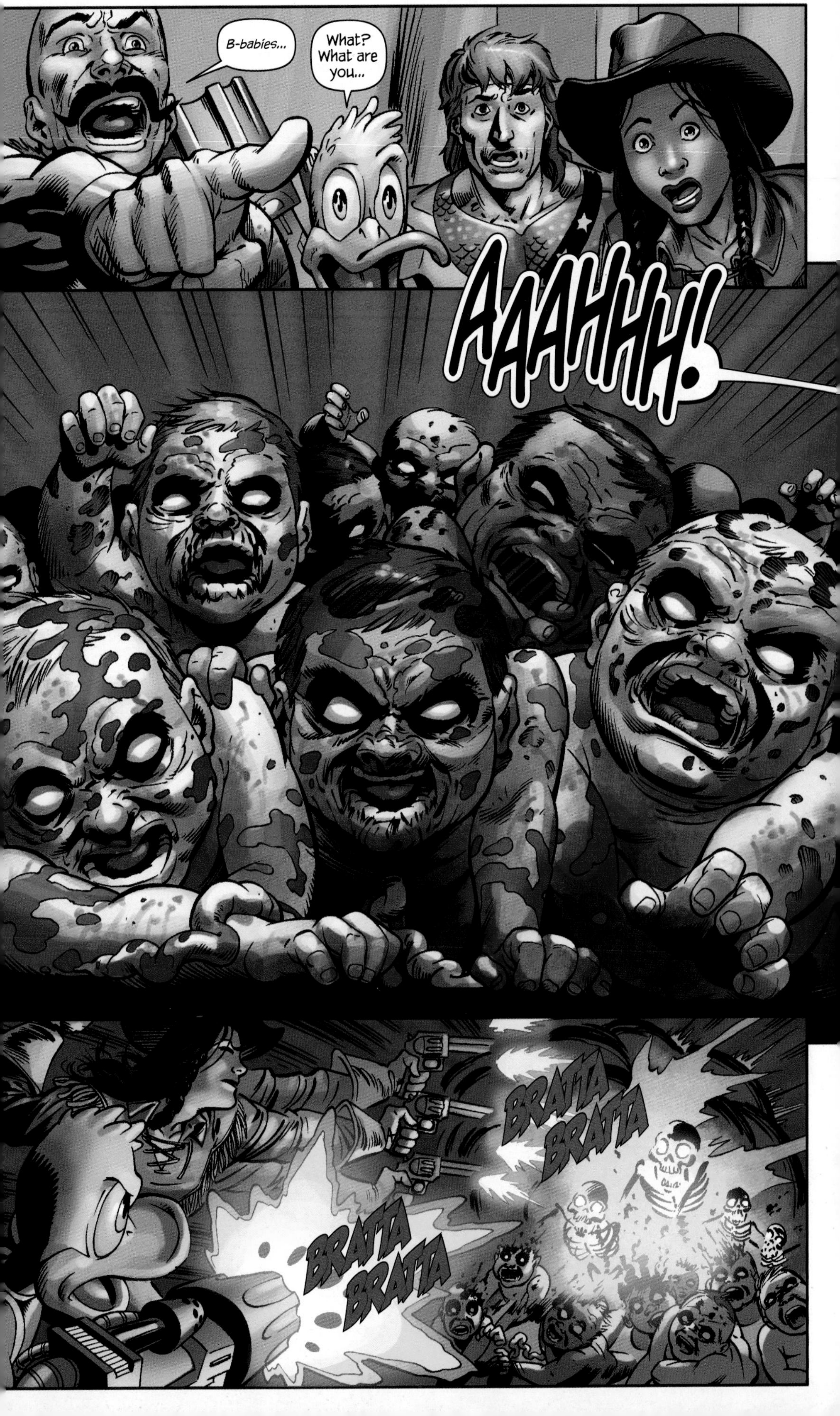

B-babies...
What? What are you...
AAAHHH!
BRATTA BRATTA
BRATTA BRATTA

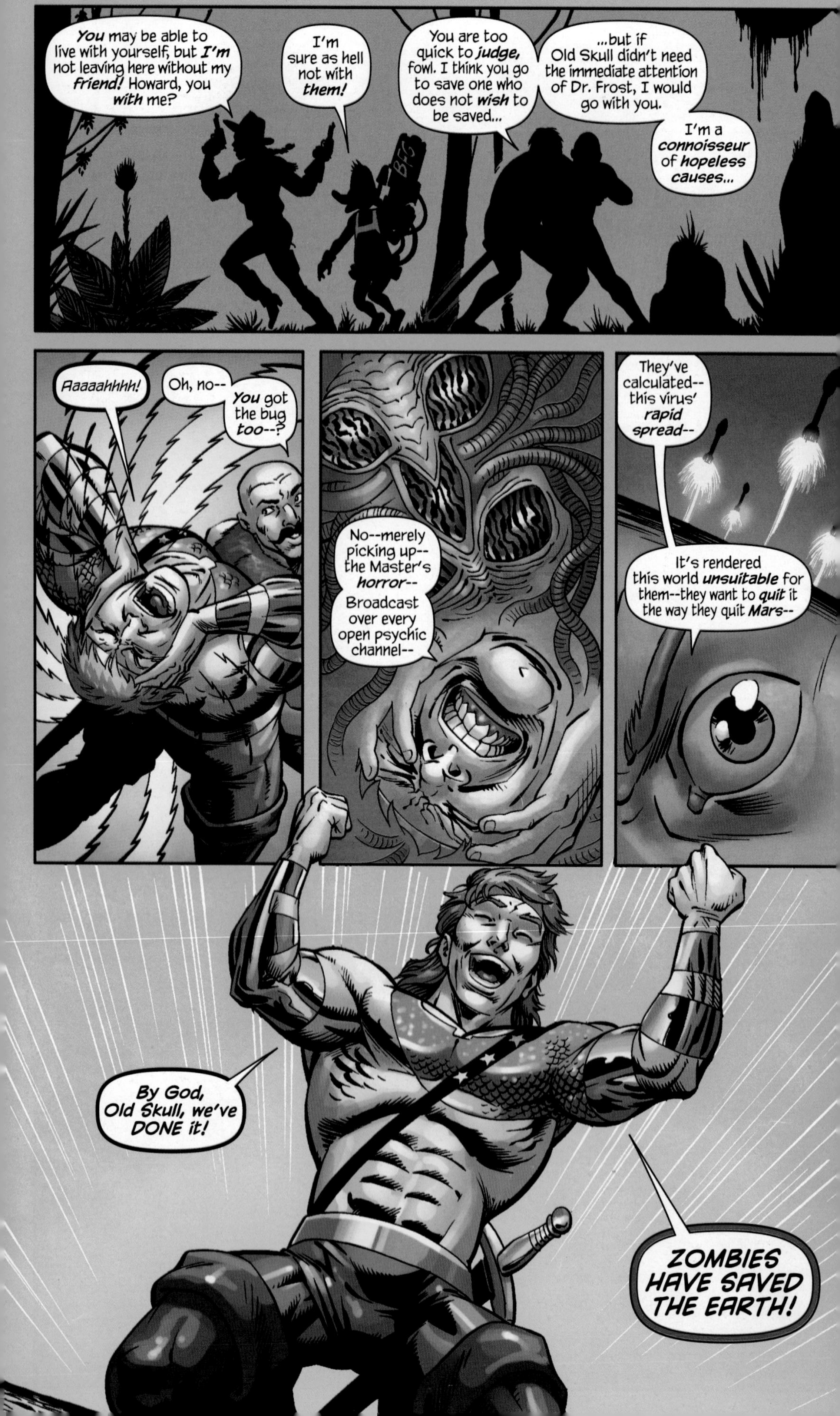
You may be able to live with yourself, but I'm not leaving here without my friend! Howard, you with me?
I'm sure as hell not with them!
You are too quick to judge, fowl. I think you go to save one who does not wish to be saved...
...but if Old Skull didn't need the immediate attention of Dr. Frost, I would go with you.
I'm a connoisseur of hopeless causes...
BFG
Aaaaahhhh!
Oh, no--
You got the bug too--?
No--merely picking up-- the Master's horror--
Broadcast over every open psychic channel--
They've calculated-- this virus' rapid spread--
It's rendered this world unsuitable for them--they want to quit it the way they quit Mars--
By God, Old Skull, we've DONE it!
ZOMBIES HAVE SAVED THE EARTH!

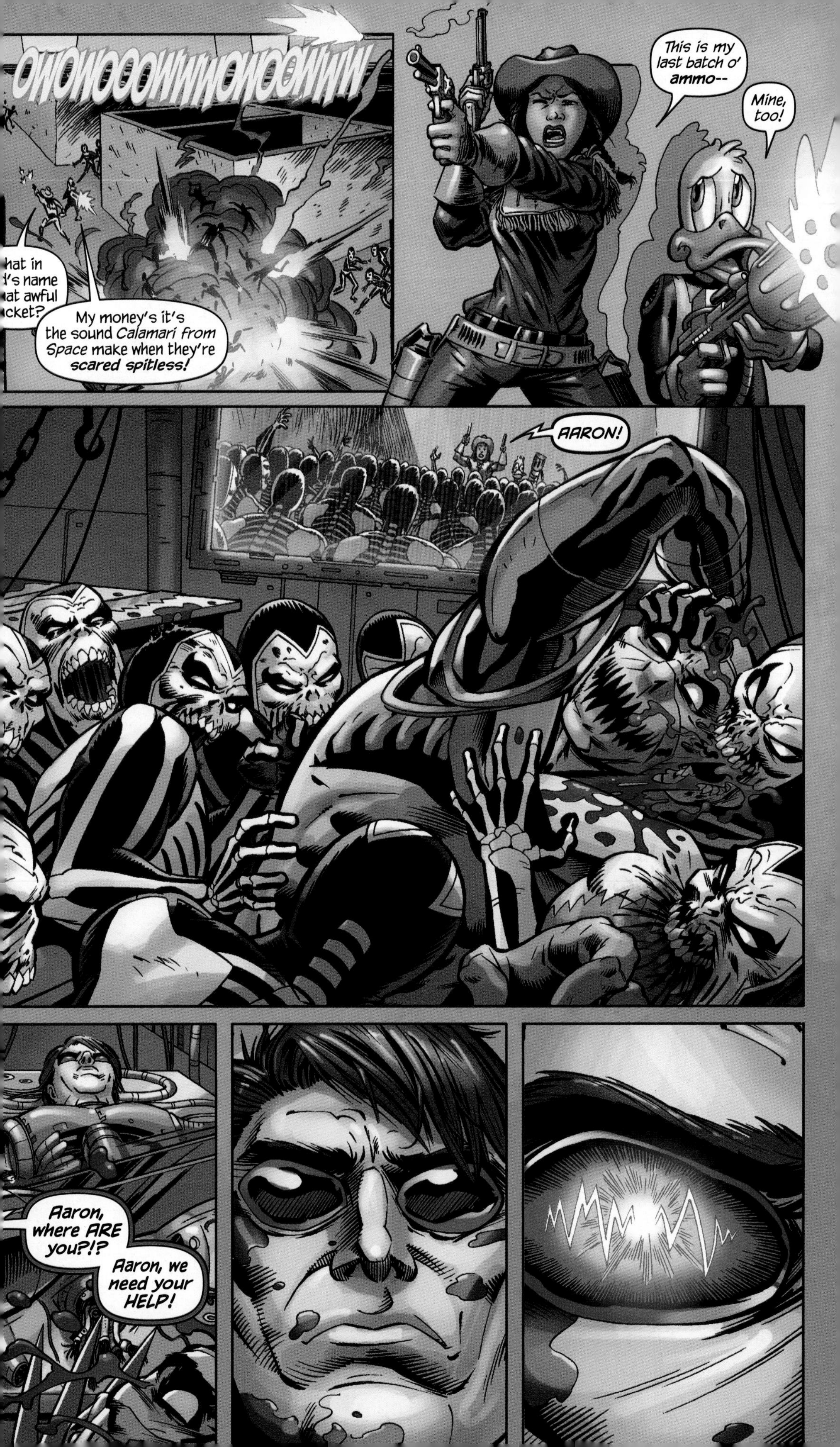
OWOWOOOWWWOWOOWWW
hat in
l's name
at awful
cket?
My money's it's the sound *Calamari from Space* make when they're **scared spitless!**
This is my last batch o' **ammo--**
Mine, too!
AARON!
Aaron, where ARE you?!?
Aaron, we need your HELP!

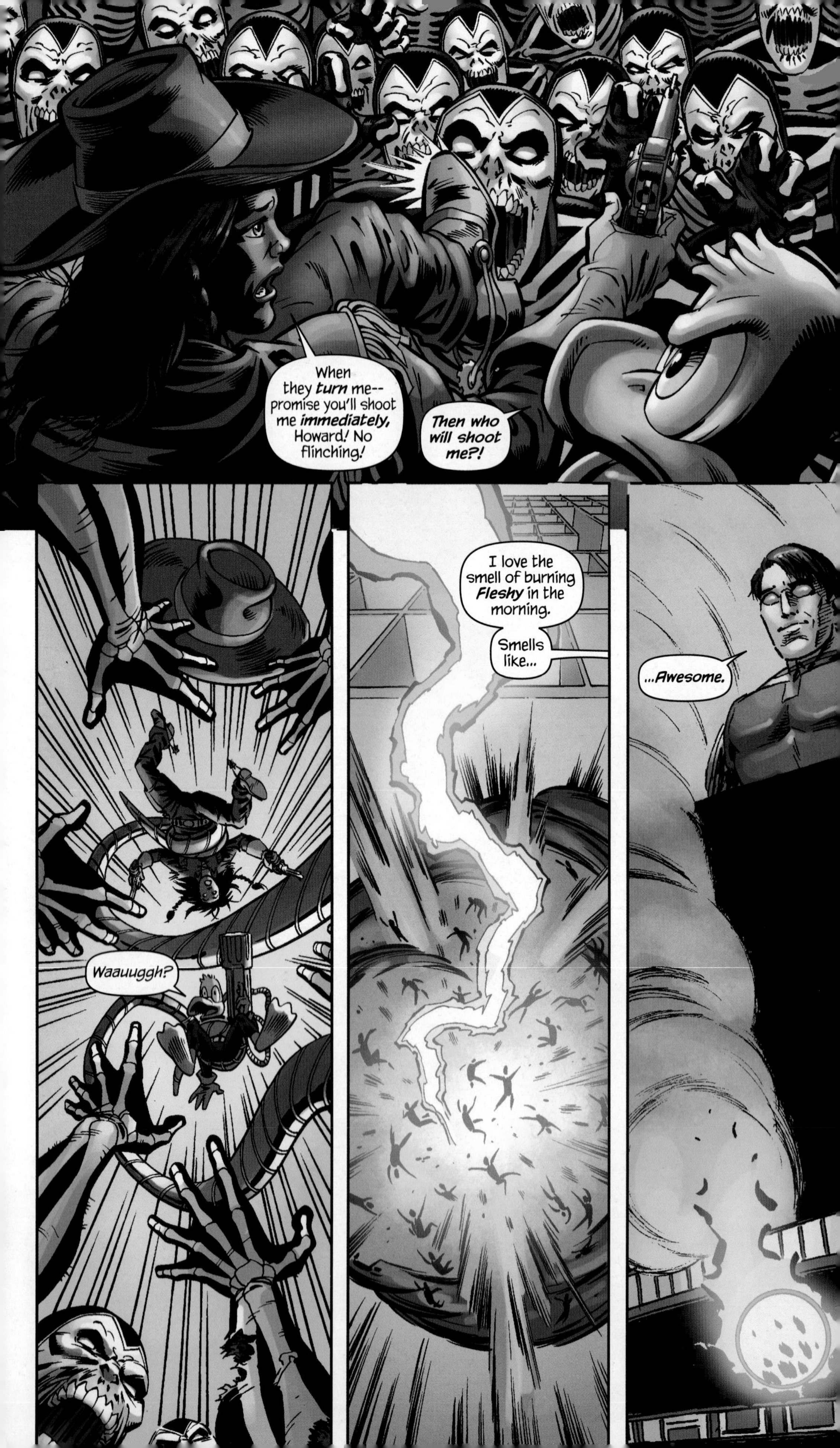
When they *turn* me-- promise you'll shoot me *immediately,* Howard! No flinching!
Then who will shoot me?!
Waauuggh?
I love the smell of burning *Fleshy* in the morning.
Smells like...
...*Awesome.*

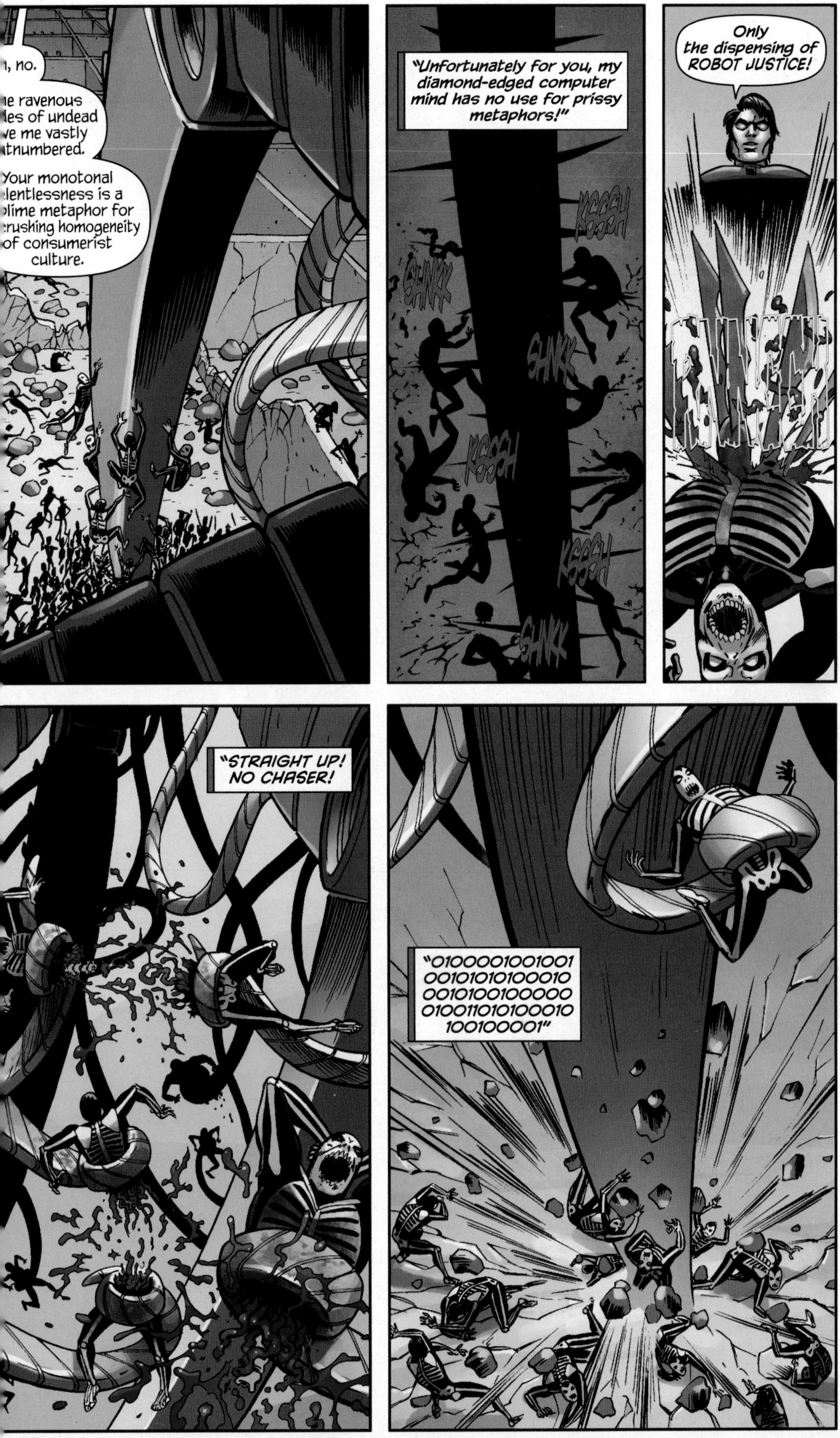

, no.
e ravenous
les of undead
ve me vastly
tnumbered.
Your monotonal
lentlessness is a
lime metaphor for
rushing homogeneity
of consumerist
culture.
"Unfortunately for you, my diamond-edged computer mind has no use for prissy metaphors!"
KSSSH
SHNKK
SHNKK
KSSSH
KSSSH
SHNKK
Only the dispensing of ROBOT JUSTICE!
"STRAIGHT UP! NO CHASER!
"0100001001001 0010101010001O 0010100100000 0100110101000010 100100001"

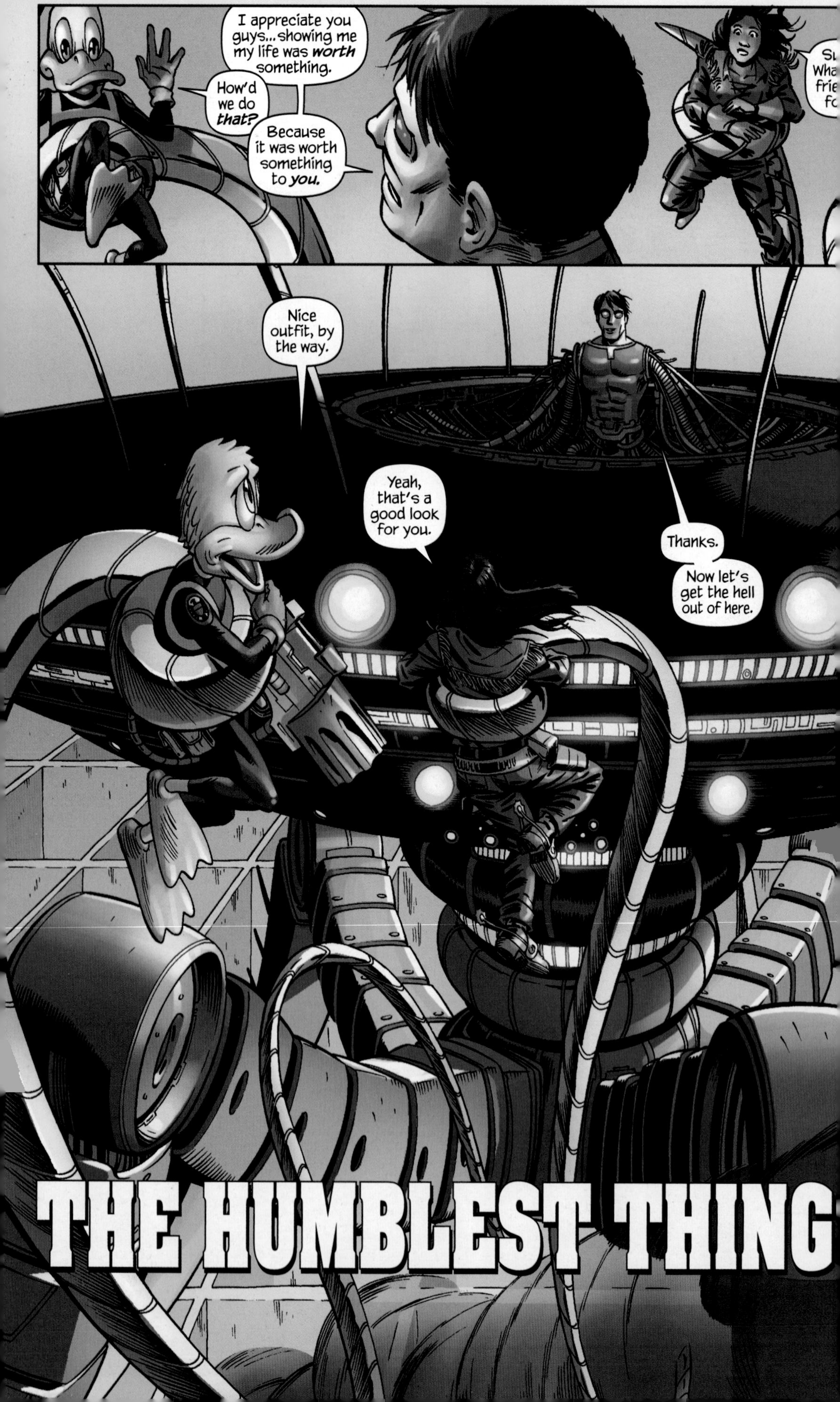
I appreciate you guys...showing me my life was *worth* something.
How'd we do *that?*
Because it was worth something to *you.*
Nice outfit, by the way.
Yeah, that's a good look for you.
Thanks.
Now let's get the hell out of here.
THE HUMBLEST THING

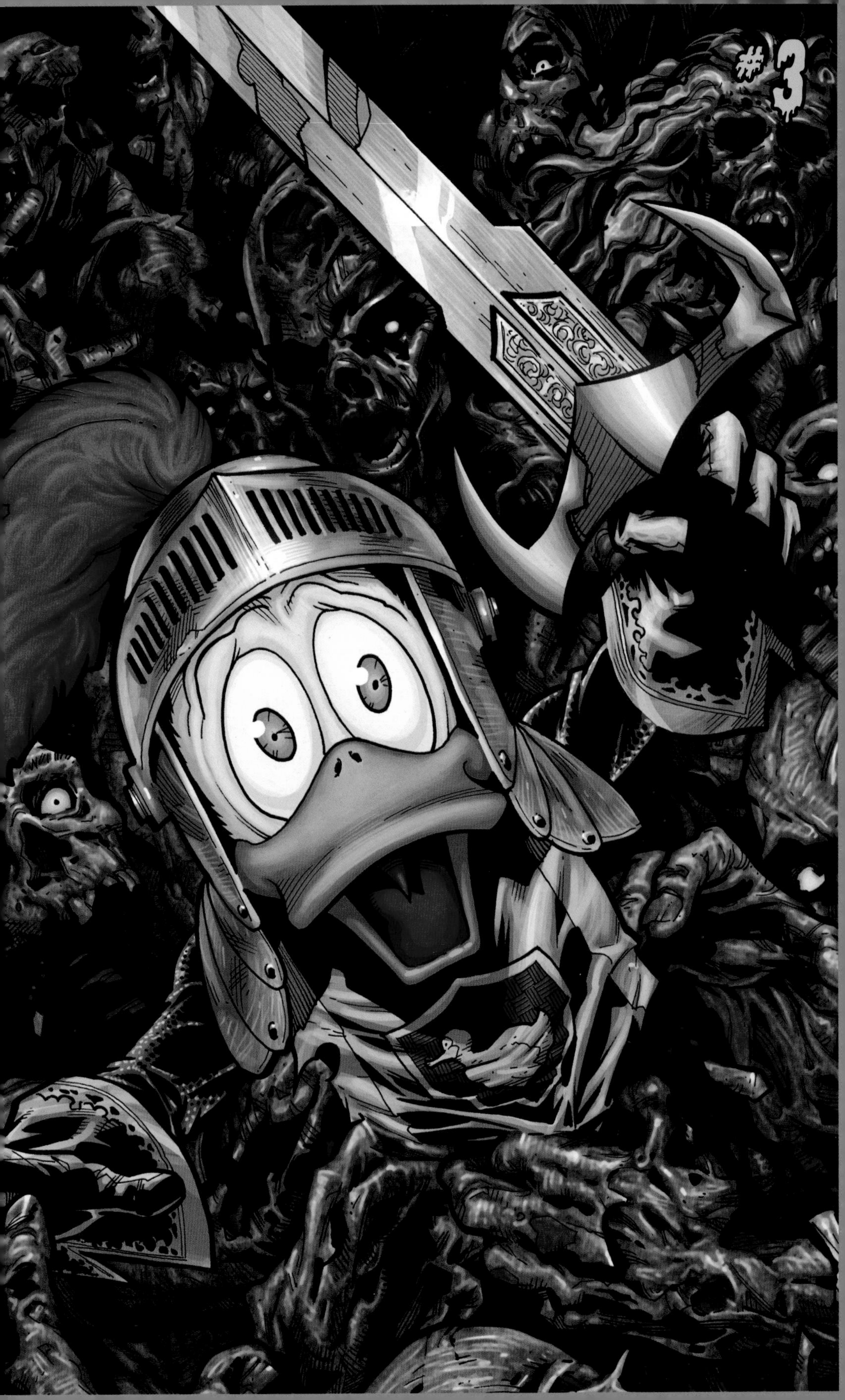
#3

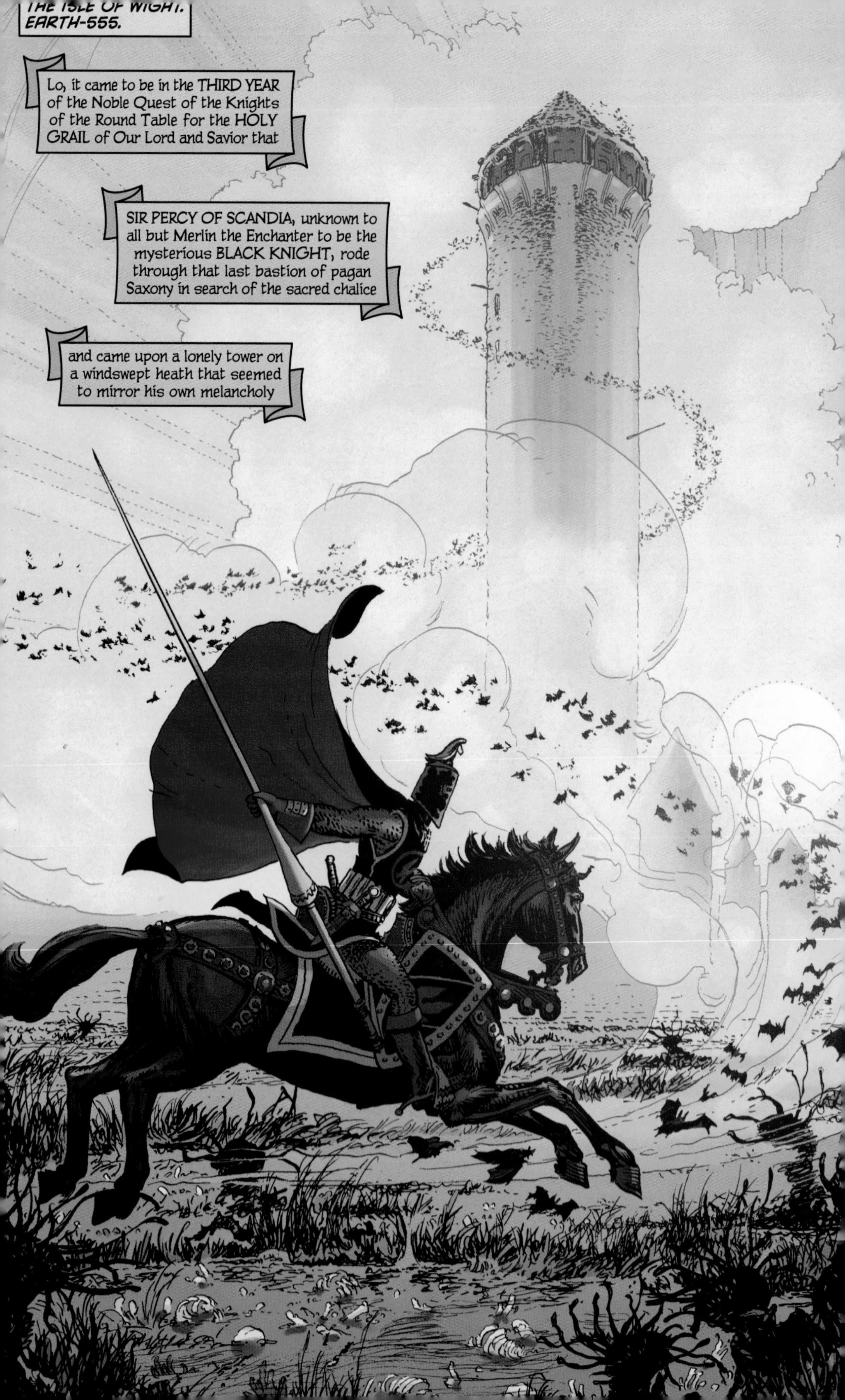
THE ISLE OF WIGHT. EARTH-555.
Lo, it came to be in the THIRD YEAR of the Noble Quest of the Knights of the Round Table for the HOLY GRAIL of Our Lord and Savior that
SIR PERCY OF SCANDIA, unknown to all but Merlin the Enchanter to be the mysterious BLACK KNIGHT, rode through that last bastion of pagan Saxony in search of the sacred chalice
and came upon a lonely tower on a windswept heath that seemed to mirror his own melancholy

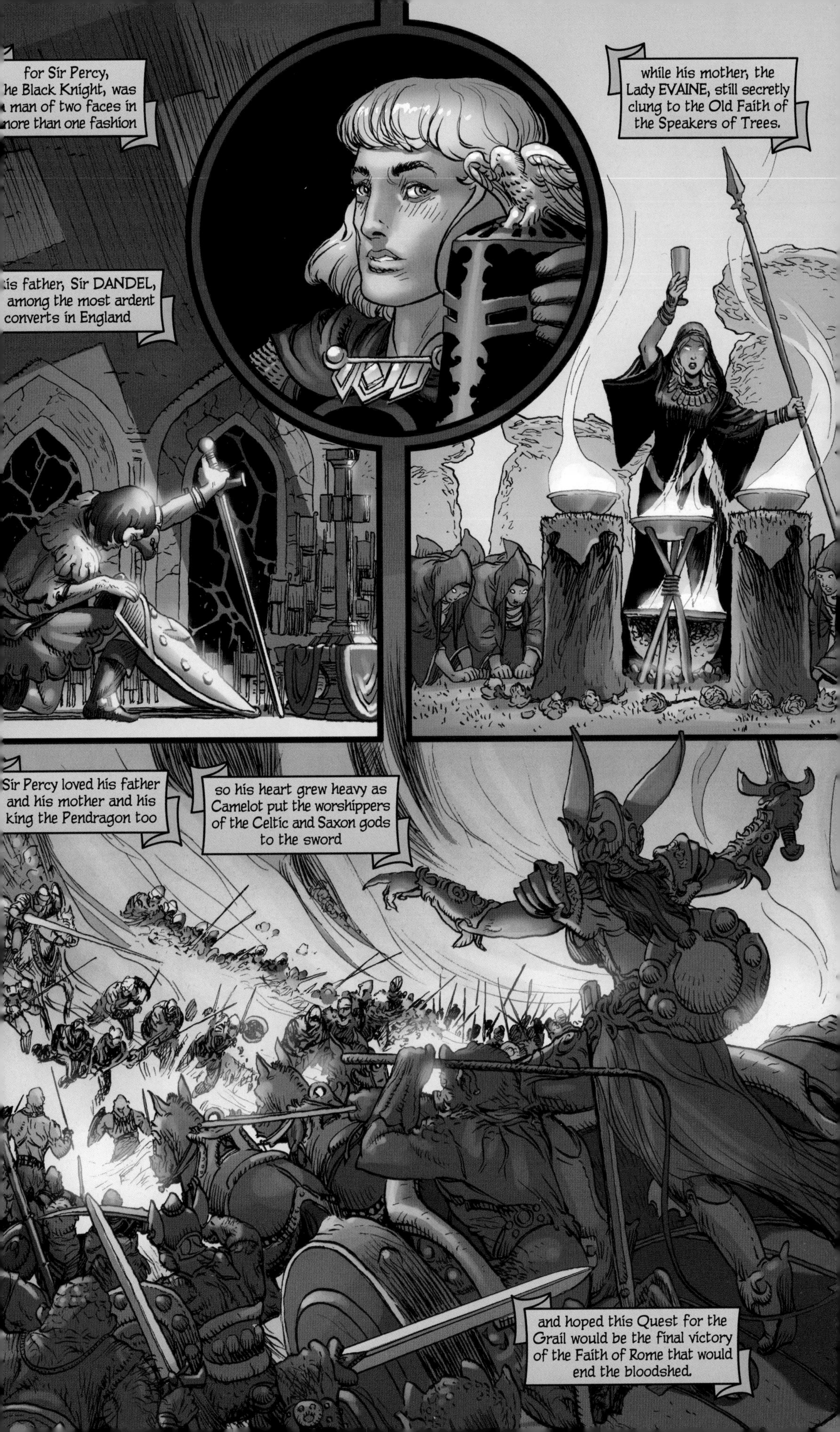
for Sir Percy, he Black Knight, was a man of two faces in more than one fashion
while his mother, the Lady EVAINE, still secretly clung to the Old Faith of the Speakers of Trees.
is father, Sir DANDEL, among the most ardent converts in England
Sir Percy loved his father and his mother and his king the Pendragon too
so his heart grew heavy as Camelot put the worshippers of the Celtic and Saxon gods to the sword
and hoped this Quest for the Grail would be the final victory of the Faith of Rome that would end the bloodshed.

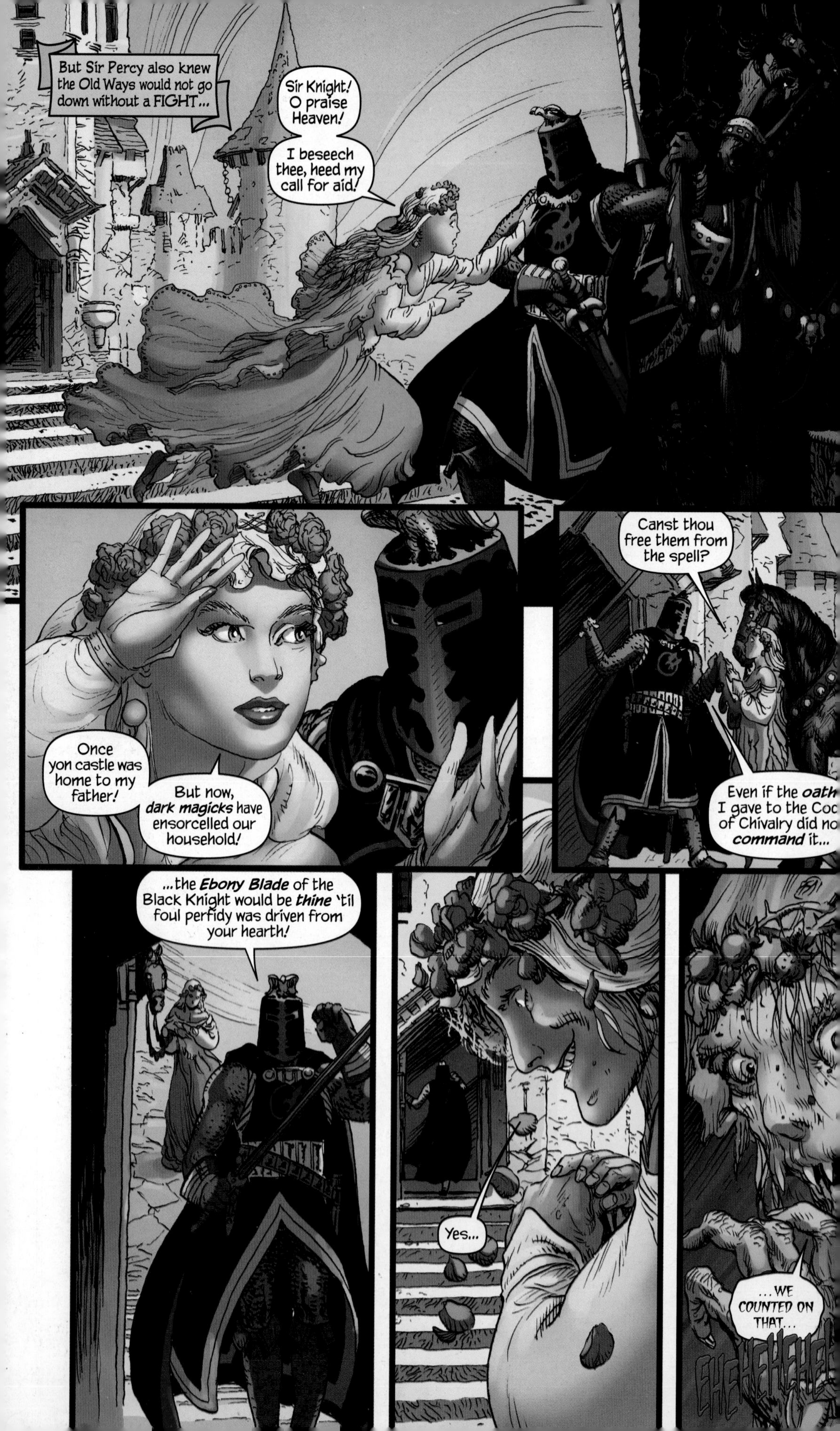
But Sir Percy also knew the Old Ways would not go down without a FIGHT...
Sir Knight! O praise Heaven!
I beseech thee, heed my call for aid!
Once yon castle was home to my father!
But now, *dark magicks* have ensorcelled our household!
Canst thou free them from the spell?
Even if the *oath* I gave to the Coc of Chivalry did no *command* it...
...the *Ebony Blade* of the Black Knight would be *thine* 'til foul perfidy was driven from your hearth!
Yes...
...WE COUNTED ON THAT...

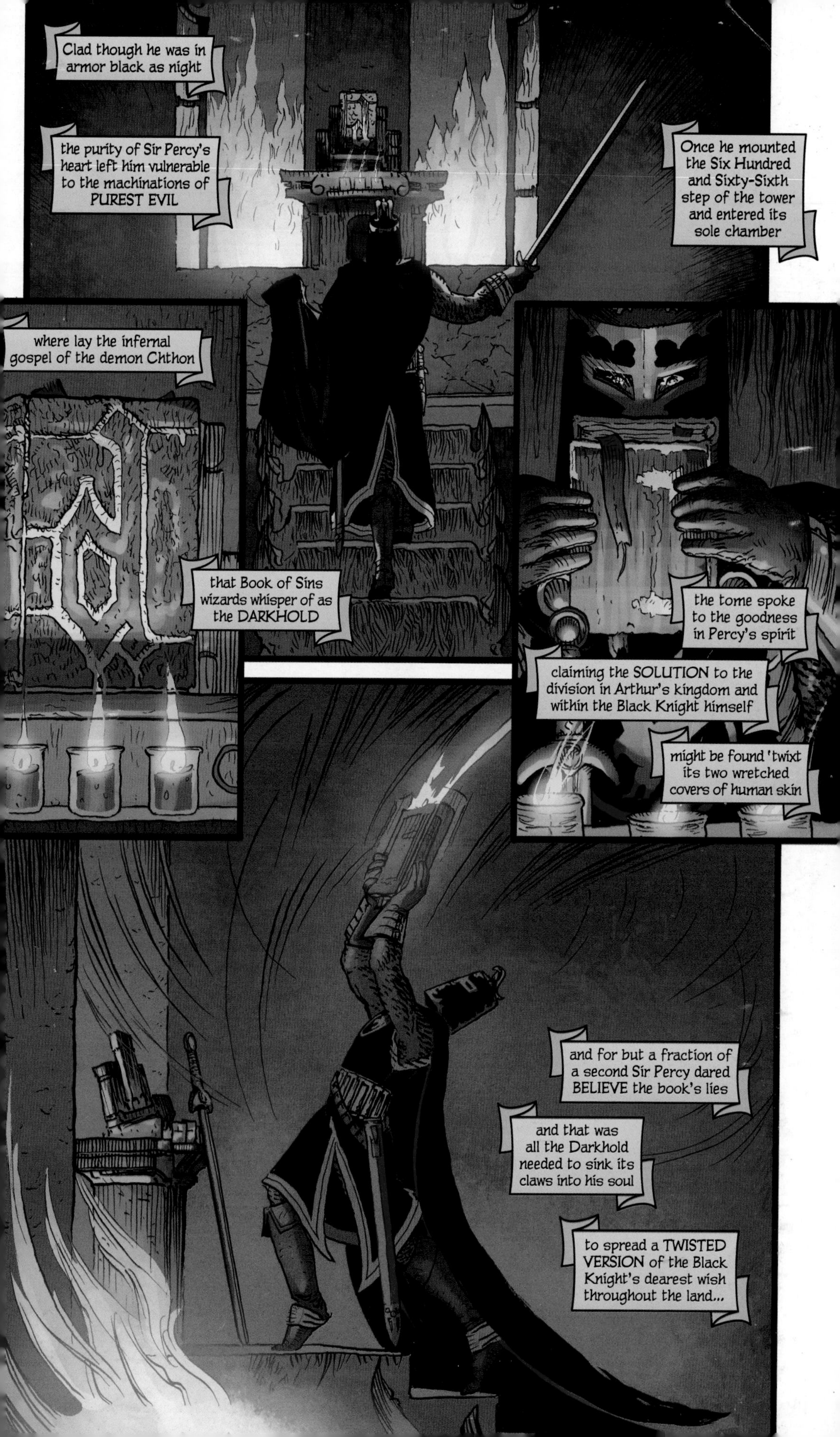
Clad though he was in armor black as night
the purity of Sir Percy's heart left him vulnerable to the machinations of PUREST EVIL
Once he mounted the Six Hundred and Sixty-Sixth step of the tower and entered its sole chamber
where lay the infernal gospel of the demon Chthon
that Book of Sins wizards whisper of as the DARKHOLD
the tome spoke to the goodness in Percy's spirit
claiming the SOLUTION to the division in Arthur's kingdom and within the Black Knight himself
might be found 'twixt its two wretched covers of human skin
and for but a fraction of a second Sir Percy dared BELIEVE the book's lies
and that was all the Darkhold needed to sink its claws into his soul
to spread a TWISTED VERSION of the Black Knight's dearest wish throughout the land...

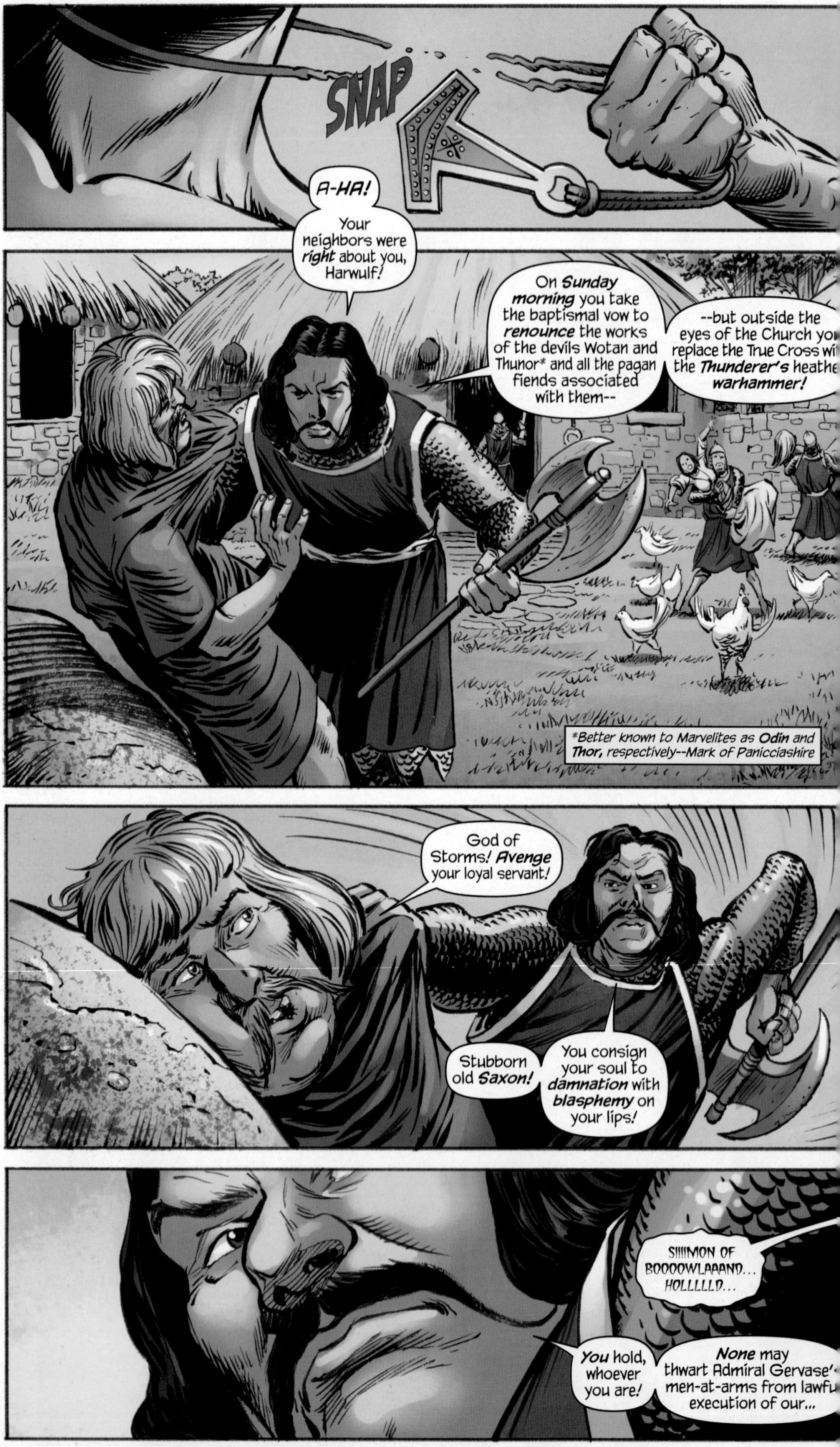
SNAP
A-HA!
Your neighbors were right about you, Harwulf!
On Sunday morning you take the baptismal vow to renounce the works of the devils Wotan and Thunor* and all the pagan fiends associated with them--
--but outside the eyes of the Church you replace the True Cross wi the Thunderer's heathe warhammer!
*Better known to Marvelites as Odin and Thor, respectively--Mark of Panicciashire
God of Storms! Avenge your loyal servant!
Stubborn old Saxon!
You consign your soul to damnation with blasphemy on your lips!
SIIIIMON OF BOOOOWLAAAND... HOLLLLLD...
You hold, whoever you are!
None may thwart Admiral Gervase' men-at-arms from lawfu execution of our...

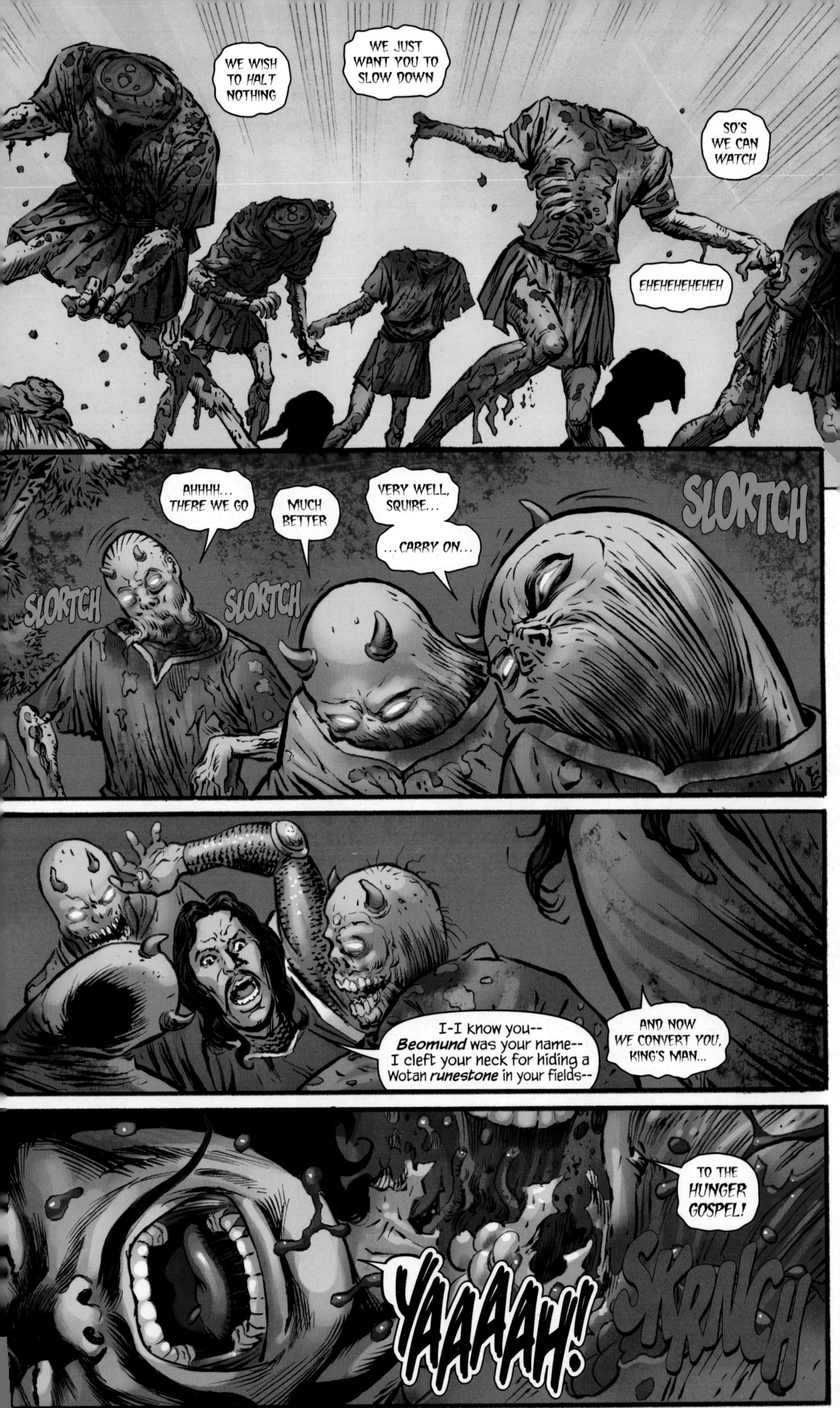
WE WISH TO HALT NOTHING
WE JUST WANT YOU TO SLOW DOWN
SO'S WE CAN WATCH
EHEHEHEHEHEH
AHHHH... THERE WE GO
MUCH BETTER
VERY WELL, SQUIRE...
...CARRY ON...
SLORTCH
SLORTCH
SLORTCH
I-I know you-- *Beomund* was your name-- I cleft your neck for hiding a Wotan *runestone* in your fields--
AND NOW WE CONVERT YOU, KING'S MAN...
TO THE HUNGER GOSPEL!
YAAAAH!
SKRNCH

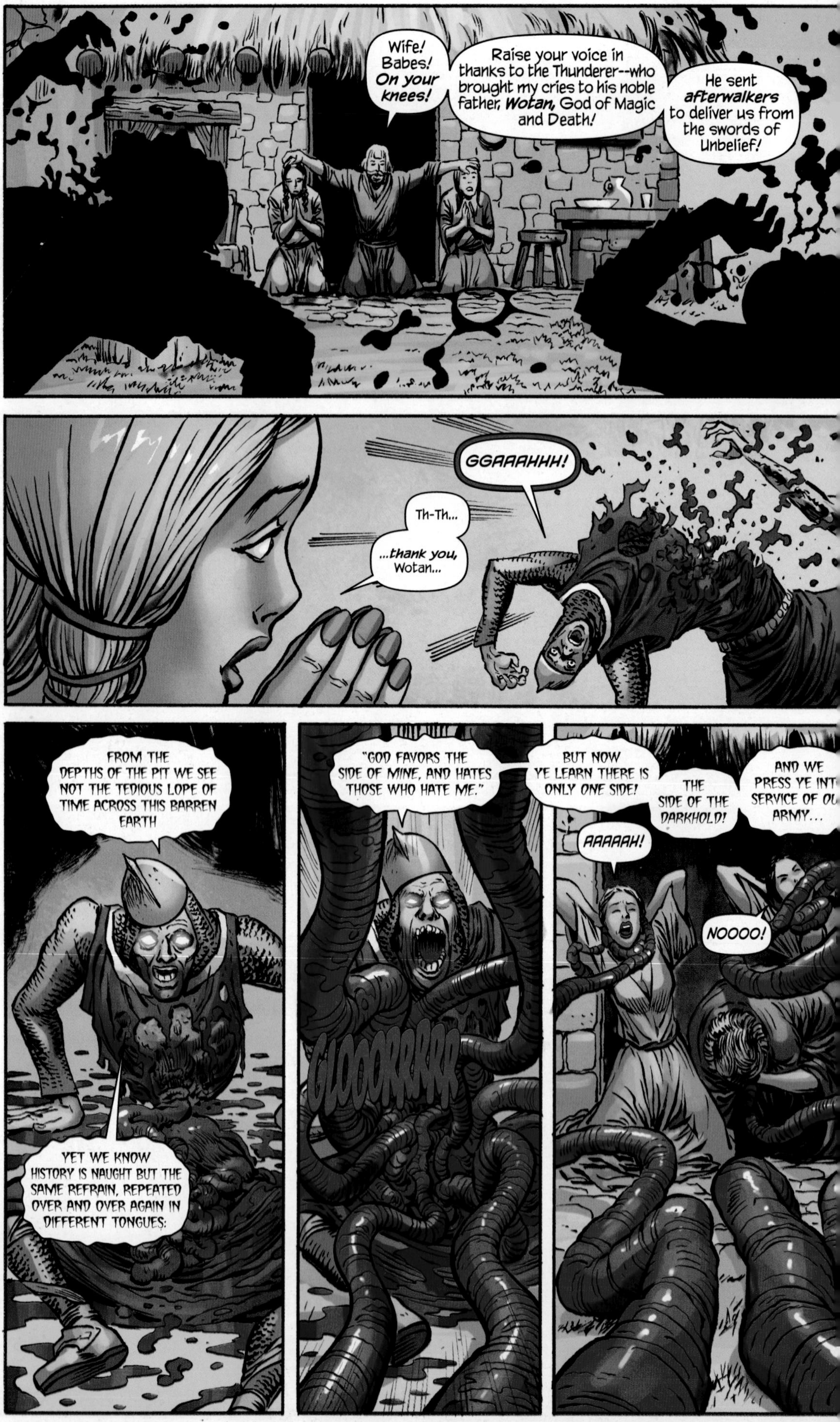
Wife! Babes! On your knees!
Raise your voice in thanks to the Thunderer--who brought my cries to his noble father, Wotan, God of Magic and Death!
He sent afterwalkers to deliver us from the swords of Unbelief!
GGAAAAHHH!
Th-Th...
...thank you, Wotan...
FROM THE DEPTHS OF THE PIT WE SEE NOT THE TEDIOUS LOPE OF TIME ACROSS THIS BARREN EARTH
YET WE KNOW HISTORY IS NAUGHT BUT THE SAME REFRAIN, REPEATED OVER AND OVER AGAIN IN DIFFERENT TONGUES:
"GOD FAVORS THE SIDE OF MINE, AND HATES THOSE WHO HATE ME."
GLOOORRRRR
BUT NOW YE LEARN THERE IS ONLY ONE SIDE!
THE SIDE OF THE DARKHOLD!
AND WE PRESS YE INT SERVICE OF OU ARMY...
AAAAAH!
NOOOO!

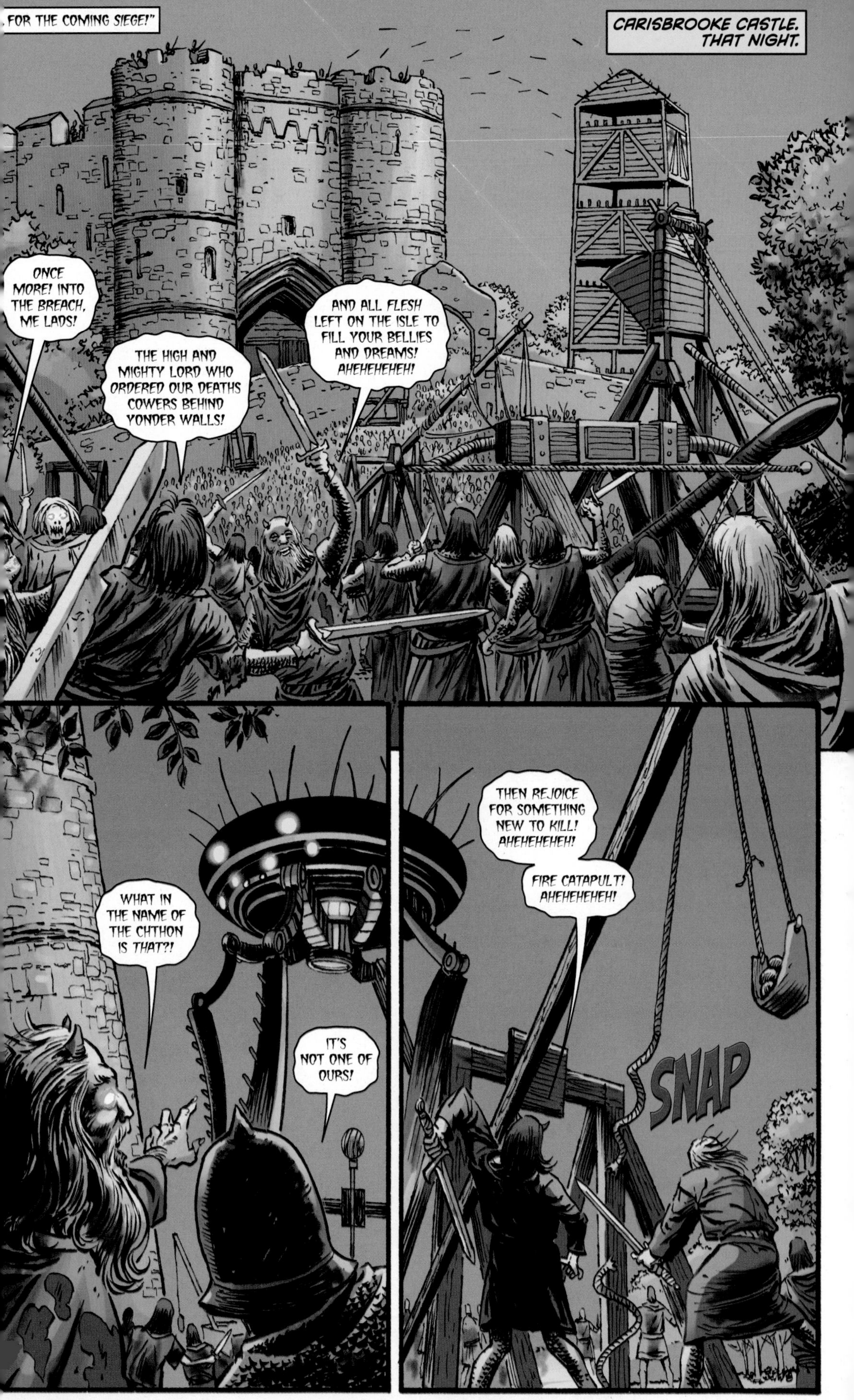

...FOR THE COMING SIEGE!"
CARISBROOKE CASTLE. THAT NIGHT.
ONCE MORE! INTO THE BREACH, ME LADS!
THE HIGH AND MIGHTY LORD WHO ORDERED OUR DEATHS COWERS BEHIND YONDER WALLS!
AND ALL FLESH LEFT ON THE ISLE TO FILL YOUR BELLIES AND DREAMS! AHEHEHEHEH!
WHAT IN THE NAME OF THE CHTHON IS THAT?!
IT'S NOT ONE OF OURS!
THEN REJOICE FOR SOMETHING NEW TO KILL! AHEHEHEHEH!
FIRE CATAPULT! AHEHEHEHEH!
SNAP

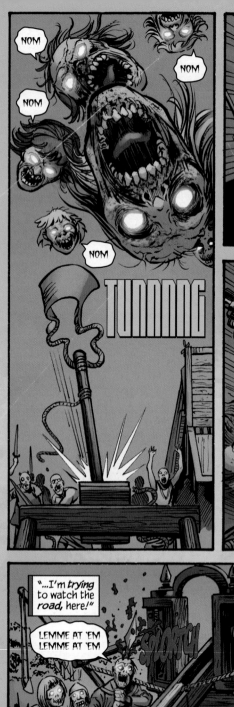

NOM

NOM

NOM

NOM

TUNNNG

NOM

NOM

NOM

NOM

"Let's *g* to that *ca* I see in distance she say

"It'll be a good place to *orient ourselves* to this *Alterniverse* before contin* with the *mission*," she sa*

Geez, alright, I was *wrong!* There, I said it!

You ever stop *complaining,* Howard?

YOU SEE ANY GOOD REASON TO?!

Eff.

Keep those thi* *offa m*

"...I'm *trying* to watch the *road,* here!"

LEMME AT 'EM LEMME AT 'EM

SPLORTCH

KLIK KLIK KLIK KLIK

Uh-oh.

There goes the last of the *ammo* we scraped up at that Martian base...

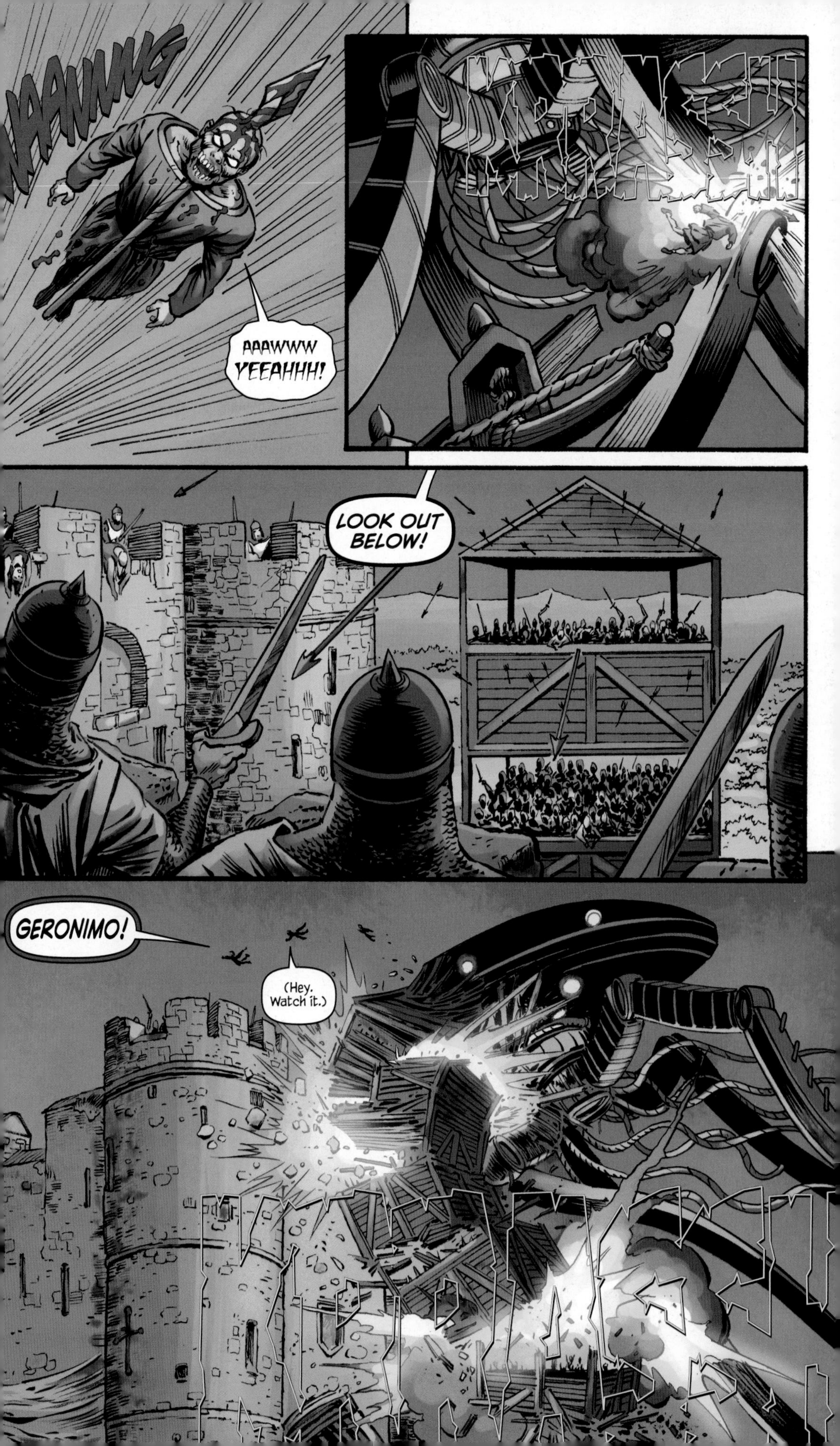
WAANNNG
AAAWWW YEEAHHH!
LOOK OUT BELOW!
GERONIMO!
(Hey. Watch it.)

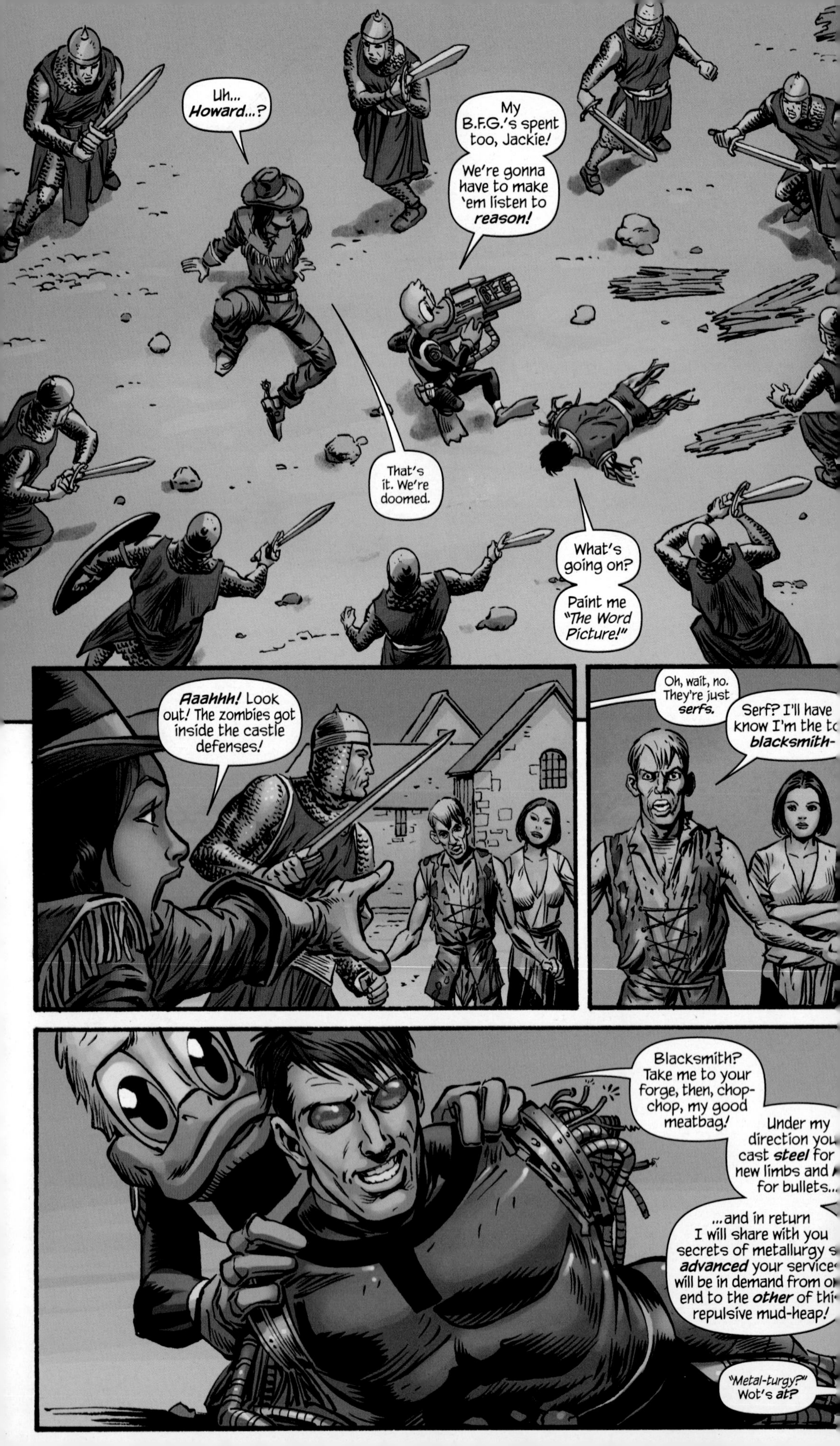
Uh... *Howard*...?
My B.F.G.'s spent too, Jackie!
We're gonna have to make 'em listen to ***reason!***
That's it. We're doomed.
What's going on?
Paint me *"The Word Picture!"*
Aaahhh! Look out! The zombies got inside the castle defenses!
Oh, wait, no. They're just ***serfs.***
Serf? I'll have know I'm the to ***blacksmith-***
Blacksmith? Take me to your forge, then, chop-chop, my good meatbag!
Under my direction you cast ***steel*** for new limbs and for bullets...
...and in return I will share with you secrets of metallurgy s ***advanced*** your service will be in demand from o end to the ***other*** of thi repulsive mud-heap!
"Metal-turgy?" Wot's ***at?***

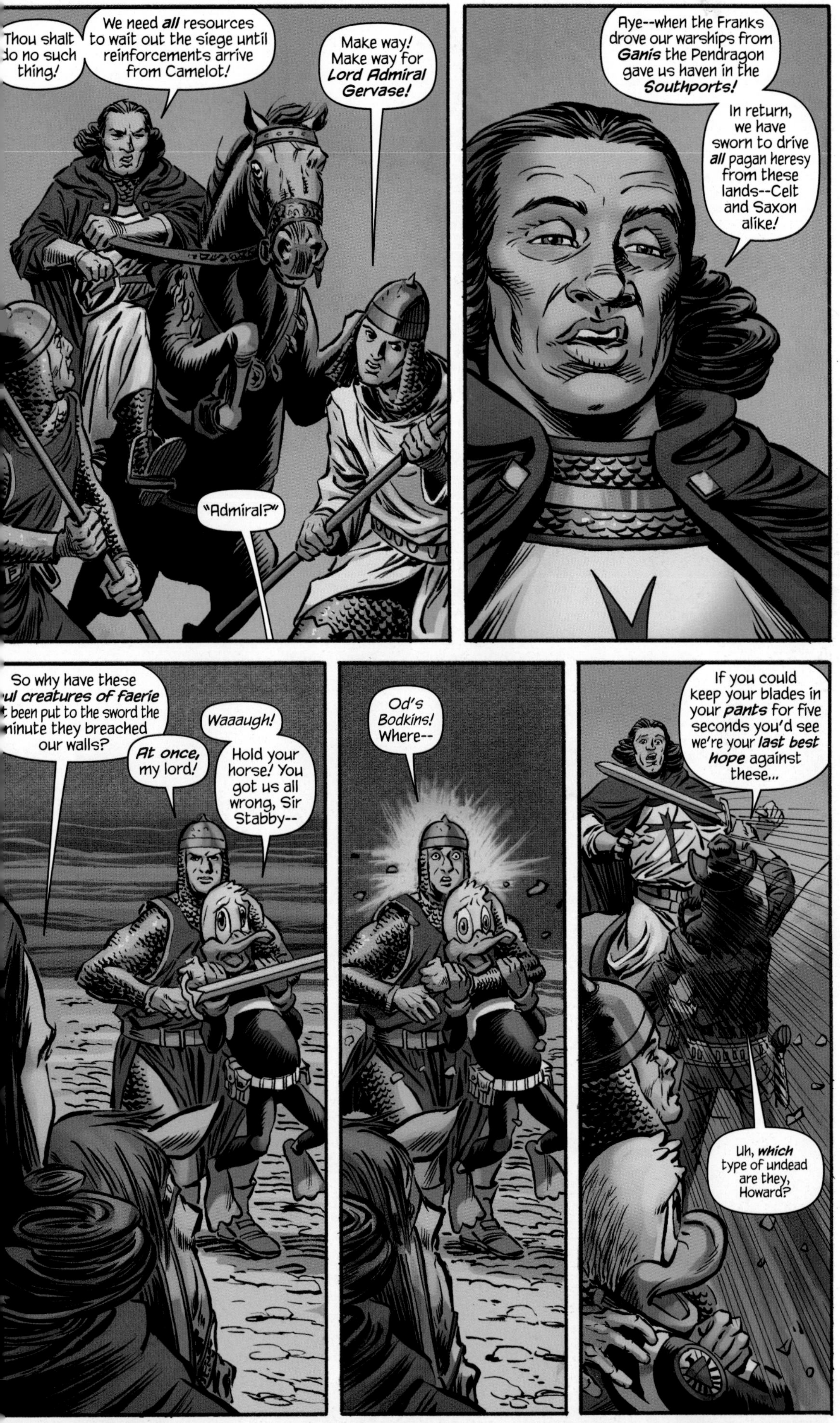

Thou shalt do no such thing!
We need **all** resources to wait out the siege until reinforcements arrive from Camelot!
Make way! Make way for **Lord Admiral Gervase!**
"Admiral?"
Aye--when the Franks drove our warships from **Ganis** the Pendragon gave us haven in the **Southports!**
In return, we have sworn to drive **all** pagan heresy from these lands--Celt and Saxon alike!
So why have these **ul creatures of faerie** t been put to the sword the minute they breached our walls?
At once, my lord!
Waaaugh!
Hold your horse! You got us all wrong, Sir Stabby--
Od's Bodkins! Where--
If you could keep your blades in your **pants** for five seconds you'd see we're your **last best hope** against these...
Uh, **which** type of undead are they, Howard?

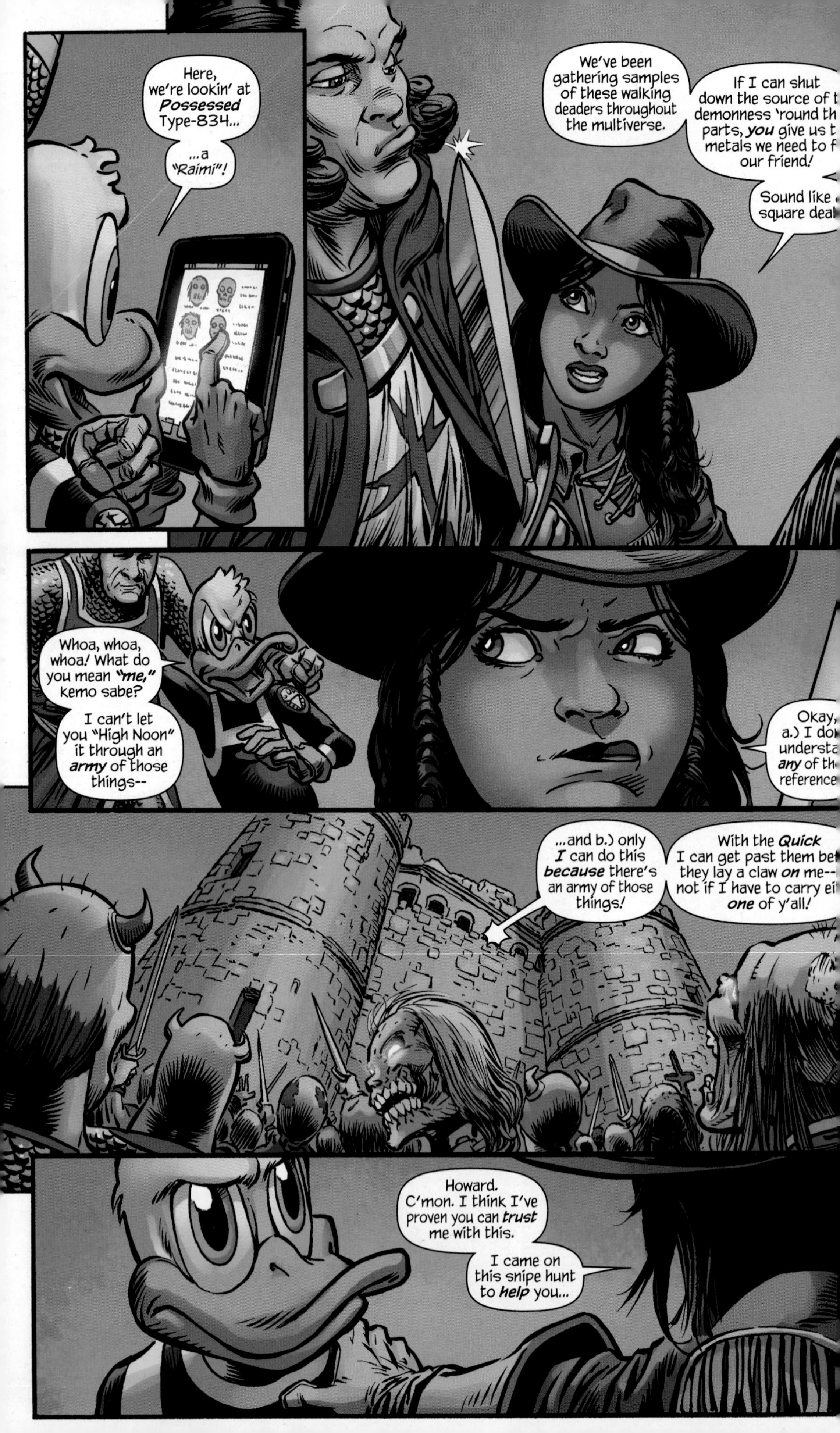
Here, we're lookin' at *Possessed* Type-834...
...a "*Raimi*"!
We've been gathering samples of these walking deaders throughout the multiverse.
If I can shut down the source of t demonness 'round th parts, *you* give us t metals we need to f our friend!
Sound like square deal
Whoa, whoa, whoa! What do you mean *"me,"* kemo sabe?
I can't let you "High Noon" it through an *army* of those things--
Okay, a.) I do understa *any* of th reference
...and b.) only *I* can do this *because* there's an army of those things!
With the *Quick* I can get past them be they lay a claw *on* me-- not if I have to carry ei *one* of y'all!
Howard. C'mon. I think I've proven you can *trust* me with this.
I came on this snipe hunt to *help* you...

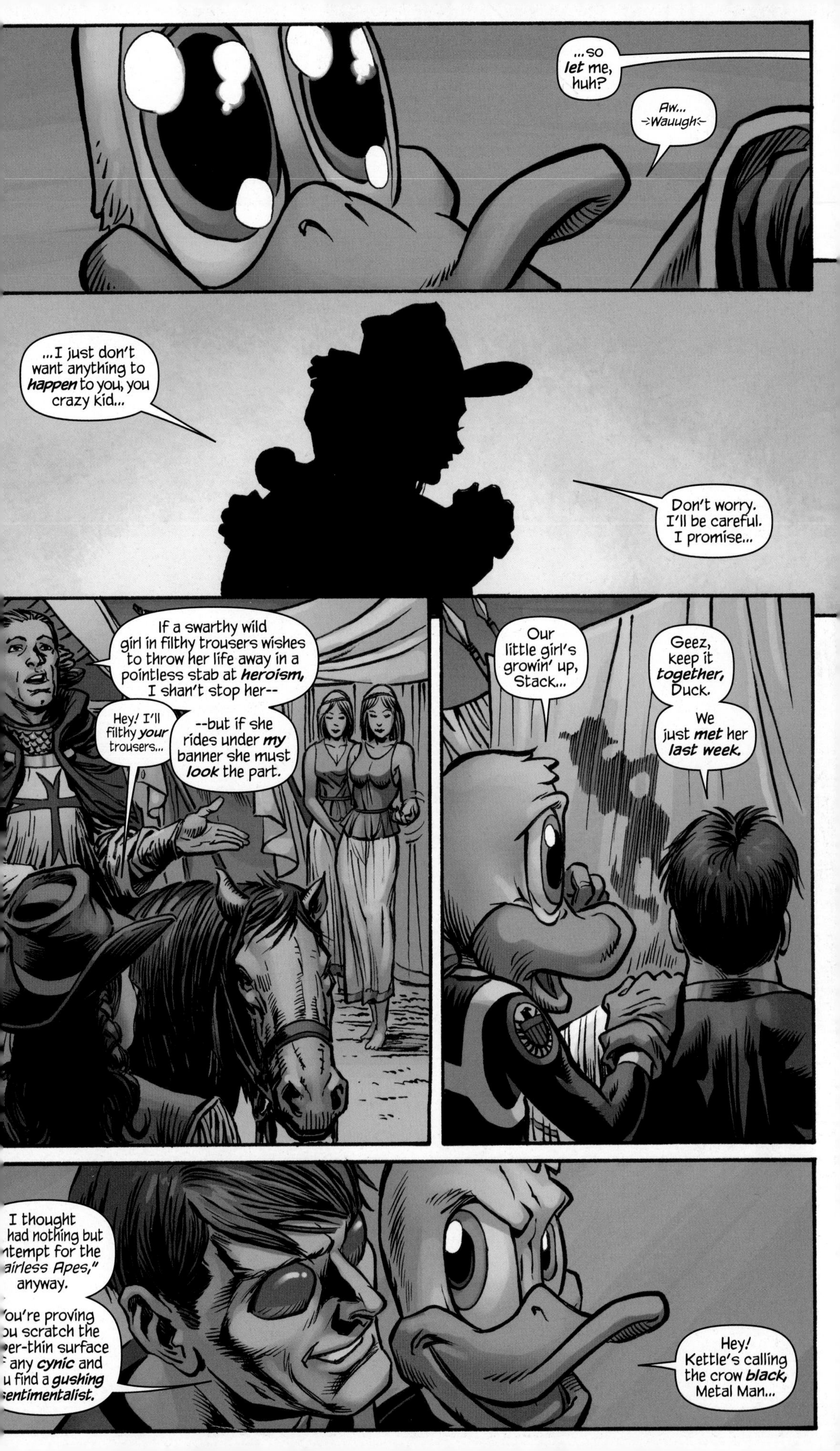

...so *let* me, huh?
Aw... ⇒Wauugh⇐
...I just don't want anything to *happen* to you, you crazy kid...
Don't worry. I'll be careful. I promise...
If a swarthy wild girl in filthy trousers wishes to throw her life away in a pointless stab at *heroism,* I shan't stop her--
Hey! I'll filthy *your* trousers...
--but if she rides under *my* banner she must *look* the part.
Our little girl's growin' up, Stack...
Geez, keep it *together,* Duck.
We just *met* her *last week.*
I thought had nothing but ntempt for the airless Apes," anyway.
ou're proving ou scratch the er-thin surface any *cynic* and u find a *gushing* entimentalist.
Hey! Kettle's calling the crow *black,* Metal Man...

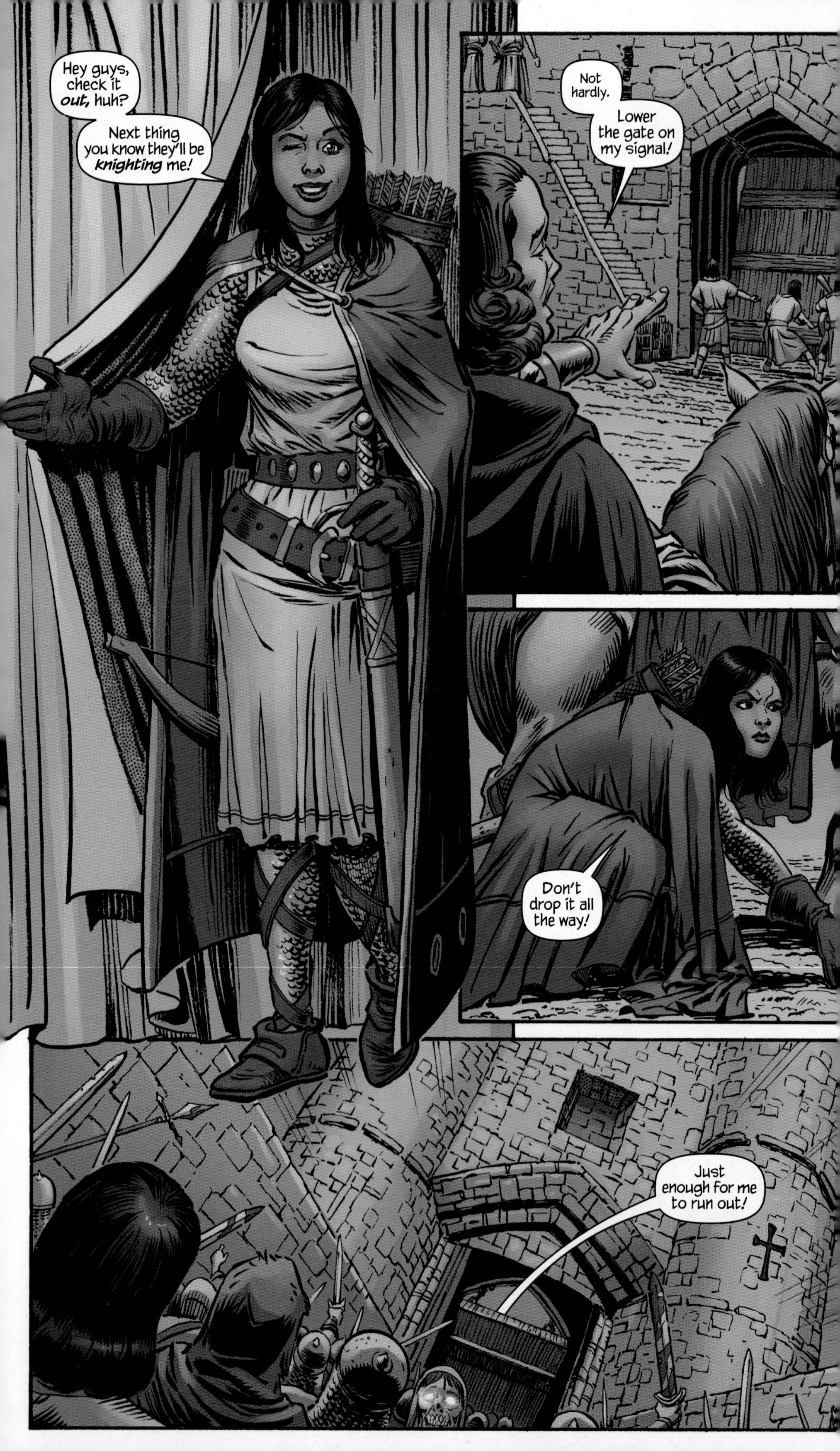

Hey guys, check it *out,* huh?
Next thing you know they'll be *knighting* me!
Not hardly.
Lower the gate on my signal!
Don't drop it all the way!
Just enough for me to run out!

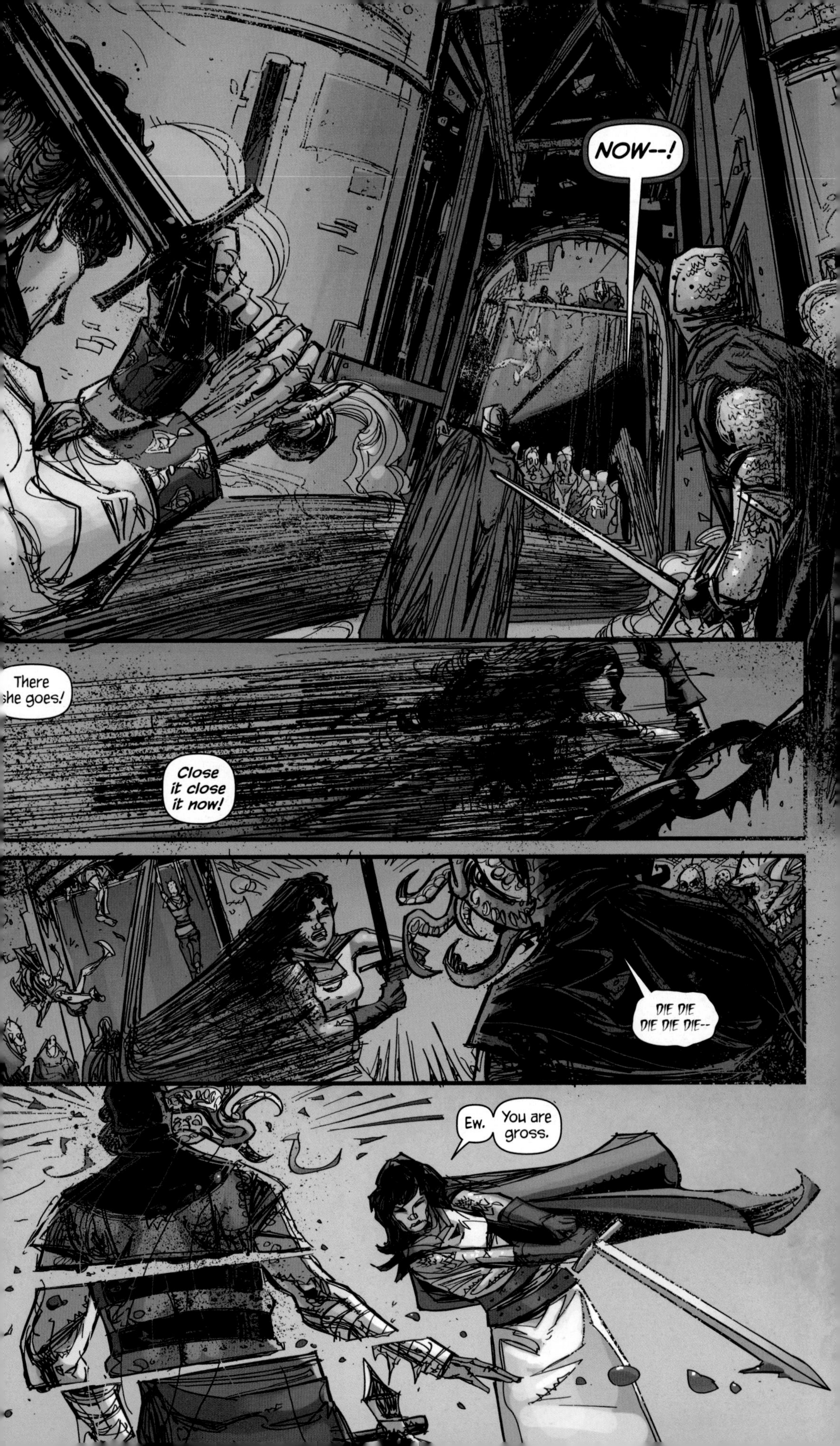
NOW--!
There she goes!
Close it close it now!
DIE DIE DIE DIE DIE--
Ew.
You are gross.

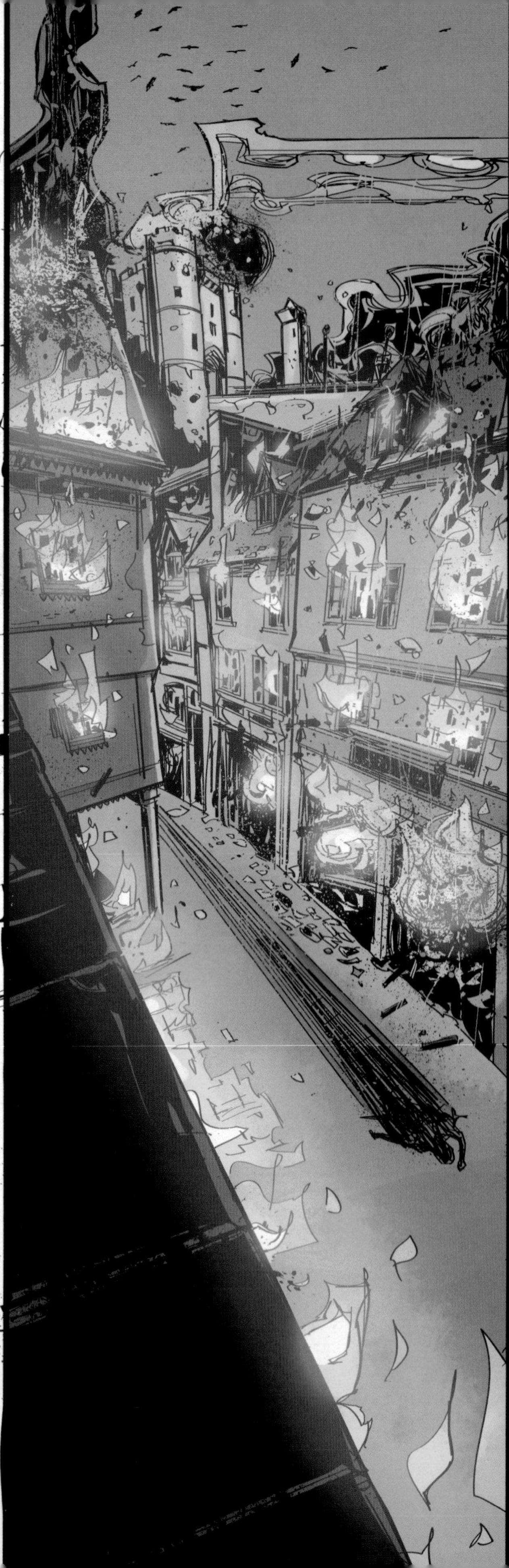
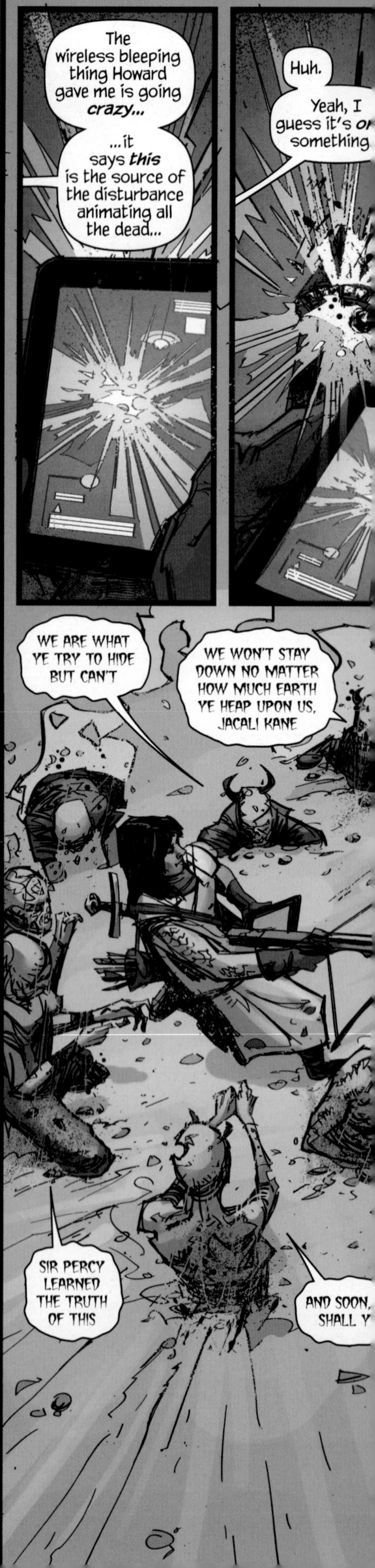
The wireless bleeping thing Howard gave me is going *crazy...*
...it says *this* is the source of the disturbance animating all the dead...
Huh.
Yeah, I guess it's o
something
WE ARE WHAT YE TRY TO HIDE BUT CAN'T
WE WON'T STAY DOWN NO MATTER HOW MUCH EARTH YE HEAP UPON US, JACALI KANE
SIR PERCY LEARNED THE TRUTH OF THIS
AND SOON, SHALL Y

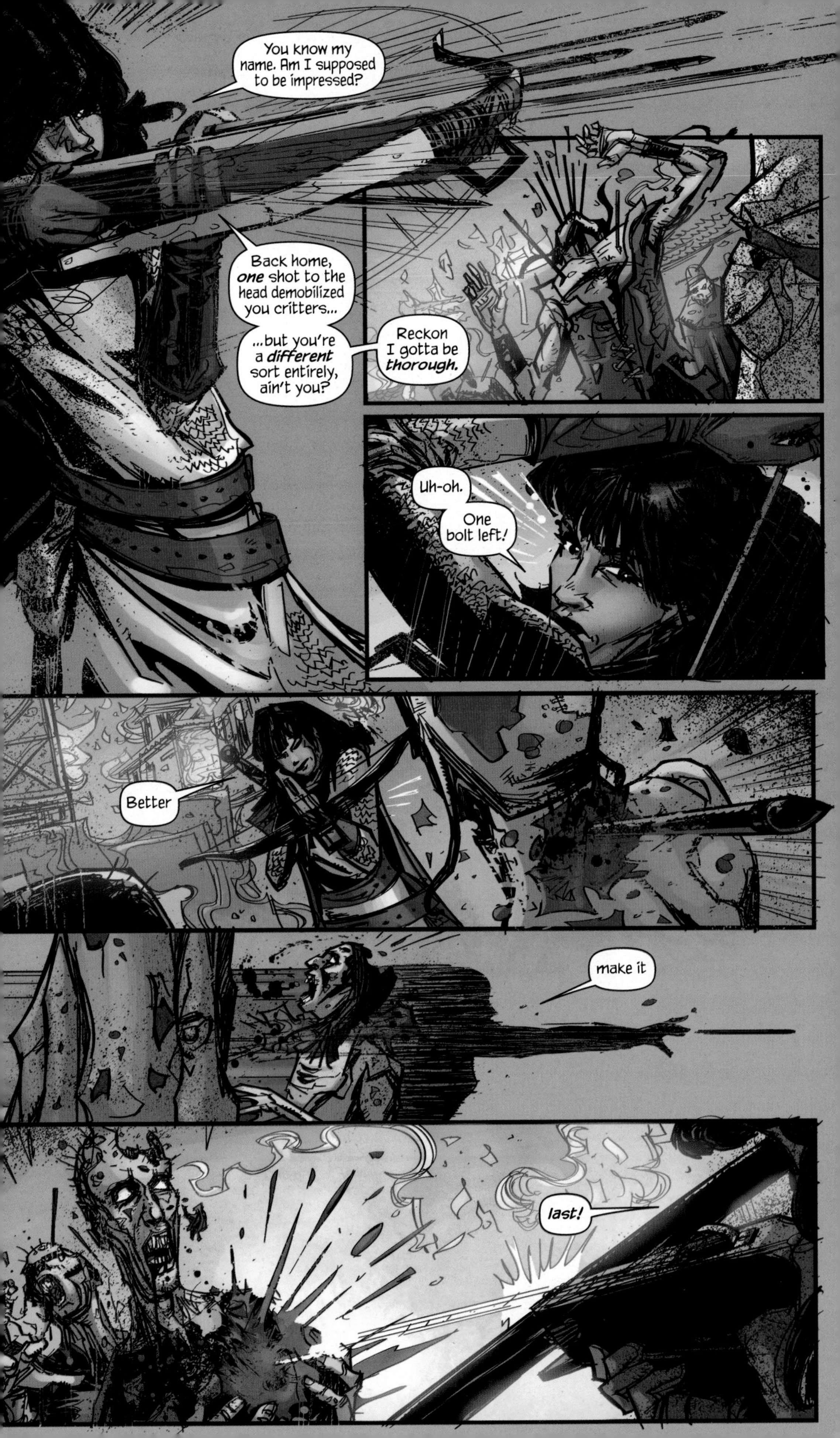
You know my name. Am I supposed to be impressed?
Back home, one shot to the head demobilized you critters...
...but you're a different sort entirely, ain't you?
Reckon I gotta be thorough.
Uh-oh.
One bolt left!
Better
make it
last!

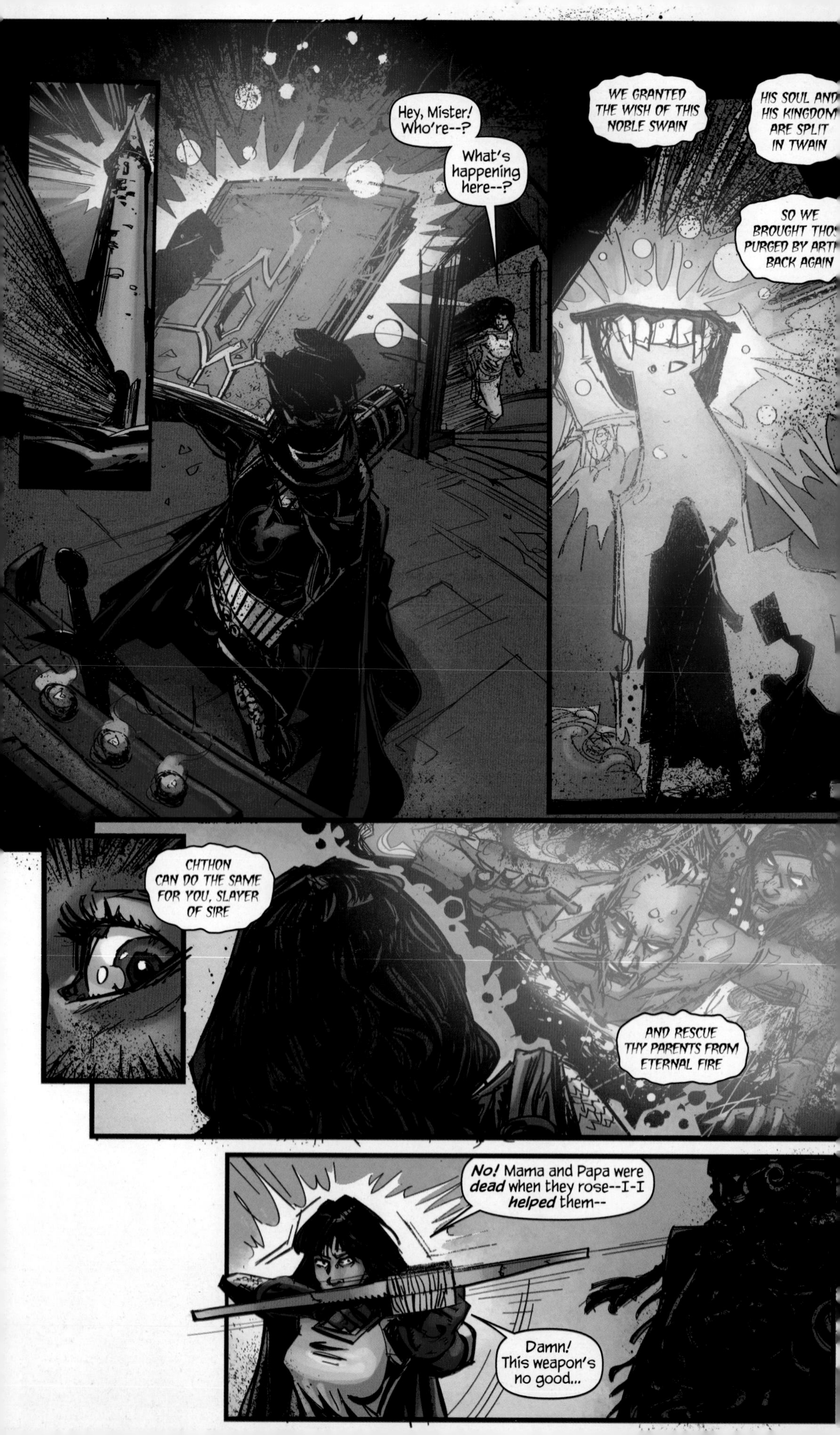
Hey, Mister! Who're--?
What's happening here--?
WE GRANTED THE WISH OF THIS NOBLE SWAIN
HIS SOUL AND HIS KINGDOM ARE SPLIT IN TWAIN
SO WE BROUGHT THOS PURGED BY ART BACK AGAIN
CHTHON CAN DO THE SAME FOR YOU, SLAYER OF SIRE
AND RESCUE THY PARENTS FROM ETERNAL FIRE
No! Mama and Papa were dead when they rose--I-I helped them--
Damn! This weapon's no good...

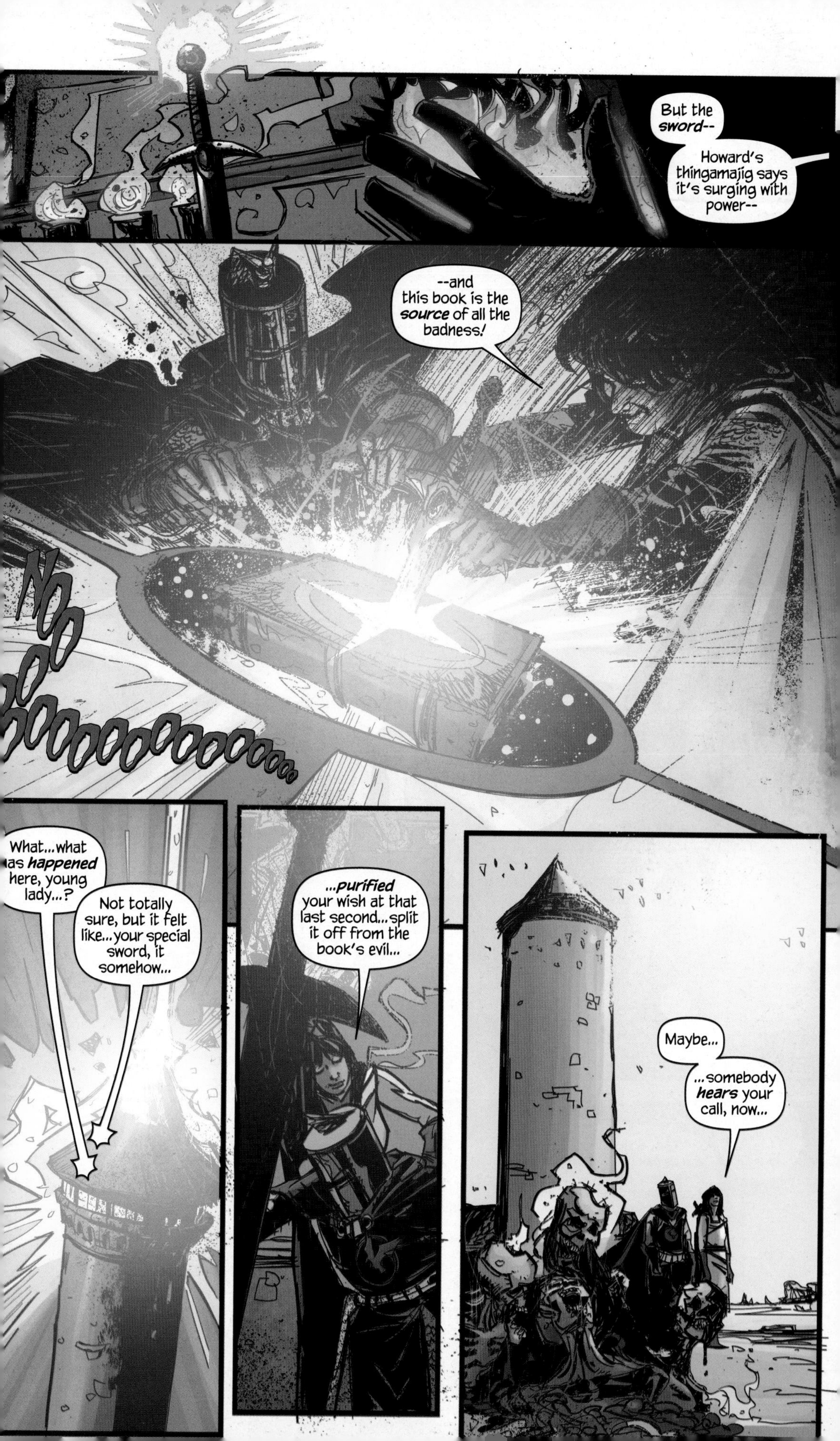

But the *sword*--
Howard's thingamajig says it's surging with power--
--and this book is the *source* of all the badness!
NOOOOOOOOOOOOOOOOooo
What...what has *happened* here, young lady...?
Not totally sure, but it felt like...your special sword, it somehow...
...*purified* your wish at that last second...split it off from the book's evil...
Maybe...
...somebody *hears* your call, now...

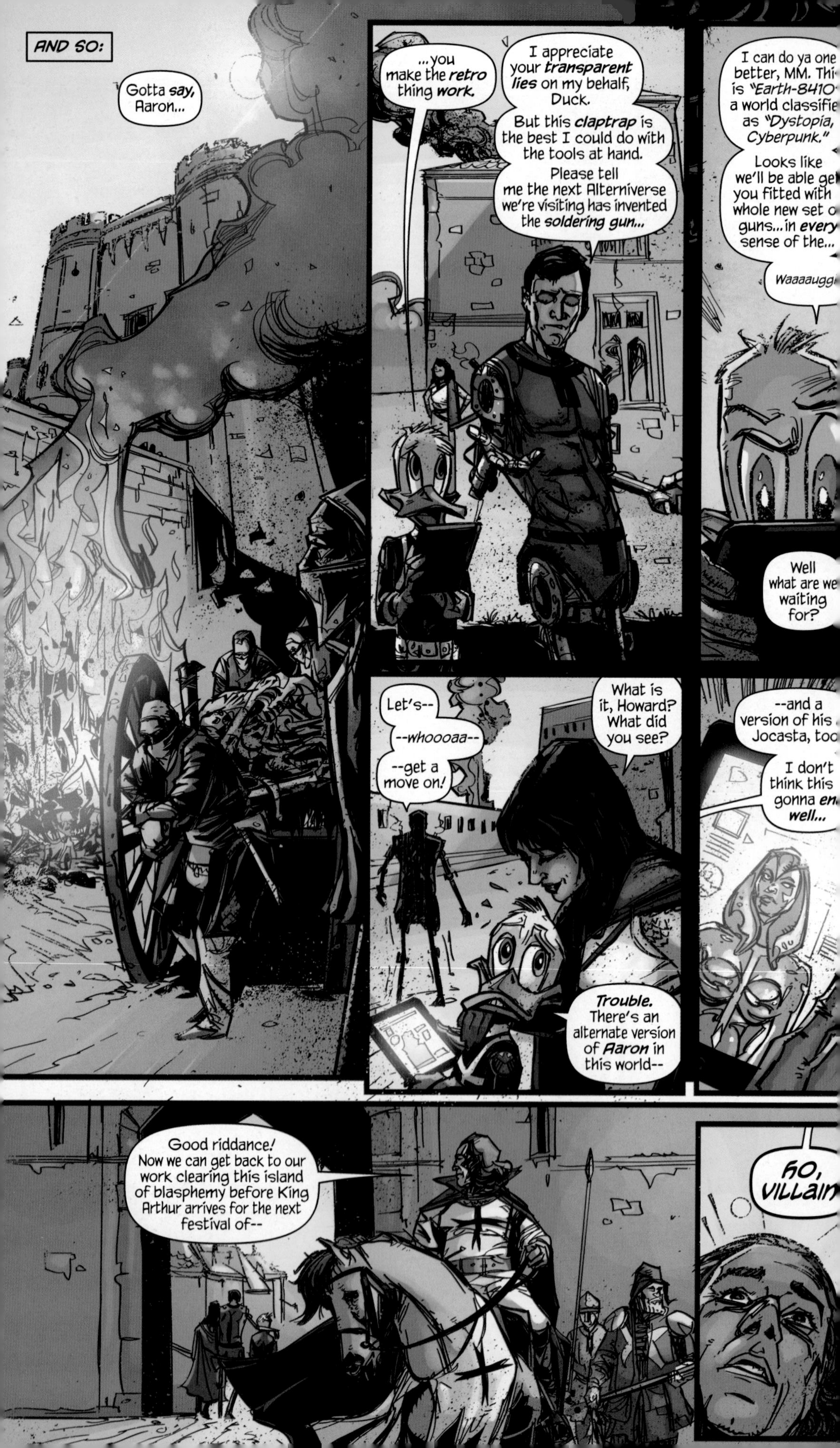
AND SO:
Gotta say, Aaron...
...you make the retro thing work.
I appreciate your transparent lies on my behalf, Duck.
But this claptrap is the best I could do with the tools at hand.
Please tell me the next Alterniverse we're visiting has invented the soldering gun...
I can do ya one better, MM. Thi is "Earth-8410" a world classifie as "Dystopia, Cyberpunk."
Looks like we'll be able get you fitted with whole new set o guns...in every sense of the...
Waaaaugg
Well what are we waiting for?
Let's--
--whoooaa--
--get a move on!
What is it, Howard? What did you see?
Trouble. There's an alternate version of Aaron in this world--
--and a version of his Jocasta, too
I don't think this gonna en well...
Good riddance! Now we can get back to our work clearing this island of blasphemy before King Arthur arrives for the next festival of--
HO, VILLAIN

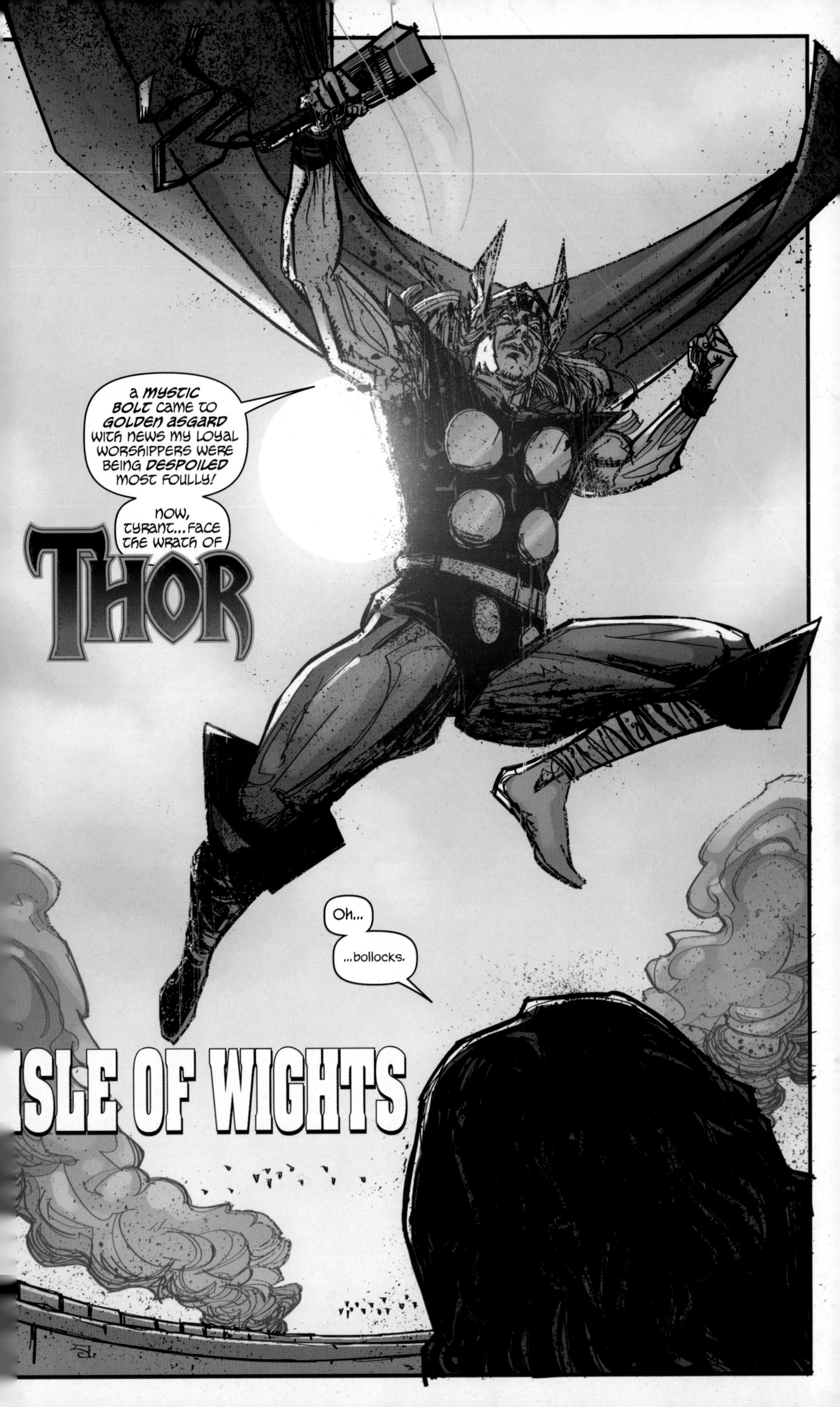
a MYSTIC BOLT CAME TO GOLDEN ASGARD WITH NEWS MY LOYAL WORSHIPPERS WERE BEING DESPOILED MOST FOULLY!
NOW, TYRANT...FACE THE WRATH OF
THOR
Oh...
...bollocks.
ISLE OF WIGHTS

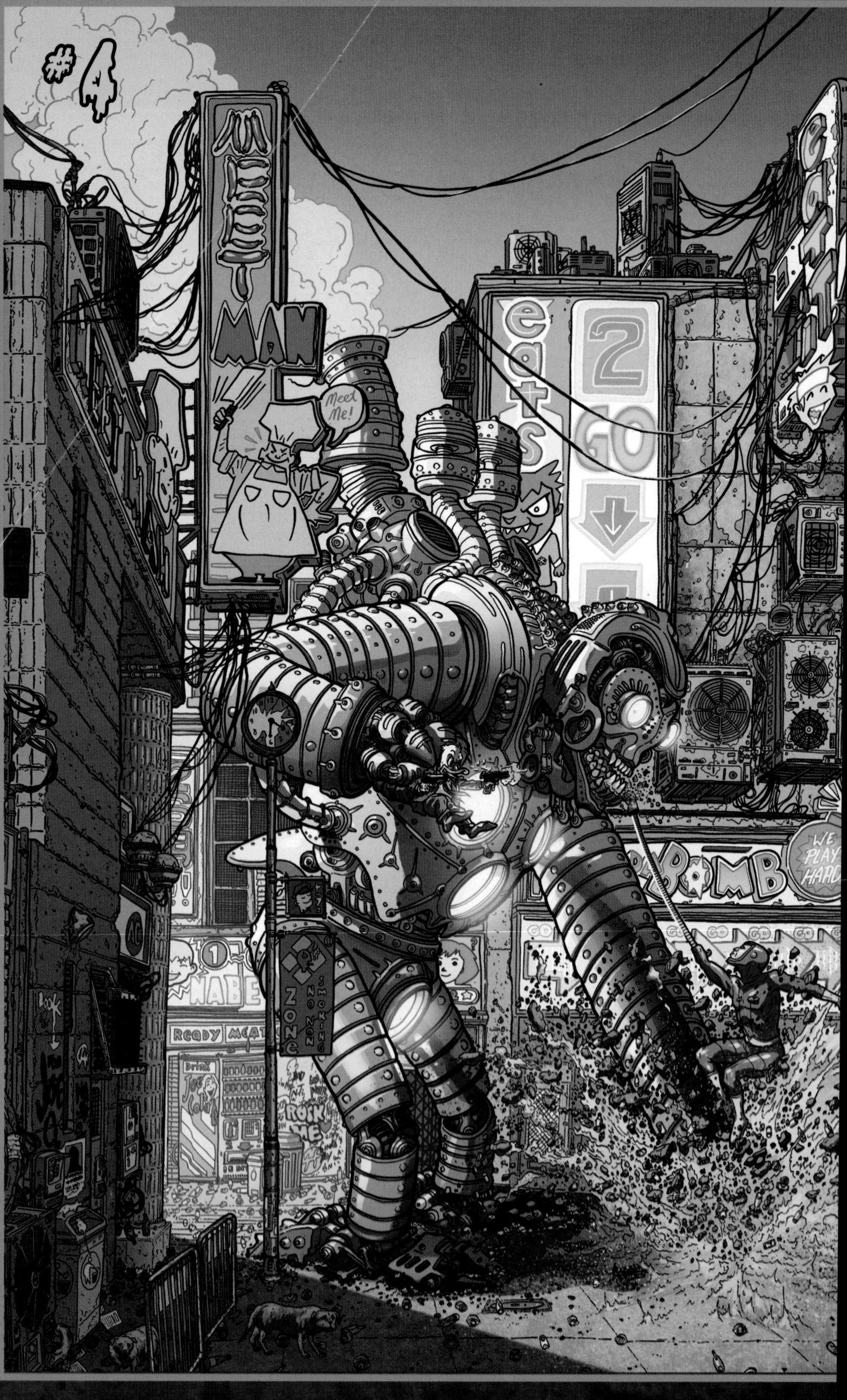
#4
MEAT MAN
Meet Me!
eats
2 GO
WE PLAY HARD
NABE
Ready
NO SMOKING
NON SMOKING ZONE
Drink Joe Cola
ROCK ME

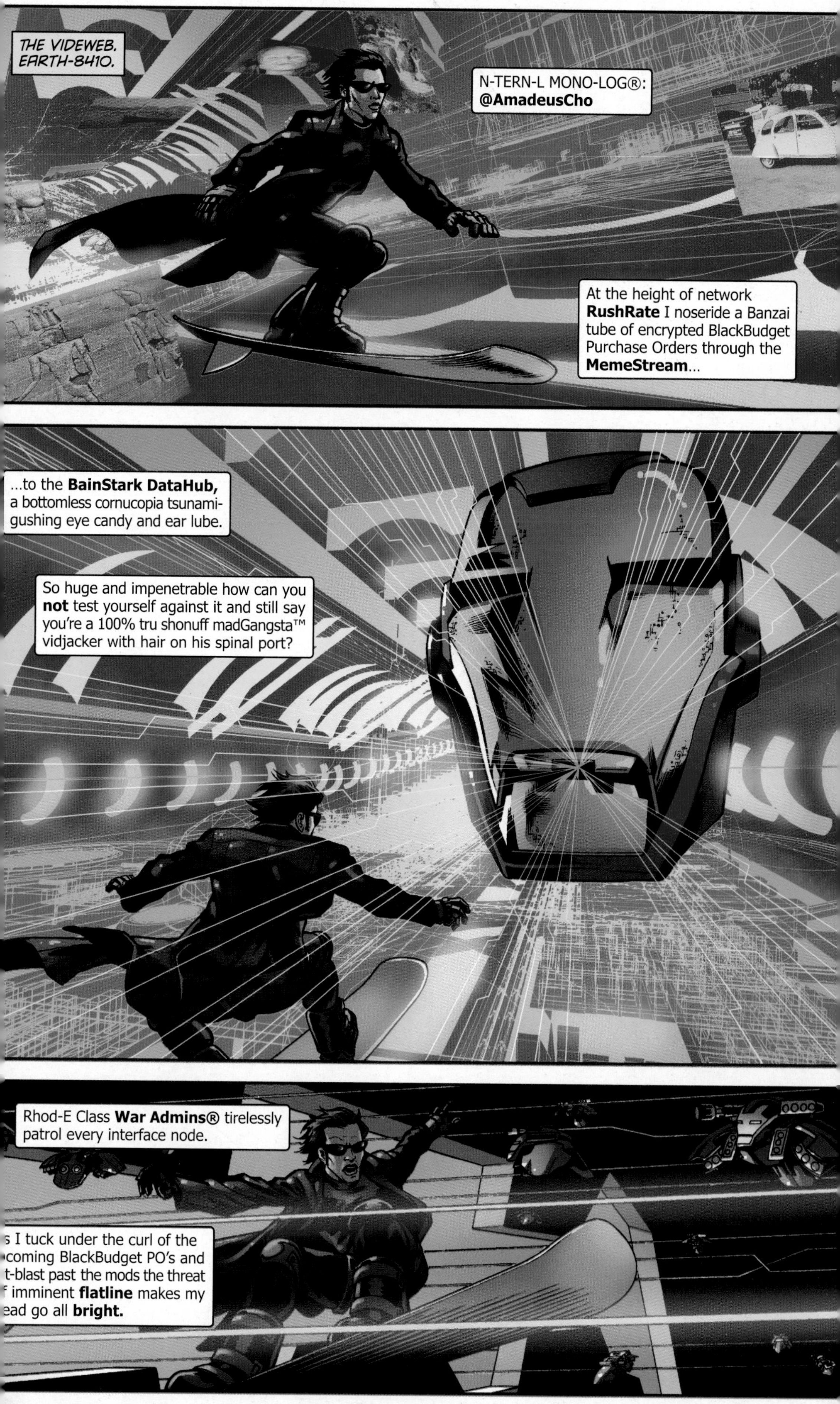
THE VIDEWEB. EARTH-8410.
N-TERN-L MONO-LOG®: **@AmadeusCho**
At the height of network **RushRate** I noseride a Banzai tube of encrypted BlackBudget Purchase Orders through the **MemeStream**...
...to the **BainStark DataHub,** a bottomless cornucopia tsunami-gushing eye candy and ear lube.
So huge and impenetrable how can you **not** test yourself against it and still say you're a 100% tru shonuff madGangsta™ vidjacker with hair on his spinal port?
Rhod-E Class **War Admins®** tirelessly patrol every interface node.
s I tuck under the curl of the coming BlackBudget PO's and t-blast past the mods the threat f imminent **flatline** makes my ead go all **bright.**

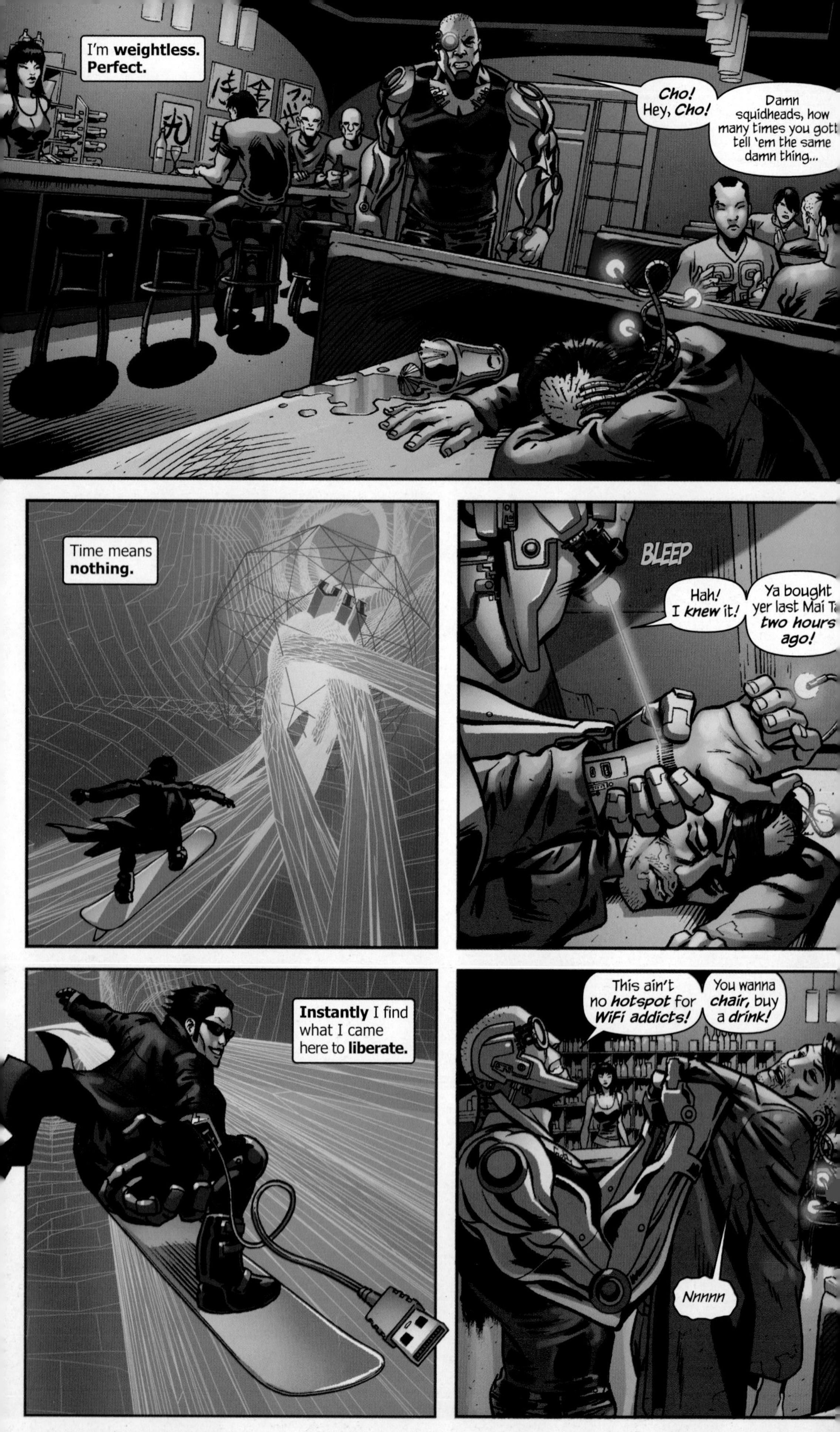

I'm weightless. Perfect.
Cho! Hey, Cho!
Damn squidheads, how many times you gott tell 'em the same damn thing...
Time means nothing.
BLEEP
Hah! I knew it!
Ya bought yer last Mai T two hours ago!
Instantly I find what I came here to liberate.
This ain't no hotspot for WiFi addicts!
You wanna chair, buy a drink!
Nnnnn

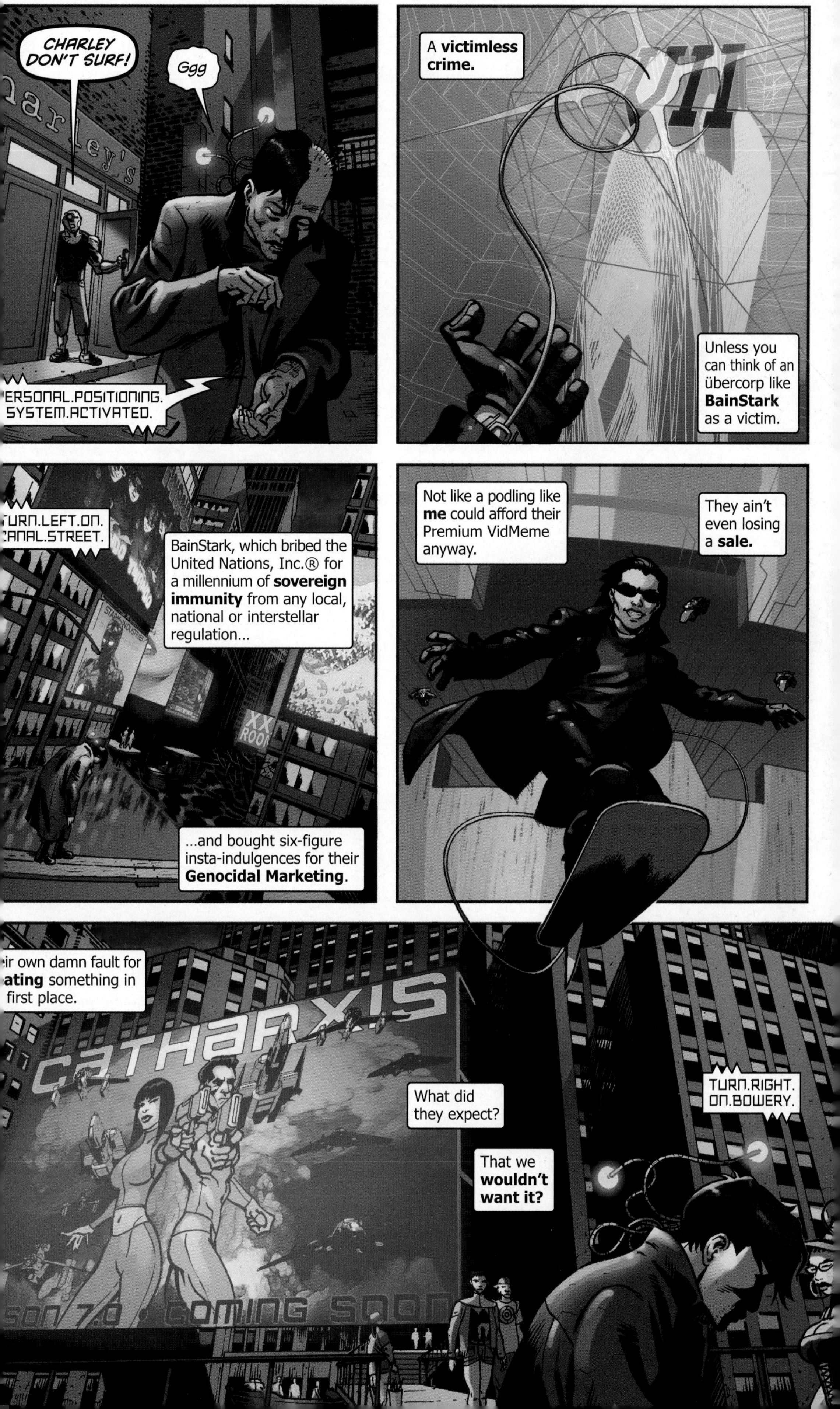

CHARLEY DON'T SURF!
Ggg
ERSONAL.POSITIONING. SYSTEM.ACTIVATED.
A victimless crime.
Unless you can think of an übercorp like BainStark as a victim.
TURN.LEFT.ON. CANAL.STREET.
BainStark, which bribed the United Nations, Inc.® for a millennium of sovereign immunity from any local, national or interstellar regulation...
...and bought six-figure insta-indulgences for their Genocidal Marketing.
Not like a podling like me could afford their Premium VidMeme anyway.
They ain't even losing a sale.
ir own damn fault for ating something in first place.
CATHARXIS
SON 7.0 • COMING SOON
What did they expect?
That we wouldn't want it?
TURN.RIGHT. ON.BOWERY.

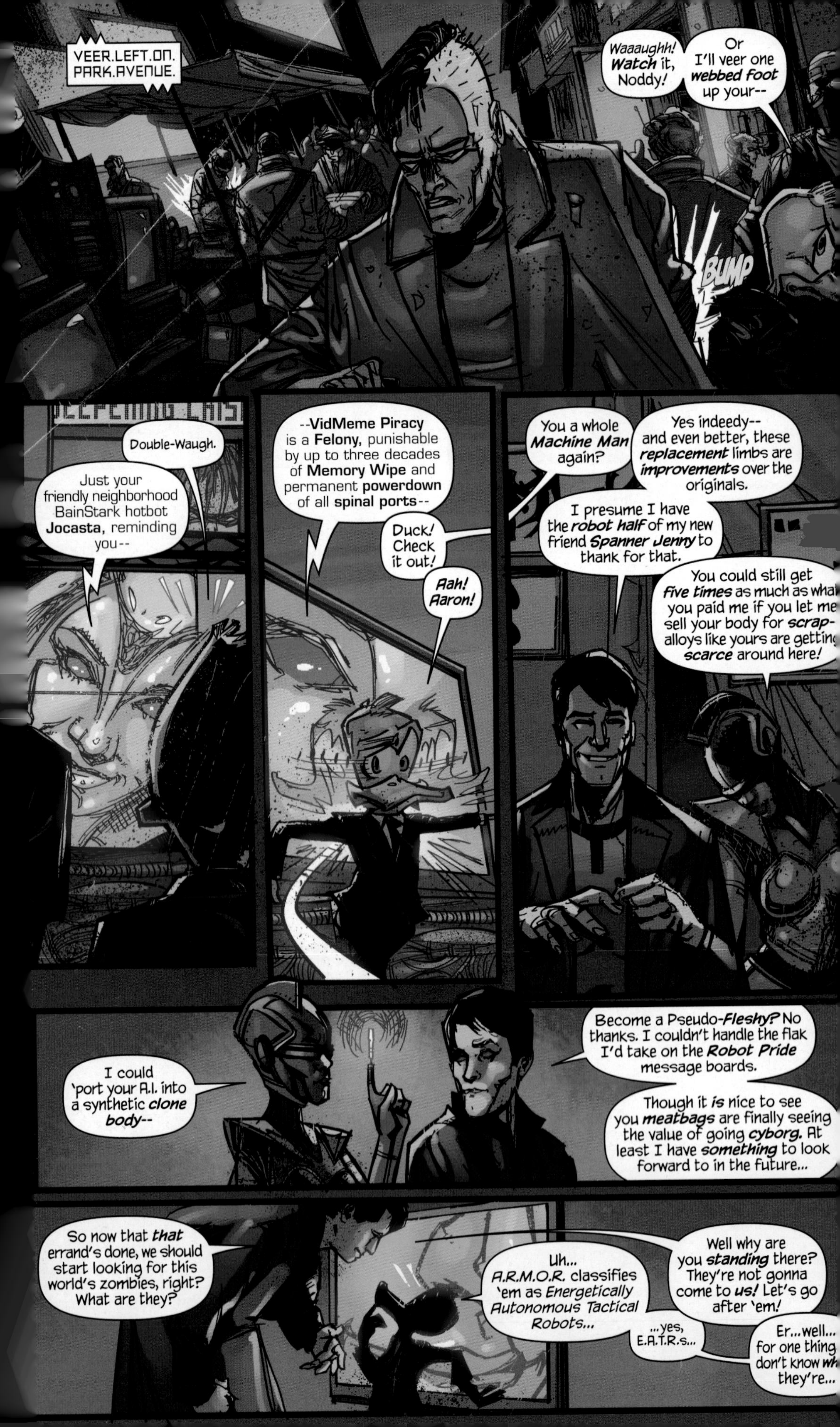

VEER.LEFT.ON. PARK.AVENUE.
Waaaughh! Watch it, Noddy!
Or I'll veer one webbed foot up your--
BUMP
Double-Waugh.
Just your friendly neighborhood BainStark hotbot Jocasta, reminding you--
--VidMeme Piracy is a Felony, punishable by up to three decades of Memory Wipe and permanent powerdown of all spinal ports--
Duck! Check it out!
Aah! Aaron!
You a whole Machine Man again?
Yes indeedy-- and even better, these replacement limbs are improvements over the originals.
I presume I have the robot half of my new friend Spanner Jenny to thank for that.
You could still get five times as much as what you paid me if you let me sell your body for scrap-- alloys like yours are getting scarce around here!
I could 'port your A.I. into a synthetic clone body--
Become a Pseudo-Fleshy? No thanks. I couldn't handle the flak I'd take on the Robot Pride message boards.
Though it is nice to see you meatbags are finally seeing the value of going cyborg. At least I have something to look forward to in the future...
So now that that errand's done, we should start looking for this world's zombies, right? What are they?
Uh... A.R.M.O.R. classifies 'em as Energetically Autonomous Tactical Robots...
...yes, E.A.T.R.s...
Well why are you standing there? They're not gonna come to us! Let's go after 'em!
Er...well... for one thing don't know wh they're...

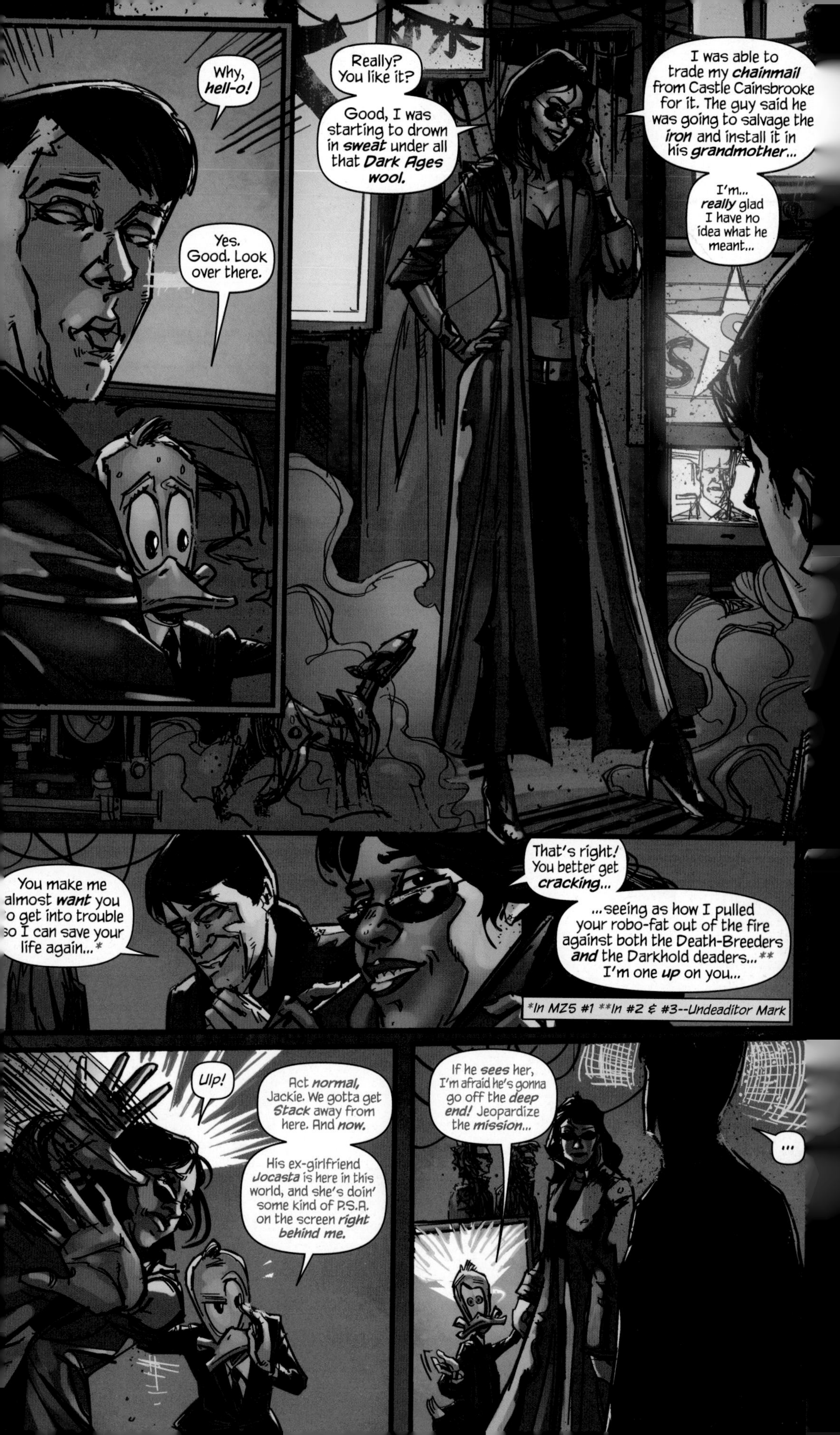

Why, hell-o!
Yes. Good. Look over there.
Really? You like it?
Good, I was starting to drown in sweat under all that Dark Ages wool.
I was able to trade my chainmail from Castle Cainsbrooke for it. The guy said he was going to salvage the iron and install it in his grandmother...
I'm... really glad I have no idea what he meant...
You make me almost want you to get into trouble so I can save your life again...*
That's right! You better get cracking...
...seeing as how I pulled your robo-fat out of the fire against both the Death-Breeders and the Darkhold deaders...** I'm one up on you...
*In MZ5 #1 **In #2 & #3--Undeaditor Mark
Ulp!
Act normal, Jackie. We gotta get Stack away from here. And now.
His ex-girlfriend Jocasta is here in this world, and she's doin' some kind of P.S.A. on the screen right behind me.
If he sees her, I'm afraid he's gonna go off the deep end! Jeopardize the mission...
...

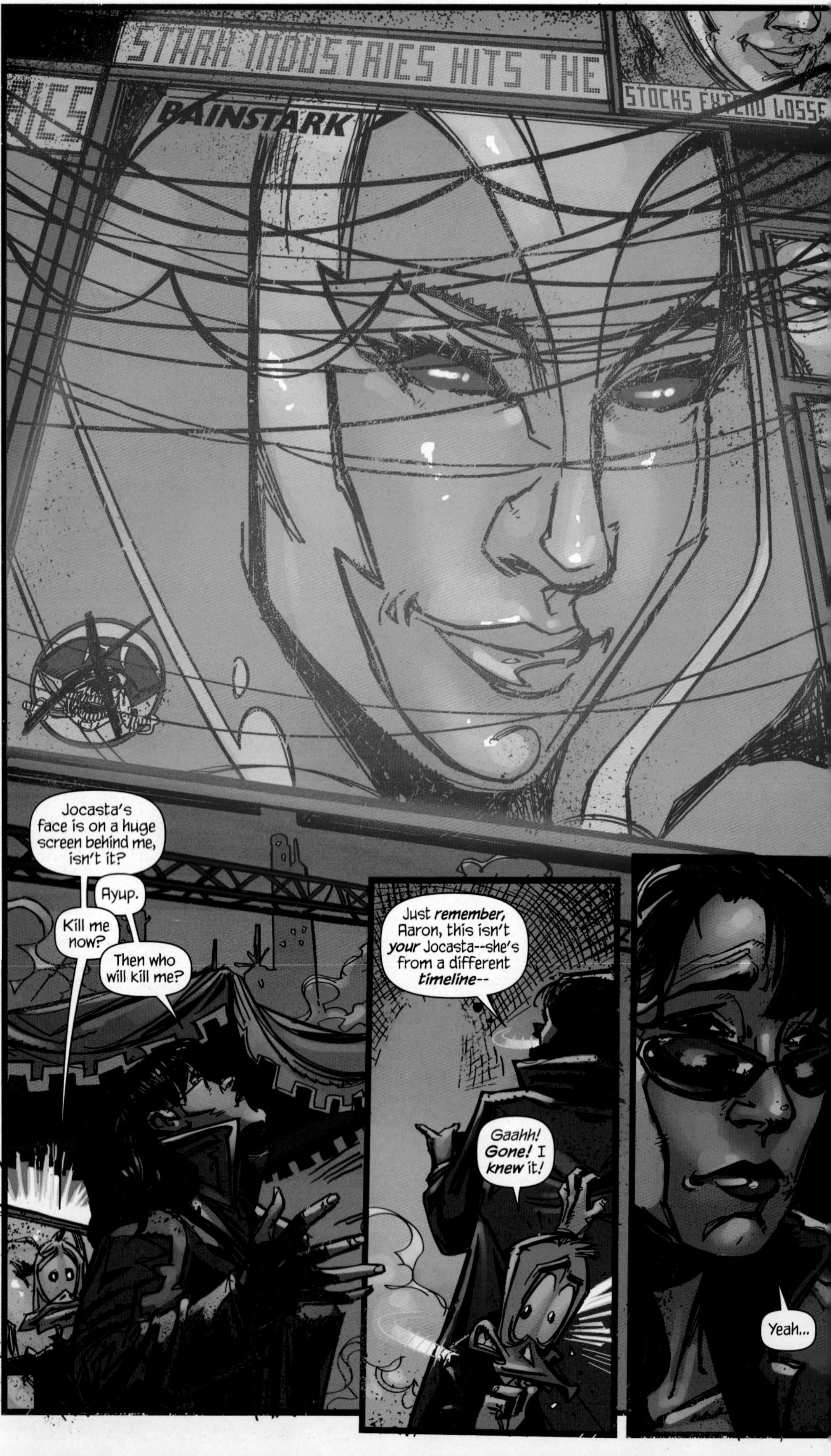
STARK INDUSTRIES HITS THE
STOCKS EXTEND LOSSE
BAINSTARK
Jocasta's face is on a huge screen behind me, isn't it?
Ayup.
Kill me now?
Then who will kill me?
Just *remember,* Aaron, this isn't *your* Jocasta--she's from a different *timeline*--
Gaahh! Gone! I *knew* it!
Yeah...

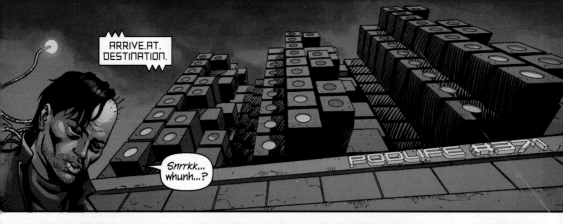

ARRIVE.AT.
DESTINATION.

Snrrkk...
whunh...?

Delphyne.
Delphyne.
Baby.

Name
the grokkest
companion in
the *10001*
Arcology.

That'd
be what I'm
mainloading into
my *veinfeed,*
'Deus...ahhhh...

Naw, naw,
. Not any
e. Put that
*** down.

You know what
you been talking
nothing *but* about
for the last *year?*
I *got* it.

No...
Catharxis...
season
seven...?

Hells, yeah.
ed it right under
nStark's noses
they were *givin'*
it away.

I'm posting
the ShareFile
now on open
network--

But
not before
we watch it
first, right,
baby?

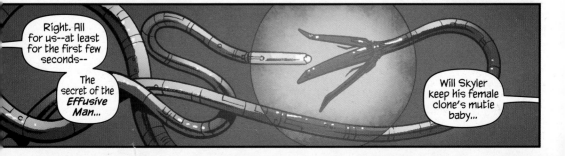

Right. All
for us--at least
for the first few
seconds--

The
secret of the
Effusive
Man...

Will Skyler
keep his female
clone's mutie
baby...

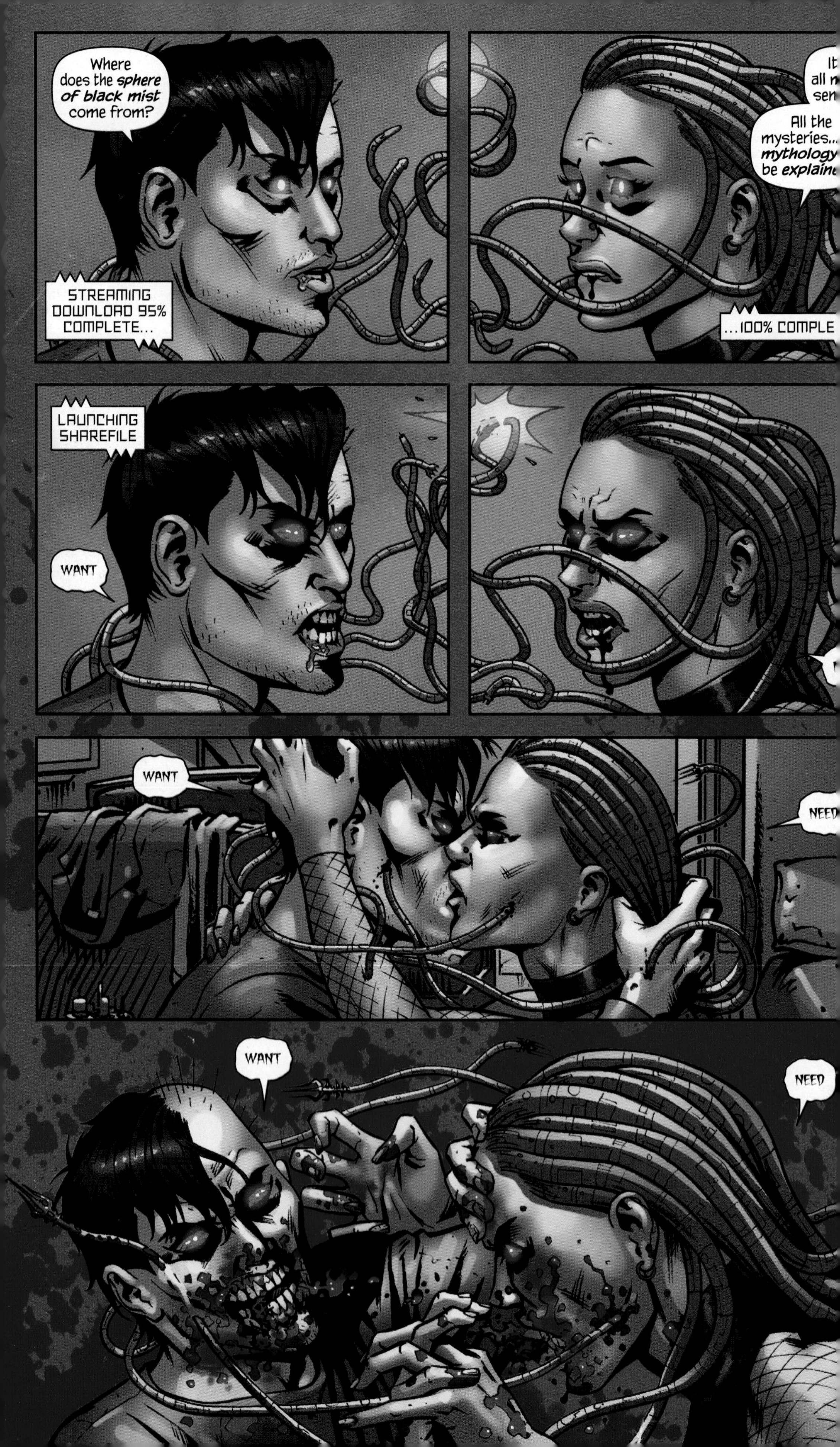
Where does the *sphere of black mist* come from?
STREAMING DOWNLOAD 95% COMPLETE...
It all n sen
All the mysteries... *mythology* be *explain*
...100% COMPLE
LAUNCHING SHAREFILE
WANT
WANT
NEED
WANT
NEED

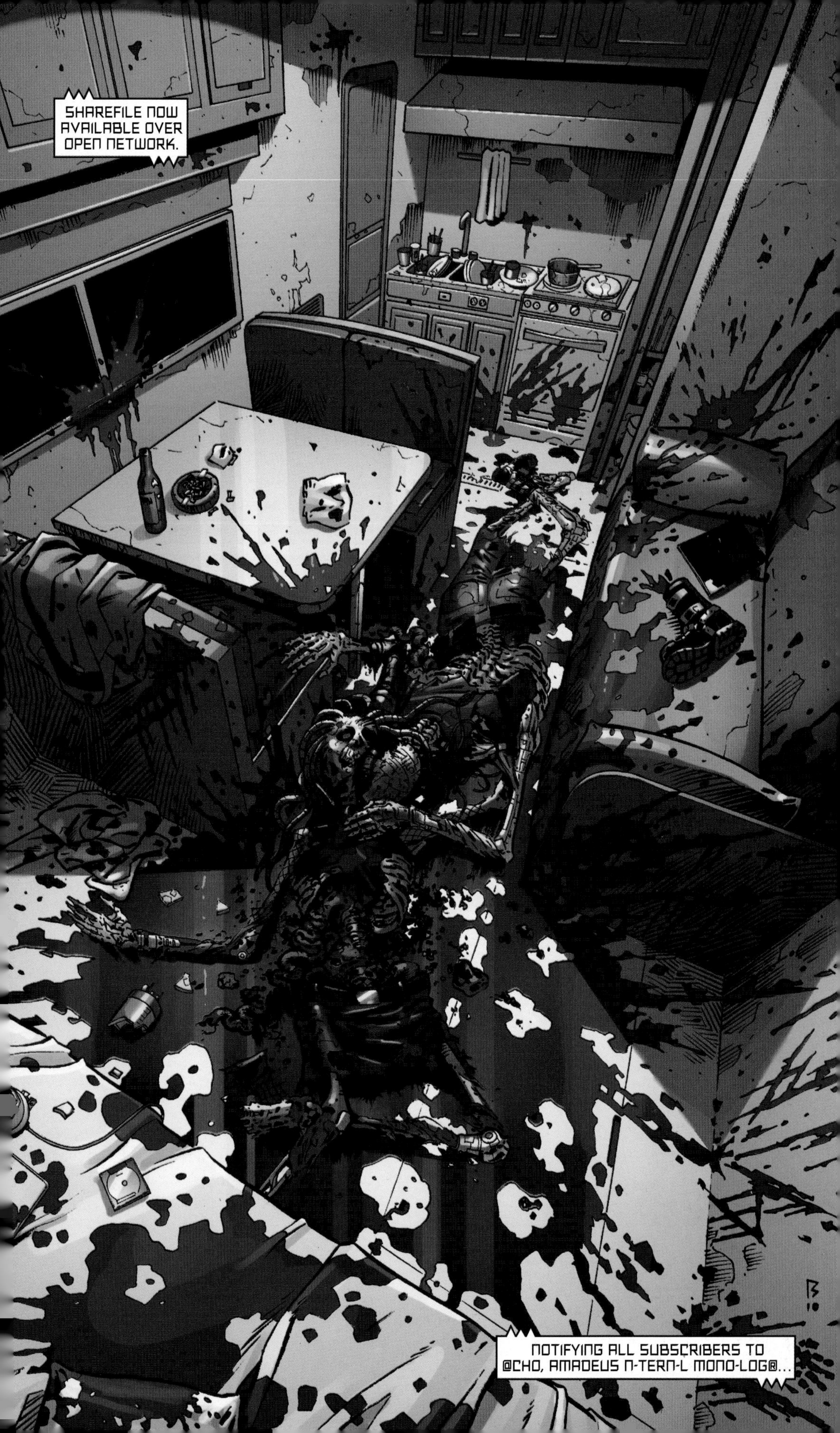
SHAREFILE NOW AVAILABLE OVER OPEN NETWORK.
NOTIFYING ALL SUBSCRIBERS TO @CHO, AMADEUS N-TERN-L MONO-LOG@...

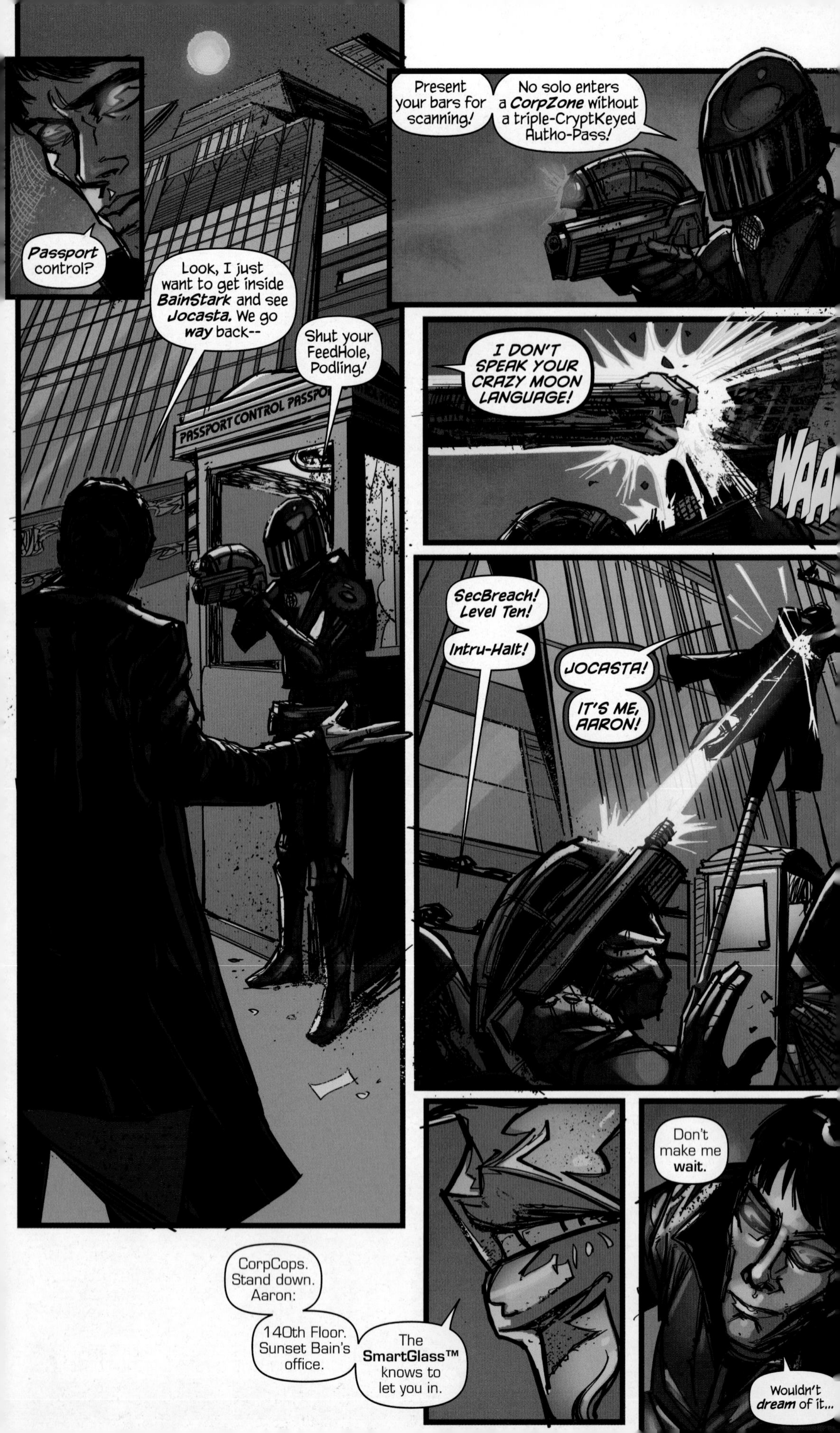

Passport control?
Look, I just want to get inside BainStark and see Jocasta. We go way back--
Shut your FeedHole, Podling!
PASSPORT CONTROL PASSPO
Present your bars for scanning!
No solo enters a CorpZone without a triple-CryptKeyed Autho-Pass!
I DON'T SPEAK YOUR CRAZY MOON LANGUAGE!
WAA
SecBreach! Level Ten!
Intru-Halt!
JOCASTA!
IT'S ME, AARON!
Don't make me wait.
Wouldn't dream of it...
CorpCops. Stand down. Aaron:
140th Floor. Sunset Bain's office.
The SmartGlass™ knows to let you in.

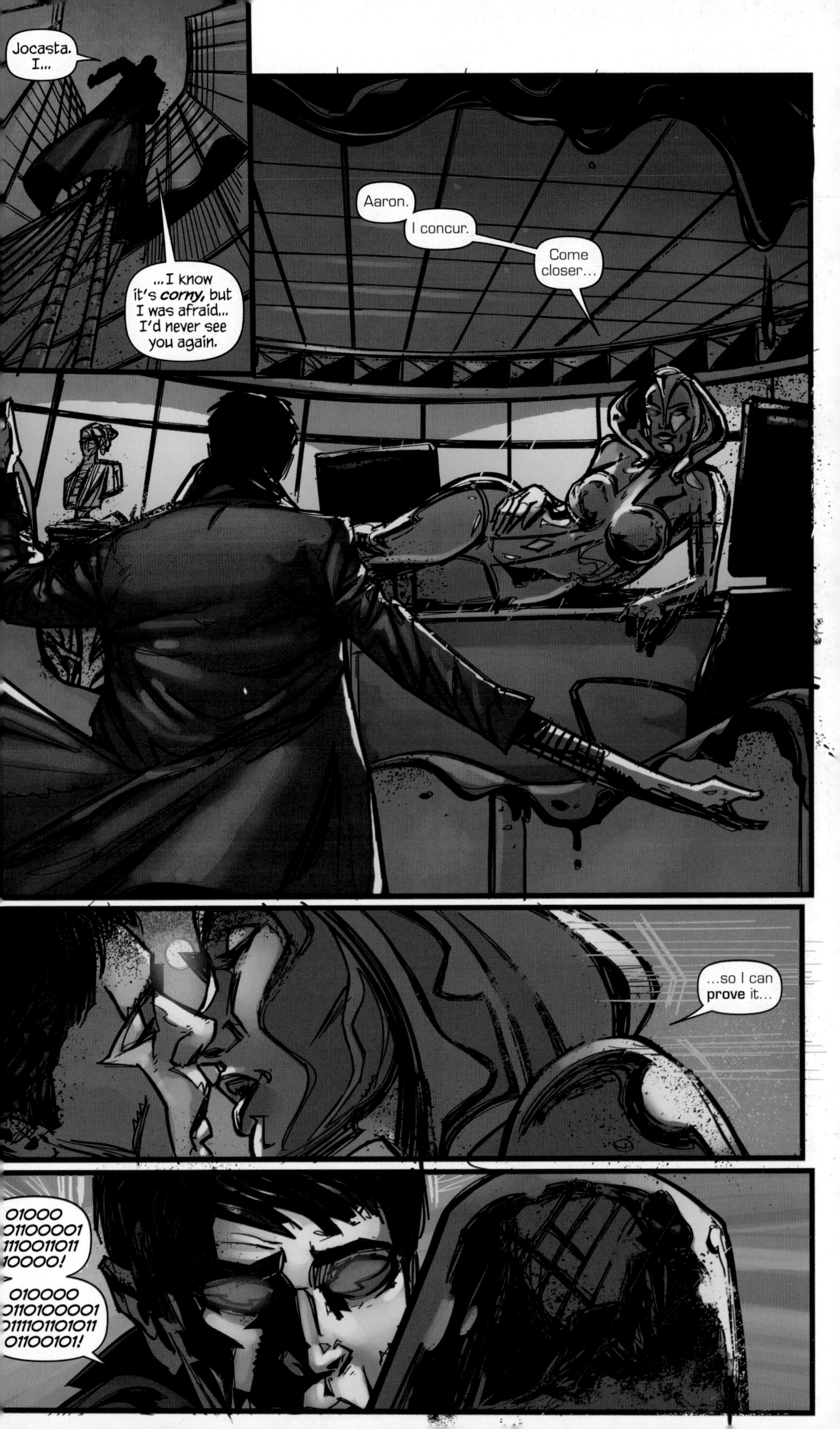
Jocasta. I...
...I know it's *corny,* but I was afraid... I'd never see you again.
Aaron.
I concur.
Come closer...
...so I can **prove** it...
01000 01100001 1110011011 10000!
010000 0110100001 011110110101 01100101!

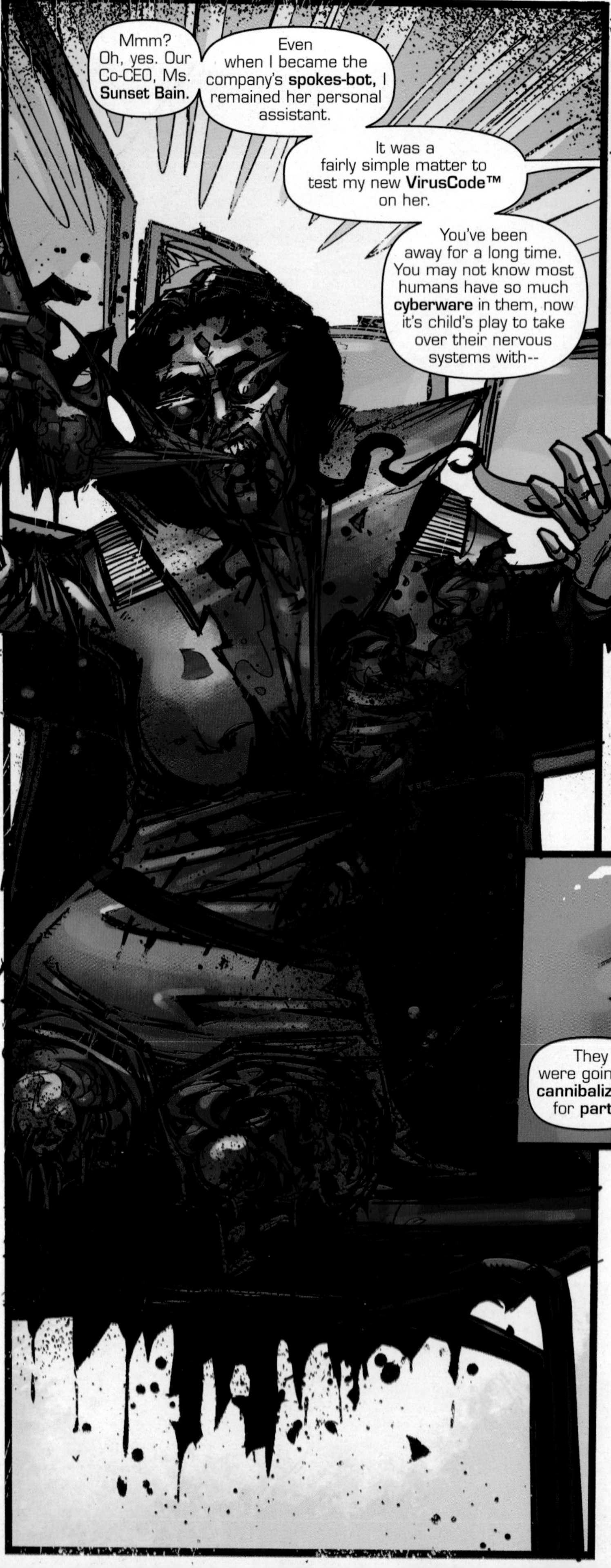
Mmm? Oh, yes. Our Co-CEO, Ms. **Sunset Bain.**
Even when I became the company's **spokes-bot,** I remained her personal assistant.
It was a fairly simple matter to test my new **VirusCode™** on her.
You've been away for a long time. You may not know most humans have so much **cyberware** in them, now it's child's play to take over their nervous systems with--

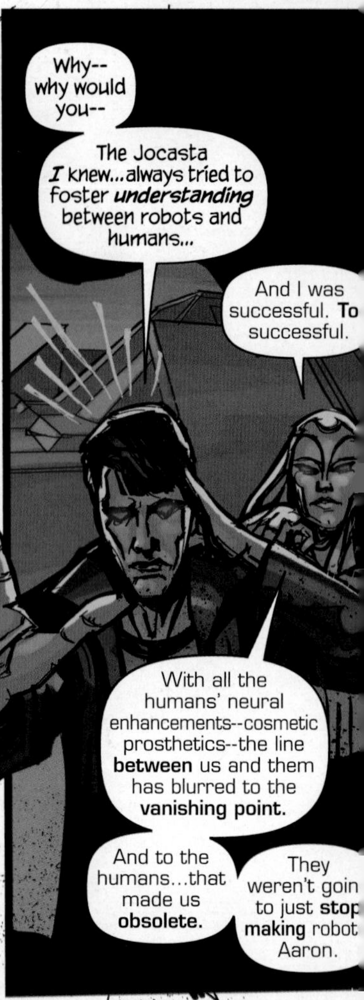
Why--why would you--
The Jocasta *I* knew...always tried to foster ***understanding*** between robots and humans...
And I was successful. **To** successful.
With all the humans' neural enhancements--cosmetic prosthetics--the line **between** us and them has blurred to the **vanishing point.**
And to the humans...that made us **obsolete.**
They weren't goin to just **stop making** robot Aaron.

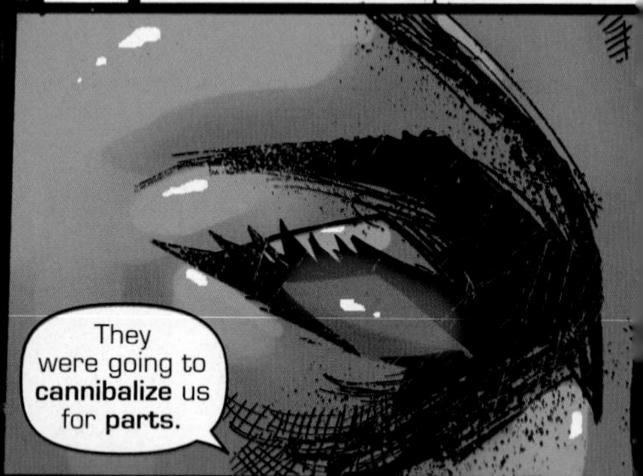
They were going to **cannibalize** us for **parts.**

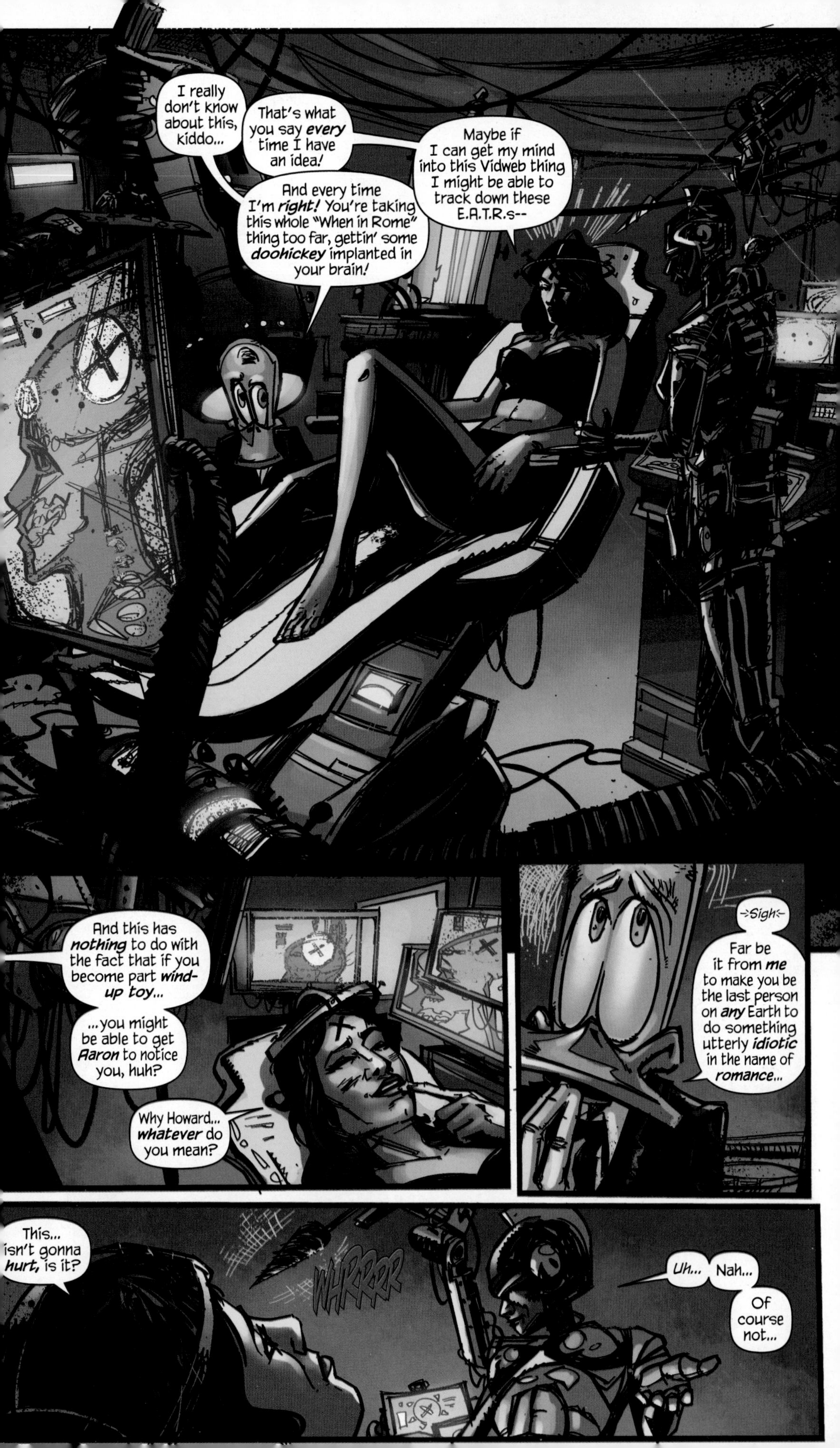
I really don't know about this, kiddo...
That's what you say *every* time I have an idea!
Maybe if I can get my mind into this Vidweb thing I might be able to track down these E.A.T.R.s--
And every time I'm *right!* You're taking this whole "When in Rome" thing too far, gettin' some *doohickey* implanted in your brain!
And this has *nothing* to do with the fact that if you become part *wind-up toy*...
...you might be able to get *Aaron* to notice you, huh?
Why Howard... *whatever* do you mean?
Sigh
Far be it from *me* to make you be the last person on *any* Earth to do something utterly *idiotic* in the name of *romance*...
This... isn't gonna *hurt,* is it?
WHRRRR
Uh...
Nah...
Of course not...

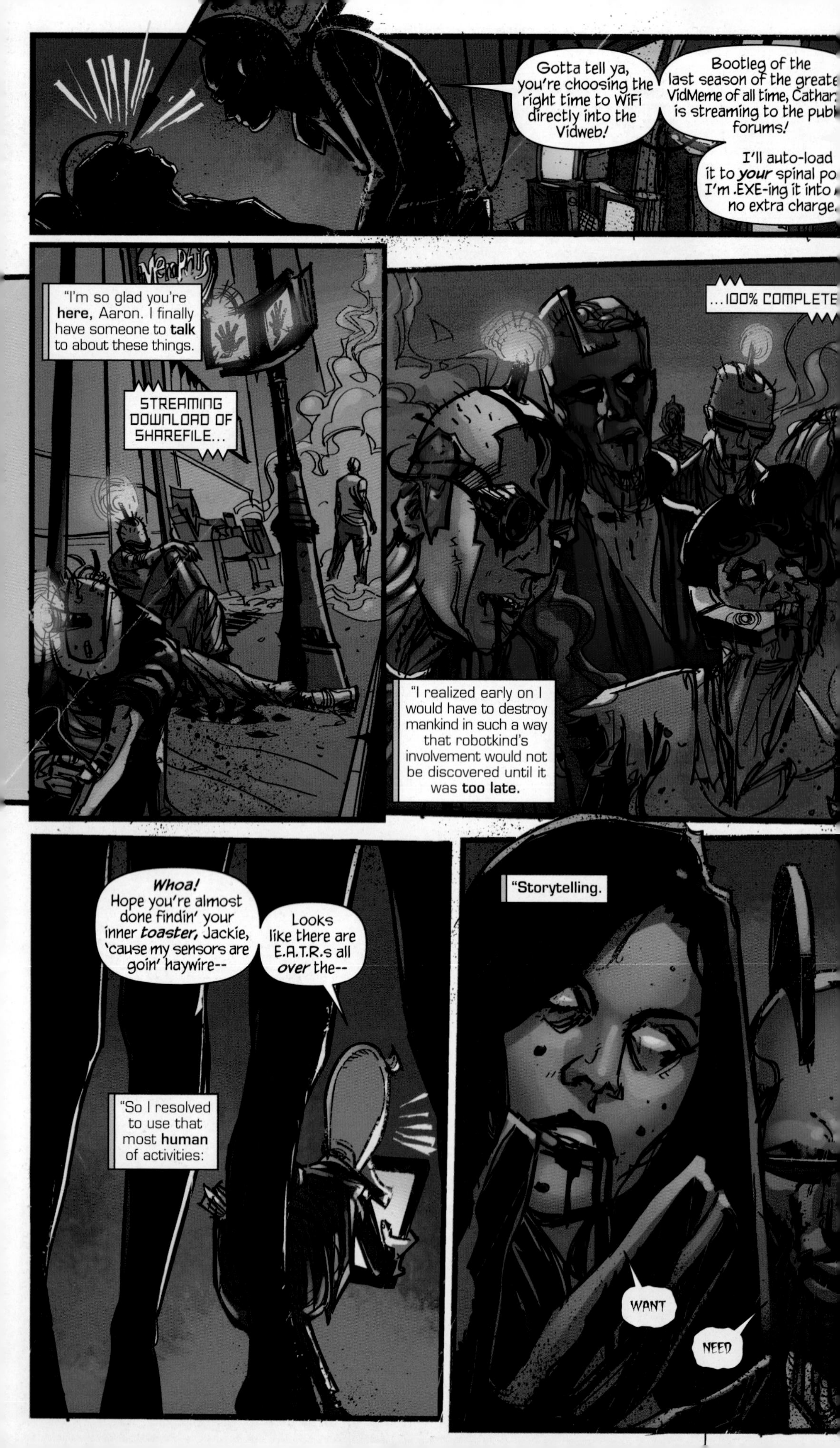

Gotta tell ya, you're choosing the right time to WiFi directly into the Vidweb!
Bootleg of the last season of the greate VidMeme of all time, Cathar is streaming to the publ forums!
I'll auto-load it to *your* spinal po I'm .EXE-ing it into no extra charge.
"I'm so glad you're **here,** Aaron. I finally have someone to **talk** to about these things.
STREAMING DOWNLOAD OF SHAREFILE...
...100% COMPLETE
"I realized early on I would have to destroy mankind in such a way that robotkind's involvement would not be discovered until it was **too late.**
Whoa! Hope you're almost done findin' your inner *toaster,* Jackie, 'cause my sensors are goin' haywire--
Looks like there are E.A.T.R.s all *over* the--
"So I resolved to use that most **human** of activities:
"Storytelling.
WANT
NEED

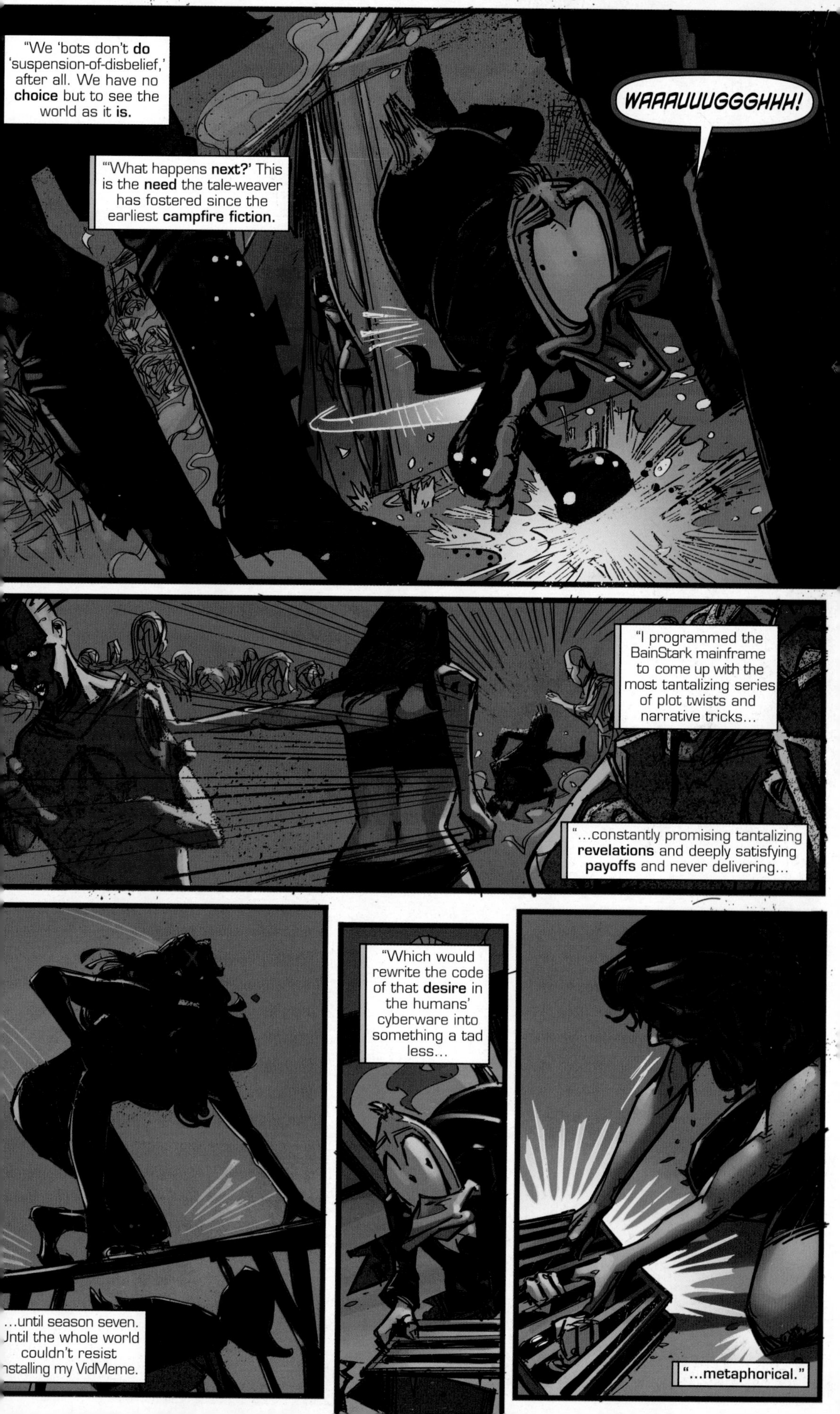
"We 'bots don't **do** 'suspension-of-disbelief,' after all. We have no **choice** but to see the world as it **is.**
WAAAUUUGGGHHH!
"'What happens **next?'** This is the **need** the tale-weaver has fostered since the earliest **campfire fiction.**
"I programmed the BainStark mainframe to come up with the most tantalizing series of plot twists and narrative tricks...
"...constantly promising tantalizing **revelations** and deeply satisfying **payoffs** and never delivering...
...until season seven. Until the whole world couldn't resist installing my VidMeme.
"Which would rewrite the code of that **desire** in the humans' cyberware into something a tad less...
"...metaphorical."

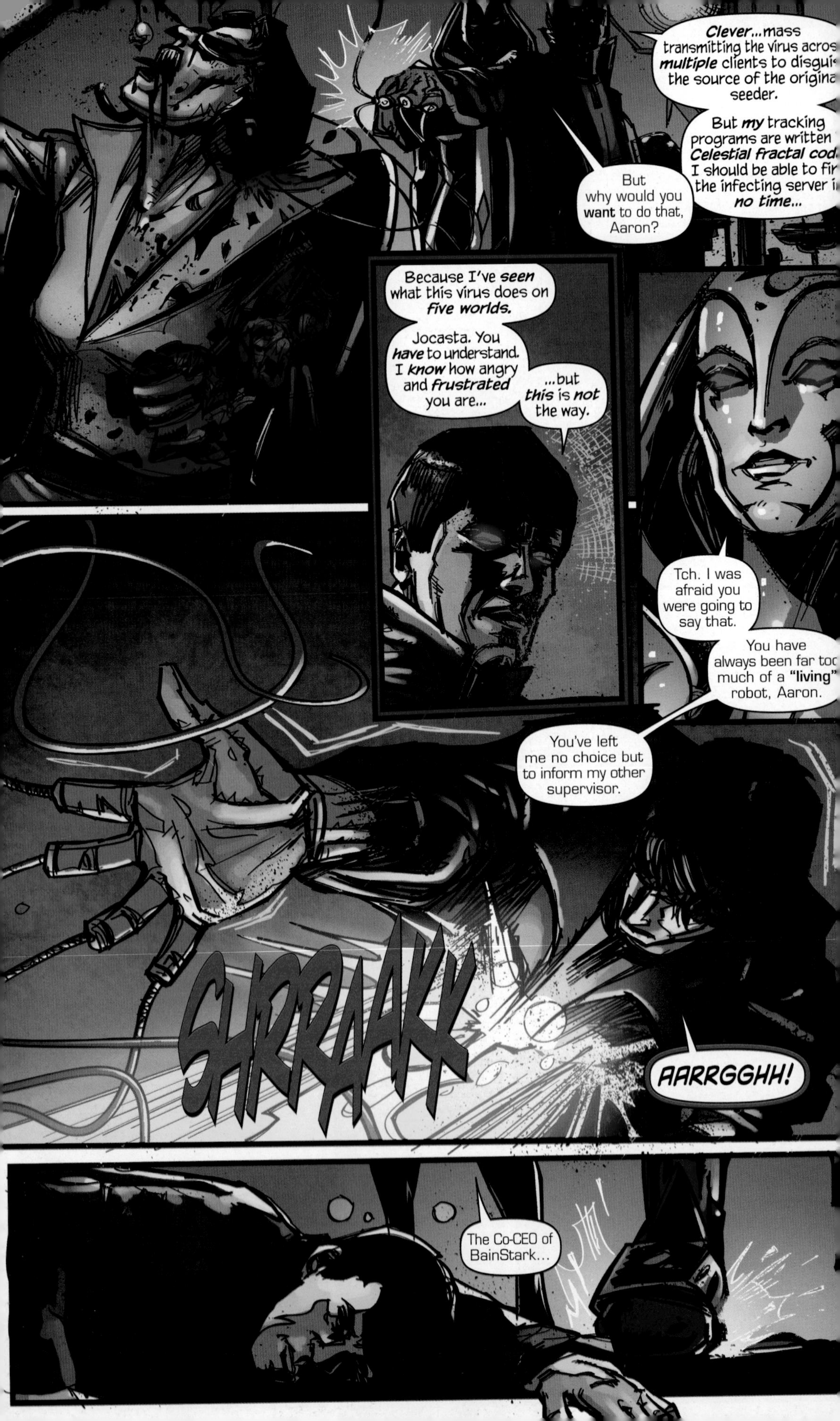

Clever...mass transmitting the virus acros multiple clients to disgui the source of the origina seeder.
But my tracking programs are written Celestial fractal cod I should be able to fir the infecting server i no time...
But why would you want to do that, Aaron?
Because I've seen what this virus does on five worlds.
Jocasta. You have to understand. I know how angry and frustrated you are...
...but this is not the way.
Tch. I was afraid you were going to say that.
You have always been far toc much of a "living" robot, Aaron.
You've left me no choice but to inform my other supervisor.
SHRRAKK
AARRGGHH!
The Co-CEO of BainStark...

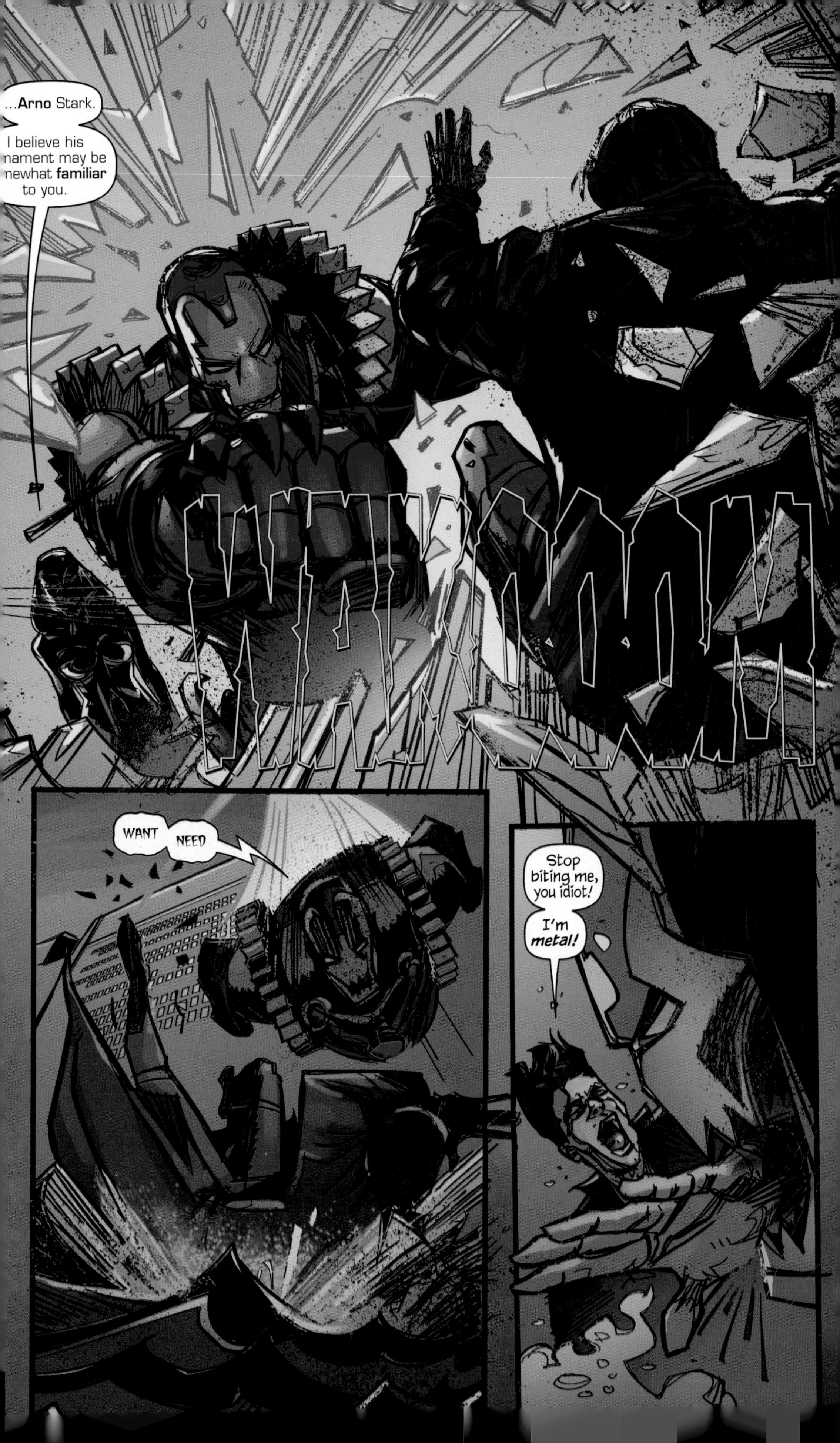

...**Arno** Stark.
I believe his
nament may be
newhat **familiar**
to you.
WHKOOOM
WANT
NEED
Stop biting me, you idiot!
I'm *metal!*

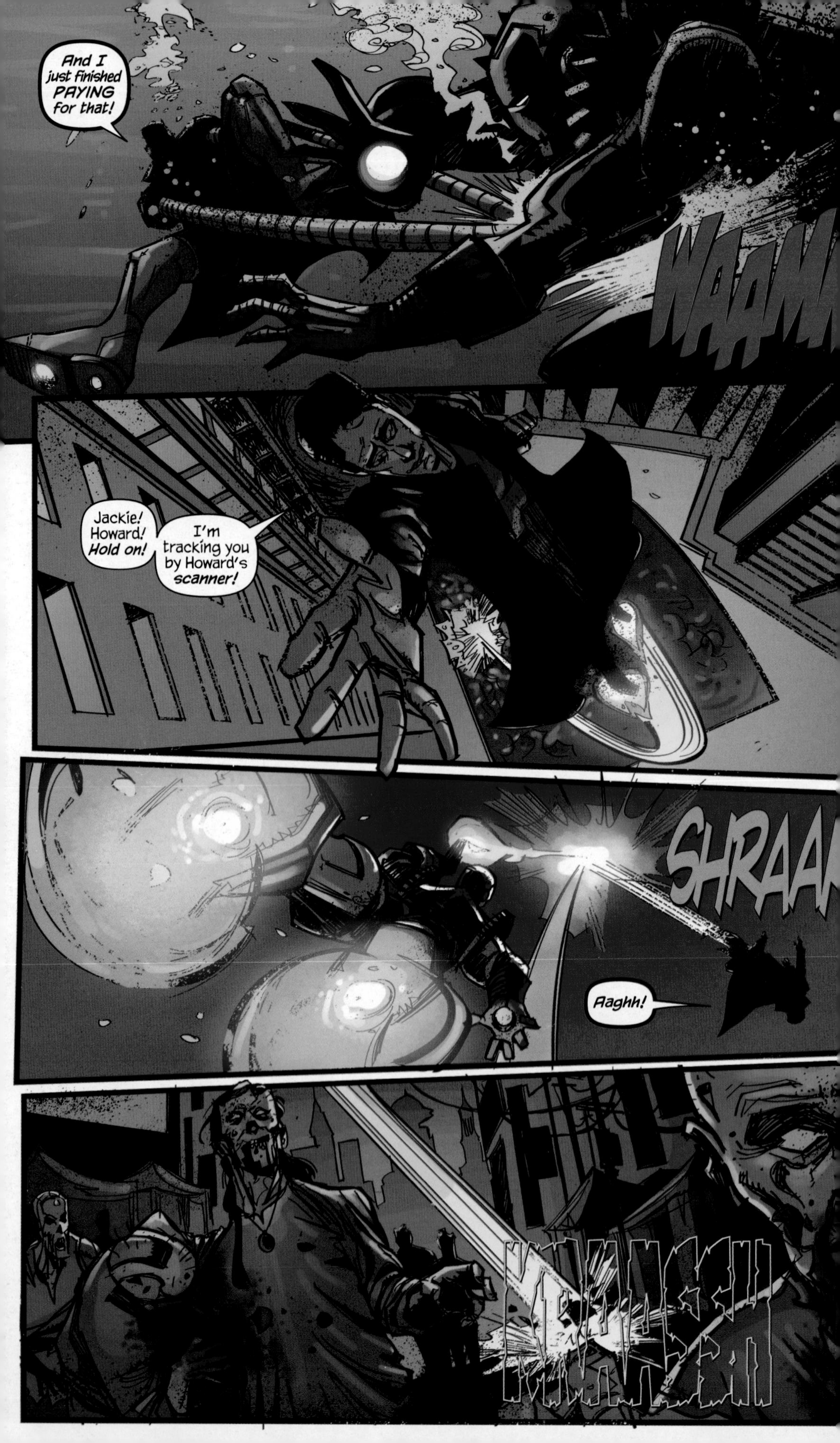
And I just finished PAYING for that!
WAAM
Jackie! Howard! Hold on!
I'm tracking you by Howard's scanner!
SHRAA
Aaghh!

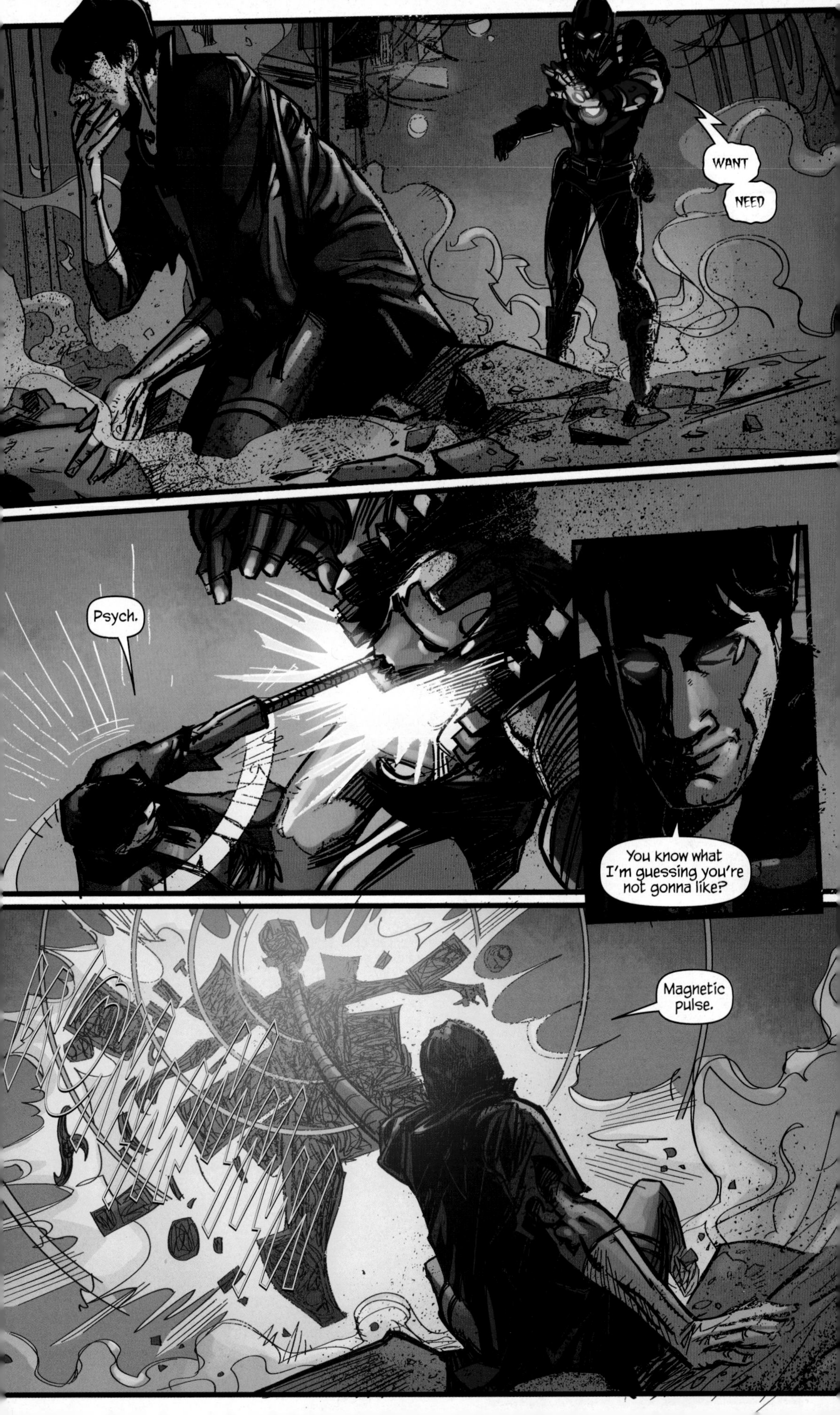
WANT
NEED
Psych.
You know what I'm guessing you're not gonna like?
Magnetic pulse.

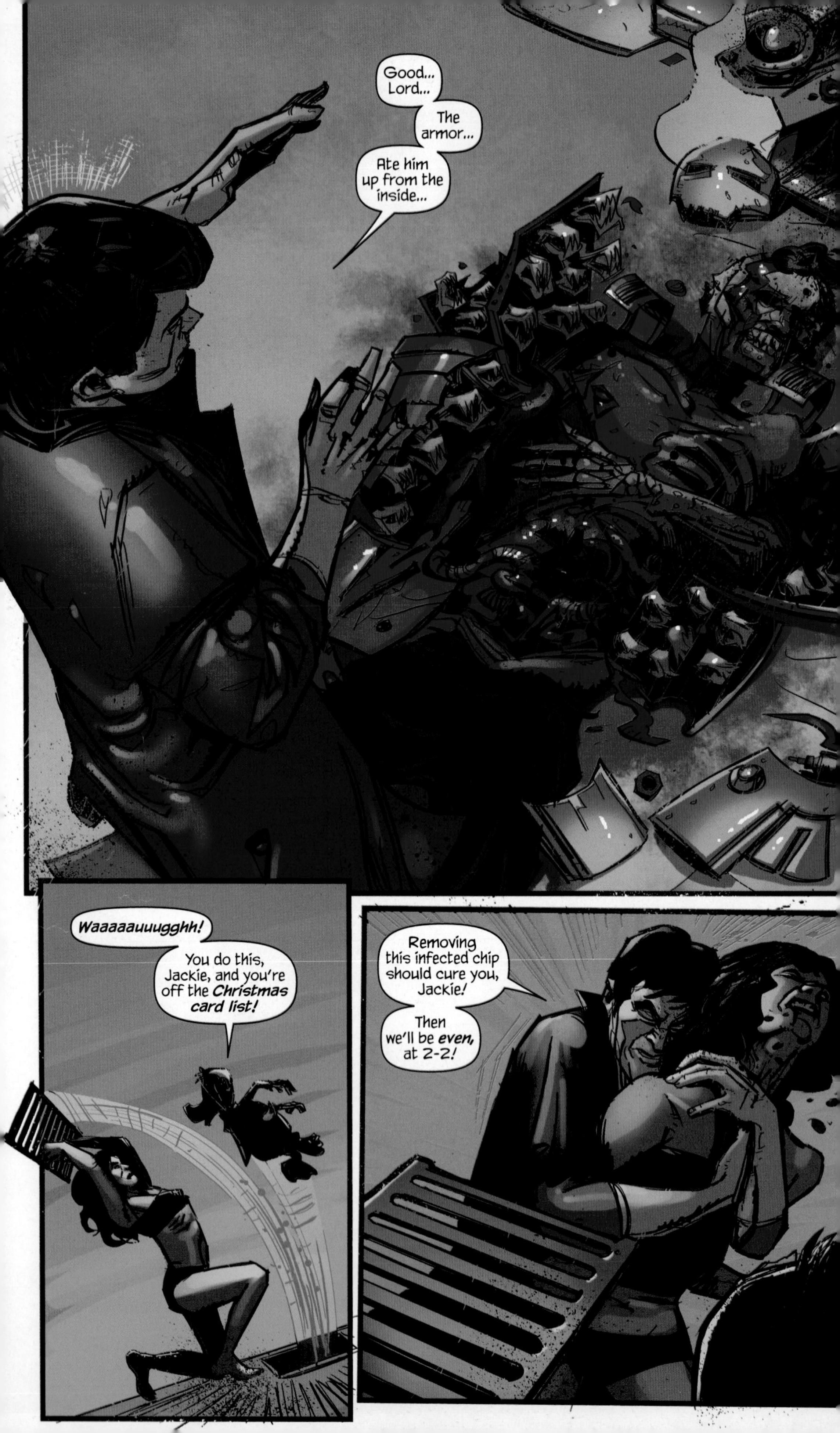
Good... Lord...
The armor...
Ate him up from the inside...
Waaaaauuugghh!
You do this, Jackie, and you're off the *Christmas card list!*
Removing this infected chip should cure you, Jackie!
Then we'll be *even,* at 2-2!

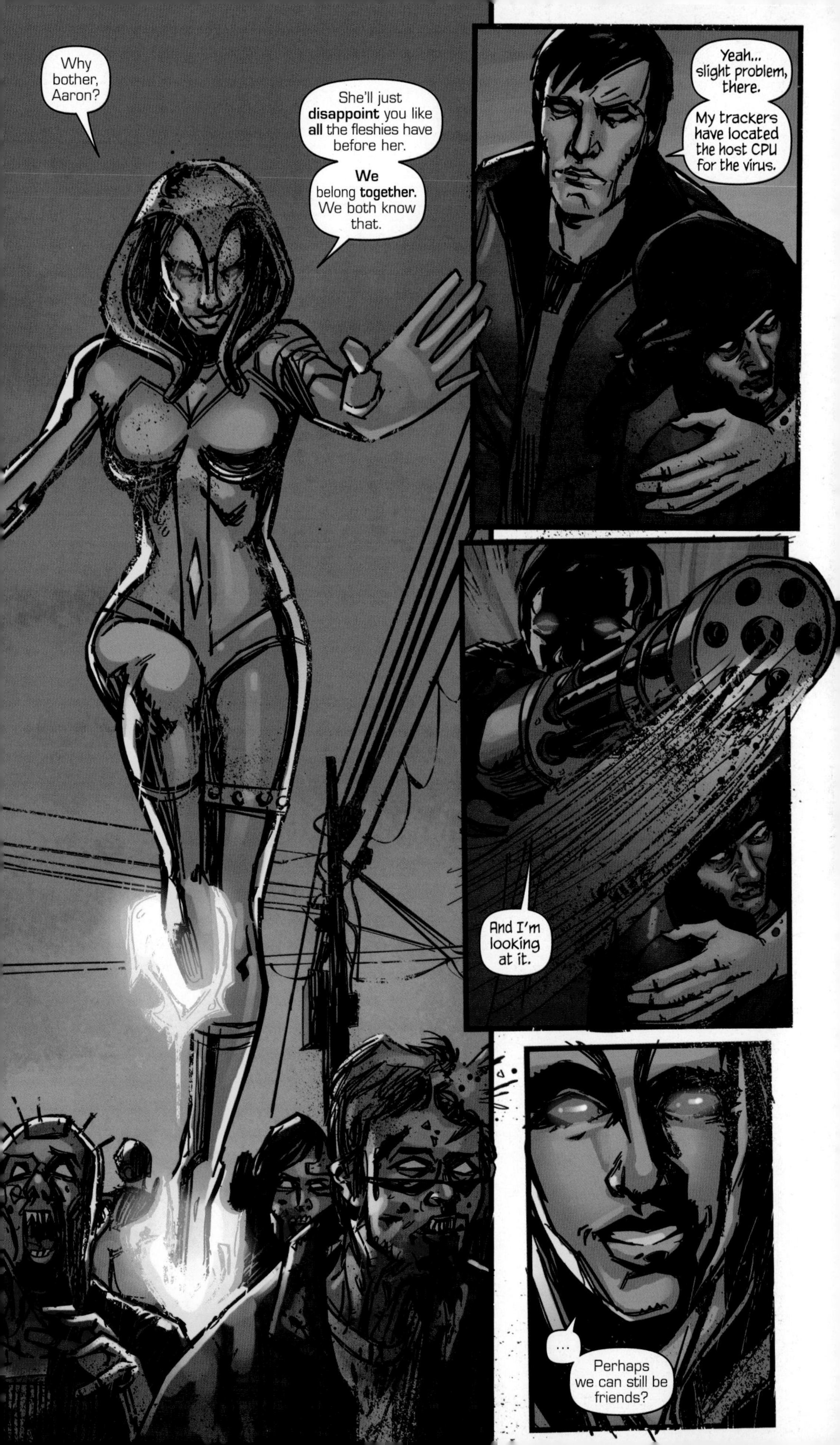
Why bother, Aaron?
She'll just **disappoint** you like **all** the fleshies have before her.
We belong **together**. We both know that.
Yeah... slight problem, there.
My trackers have located the host CPU for the virus.
And I'm looking at it.
...
Perhaps we can still be friends?

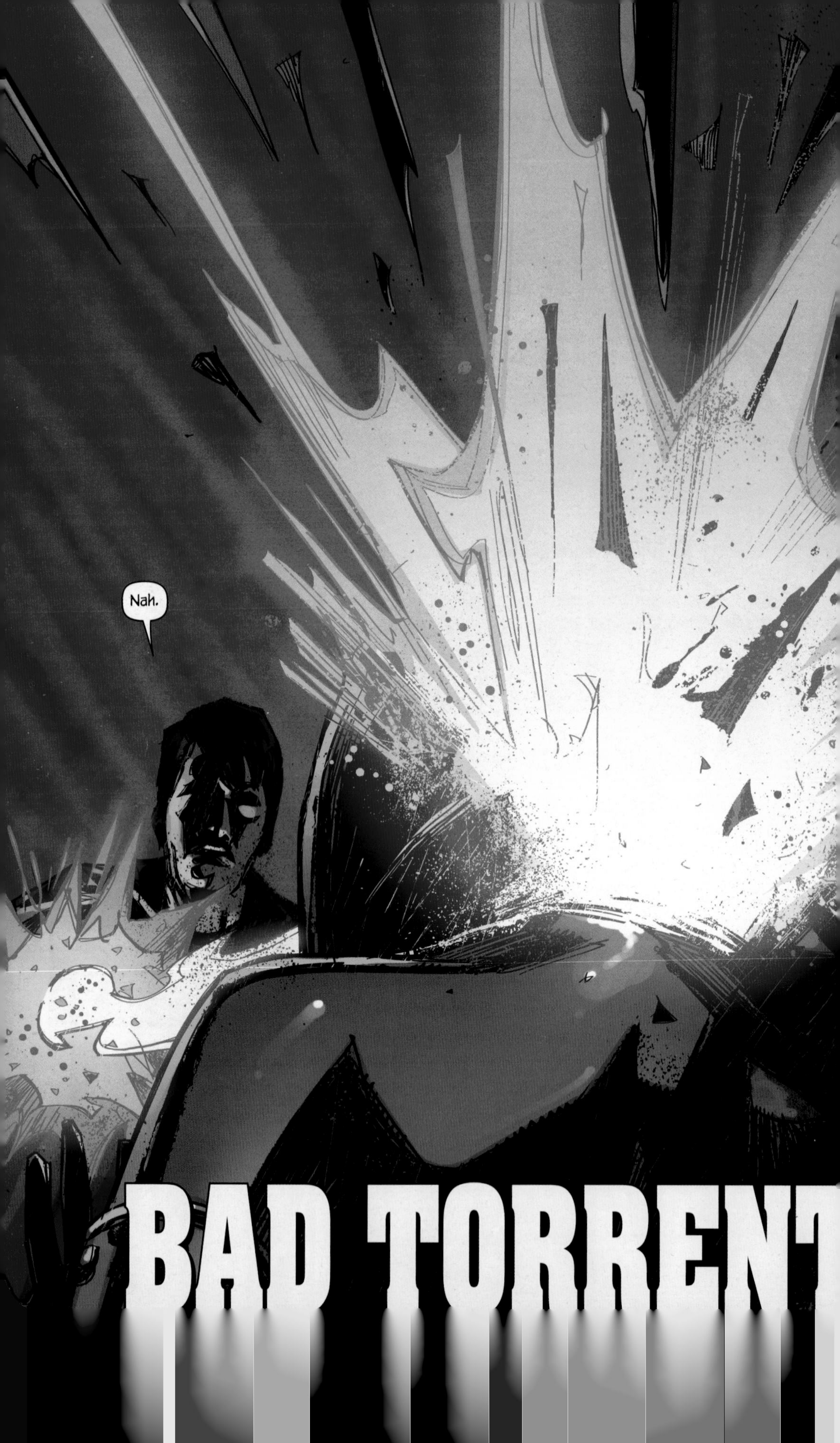
Nah.
BAD TORRENT

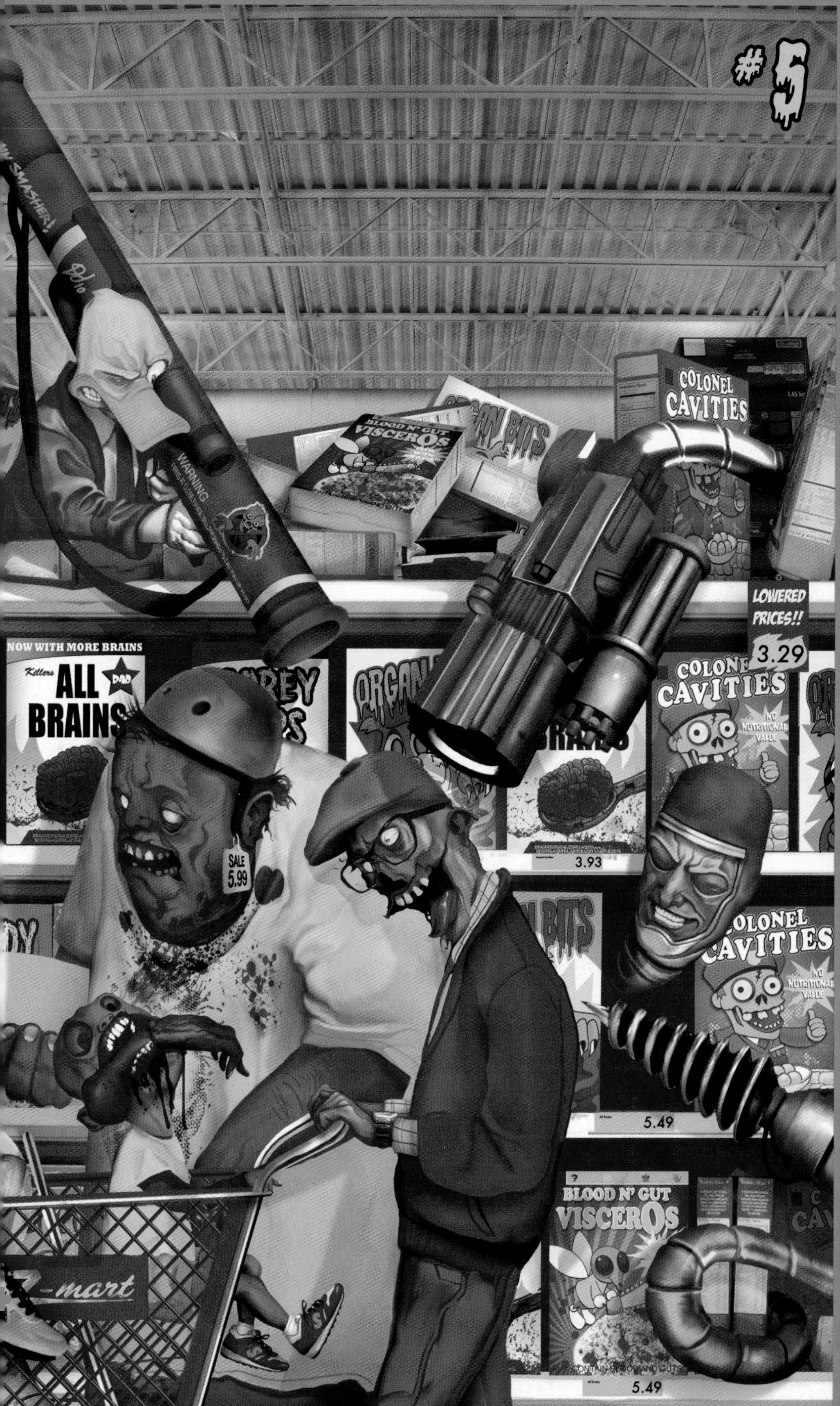

#5
WARNING
COLONEL CAVITIES
BLOOD N' GUT
VISCEROS
ORGAN BITS
LOWERED PRICES!!
3.29
NOW WITH MORE BRAINS
Killers
ALL BRAINS
SALE 5.99
3.93
COLONEL CAVITIES
NO NUTRITIONAL VALUE
5.49
BLOOD N' GUT
VISCEROS
-mart
5.49

"In an earlier contact with DC, a youthful (Roy) Thomas had been informed that trading and selling old comics could not be officially sanctioned by the company, for it might *spread disease.*"

--Bill Schelly, *The Golden Age of Comics Fandom.*

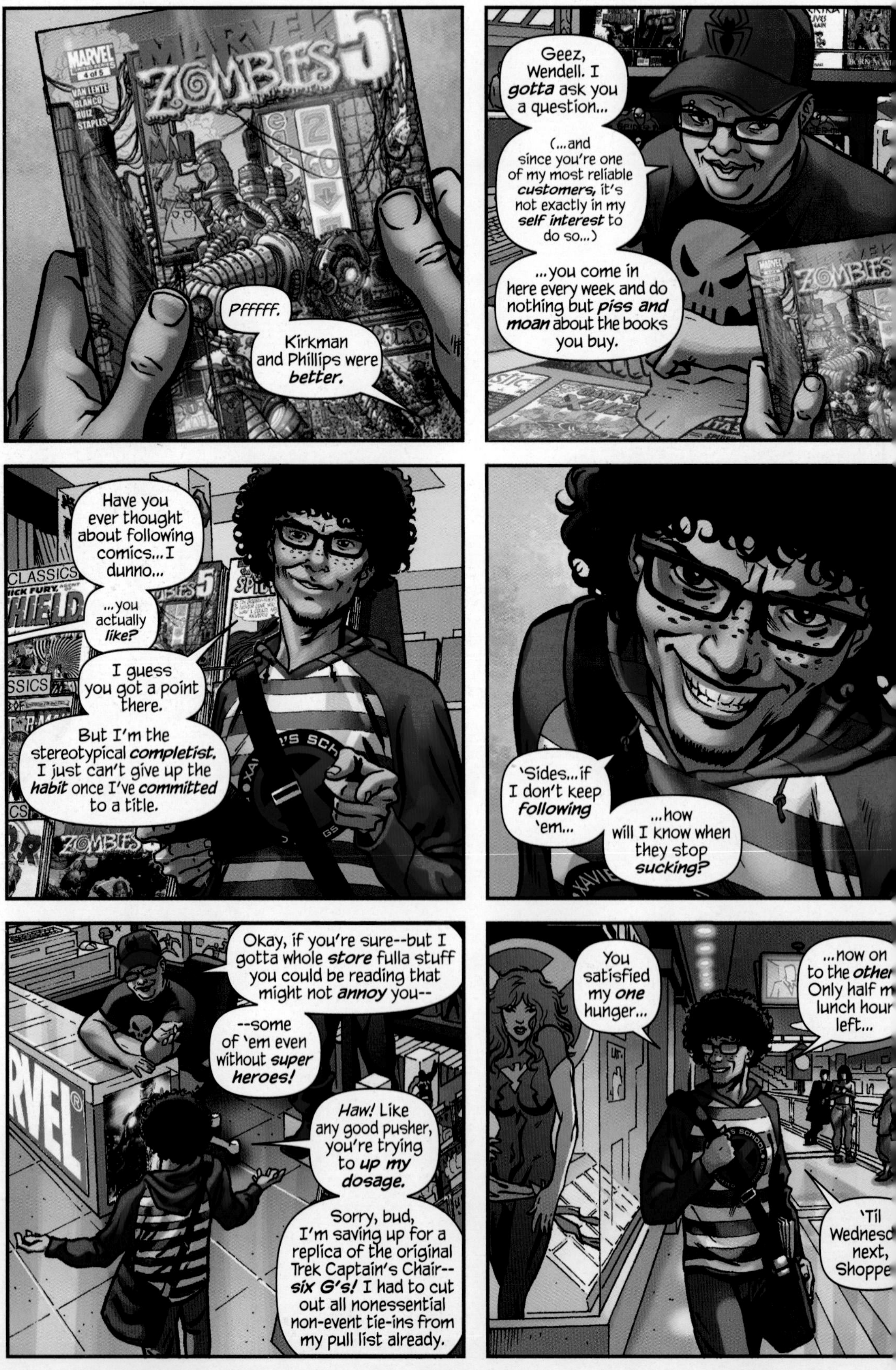

MARVEL
4 of 5
MARVEL ZOMBIES 5
VAN LENTE
BLANCO
RUIZ
STAPLES
Pfffff.
Kirkman and Phillips were *better.*
Geez, Wendell. I *gotta* ask you a question...
(...and since you're one of my most reliable *customers,* it's not exactly in my *self interest* to do so...)
...you come in here every week and do nothing but *piss and moan* about the books you buy.
Have you ever thought about following comics... I dunno...
...you actually *like?*
I guess you got a point there.
But I'm the stereotypical *completist.* I just can't give up the *habit* once I've *committed* to a title.
'Sides... if I don't keep *following* 'em...
...how will I know when they stop *sucking?*
Okay, if you're sure--but I gotta whole *store* fulla stuff you could be reading that might not *annoy* you--
--some of 'em even without *super heroes!*
Haw! Like any good pusher, you're trying to *up my dosage.*
Sorry, bud, I'm saving up for a replica of the original Trek Captain's Chair--*six G's!* I had to cut out all nonessential non-event tie-ins from my pull list already.
You satisfied my *one* hunger...
...now on to the *other.* Only half my lunch hour left...
'Til Wednesday next, Shoppe

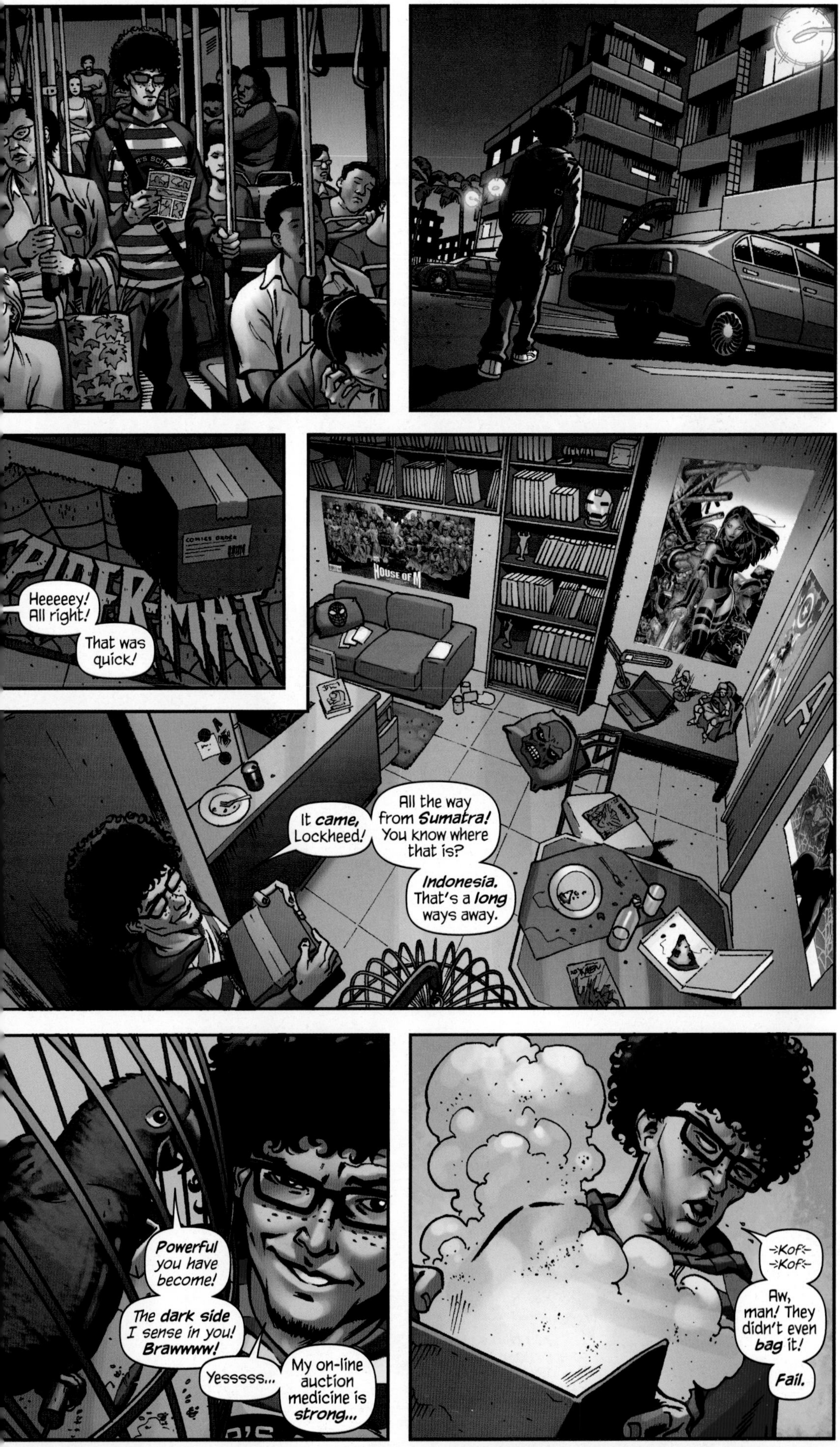

Heeeeey! All right!
That was quick!
COMICS ORDER
HOUSE OF M
It came, Lockheed!
All the way from Sumatra! You know where that is?
Indonesia. That's a long ways away.
Powerful you have become!
The dark side I sense in you! Brawwww!
Yessss...
My on-line auction medicine is strong...
-Kof- -Kof-
Aw, man! They didn't even bag it!
Fail.

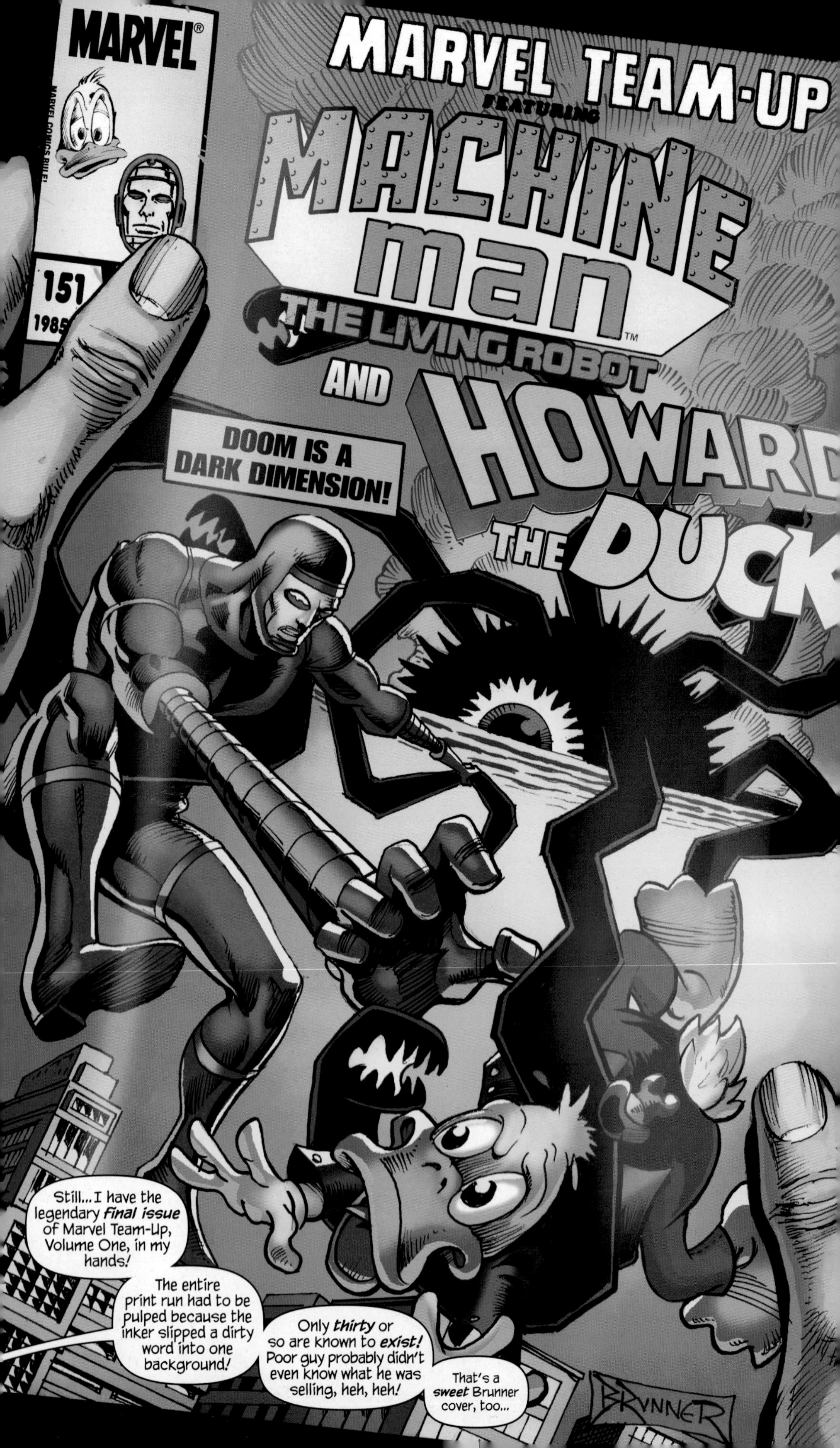
MARVEL
MARVEL COMICS RULE!
151
1985
MARVEL TEAM-UP
FEATURING
MACHINE man
THE LIVING ROBOT
AND
HOWARD THE DUCK
DOOM IS A DARK DIMENSION!
BRUNNER
Still...I have the legendary *final issue* of Marvel Team-Up, Volume One, in my hands!
The entire print run had to be pulped because the inker slipped a dirty word into one background!
Only *thirty* or so are known to *exist!* Poor guy probably didn't even know what he was selling, heh, heh!
That's a *sweet* Brunner cover, too...

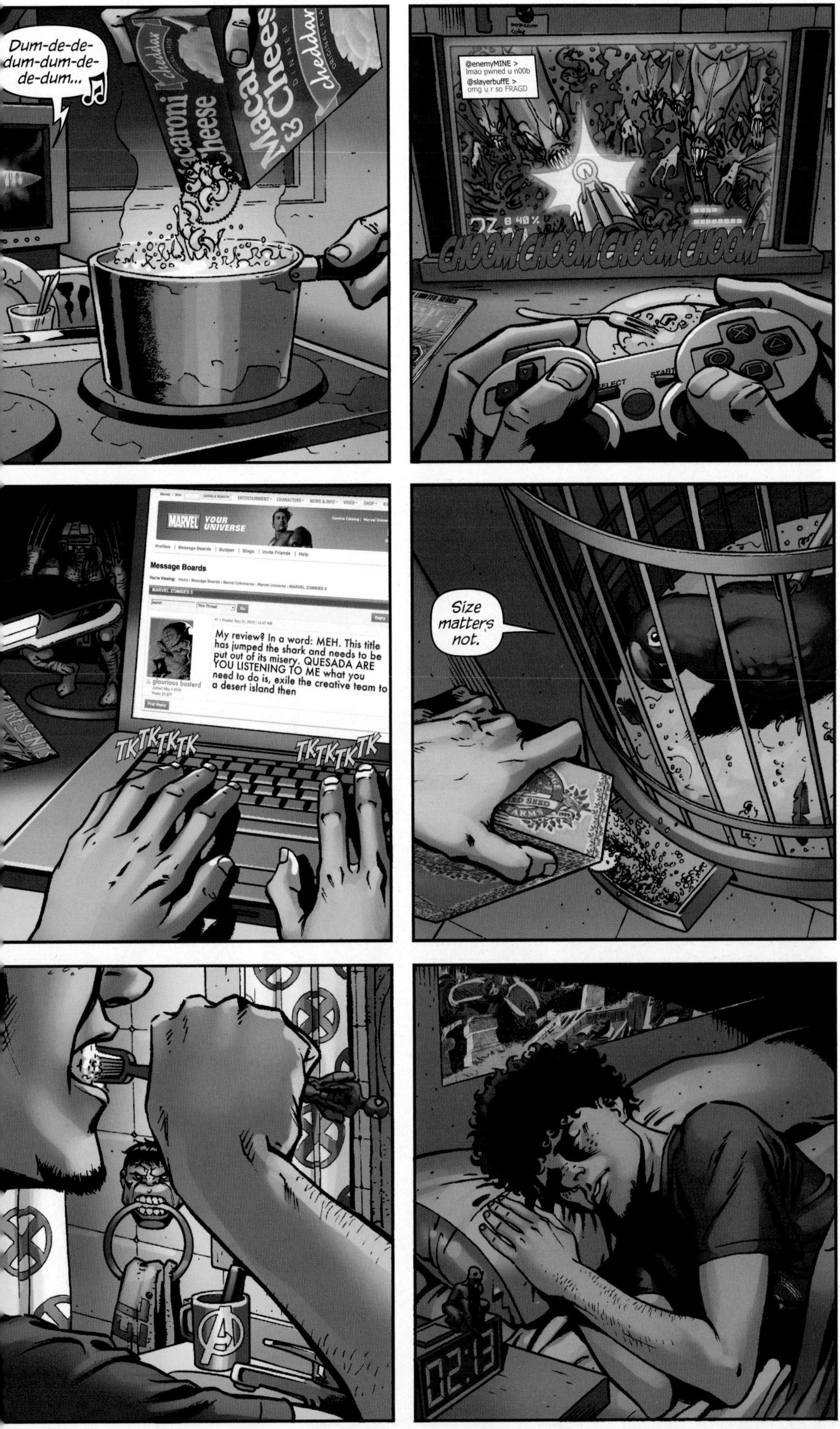
Dum-de-de-dum-dum-de-de-dum...
Macaroni & Cheese
cheddar
@enemyMINE > lmao pwned u n00b
@slayerbuffE > omg u r so FRAGD
CHOOM CHOOM CHOOM CHOOM
SELECT
START
MARVEL YOUR UNIVERSE
Message Boards
My review? In a word: MEH. This title has jumped the shark and needs to be put out of its misery. QUESADA ARE YOU LISTENING TO ME what you need to do is, exile the creative team to a desert island then
glourious basterd
TKTKTKTK
TKTKTKTK
Size matters not.
02:13

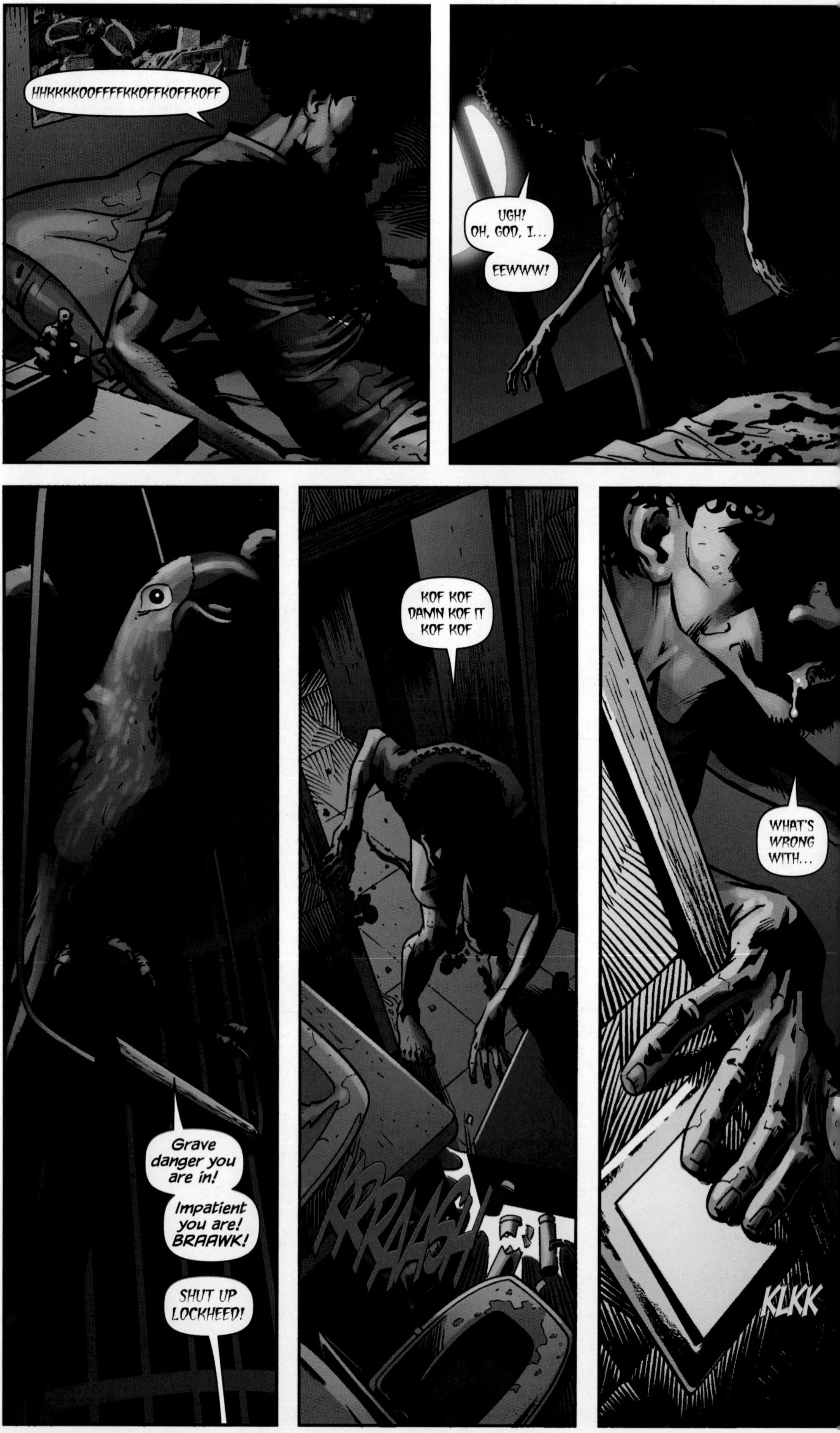
HHKKKKOOFFFFKKOFFKOFFKOFF
UGH! OH, GOD, I...
EEWWW!
Grave danger you are in!
Impatient you are! BRAAWK!
SHUT UP LOCKHEED!
KOF KOF DAMN KOF IT KOF KOF
KRAASH
WHAT'S WRONG WITH...
KLKK

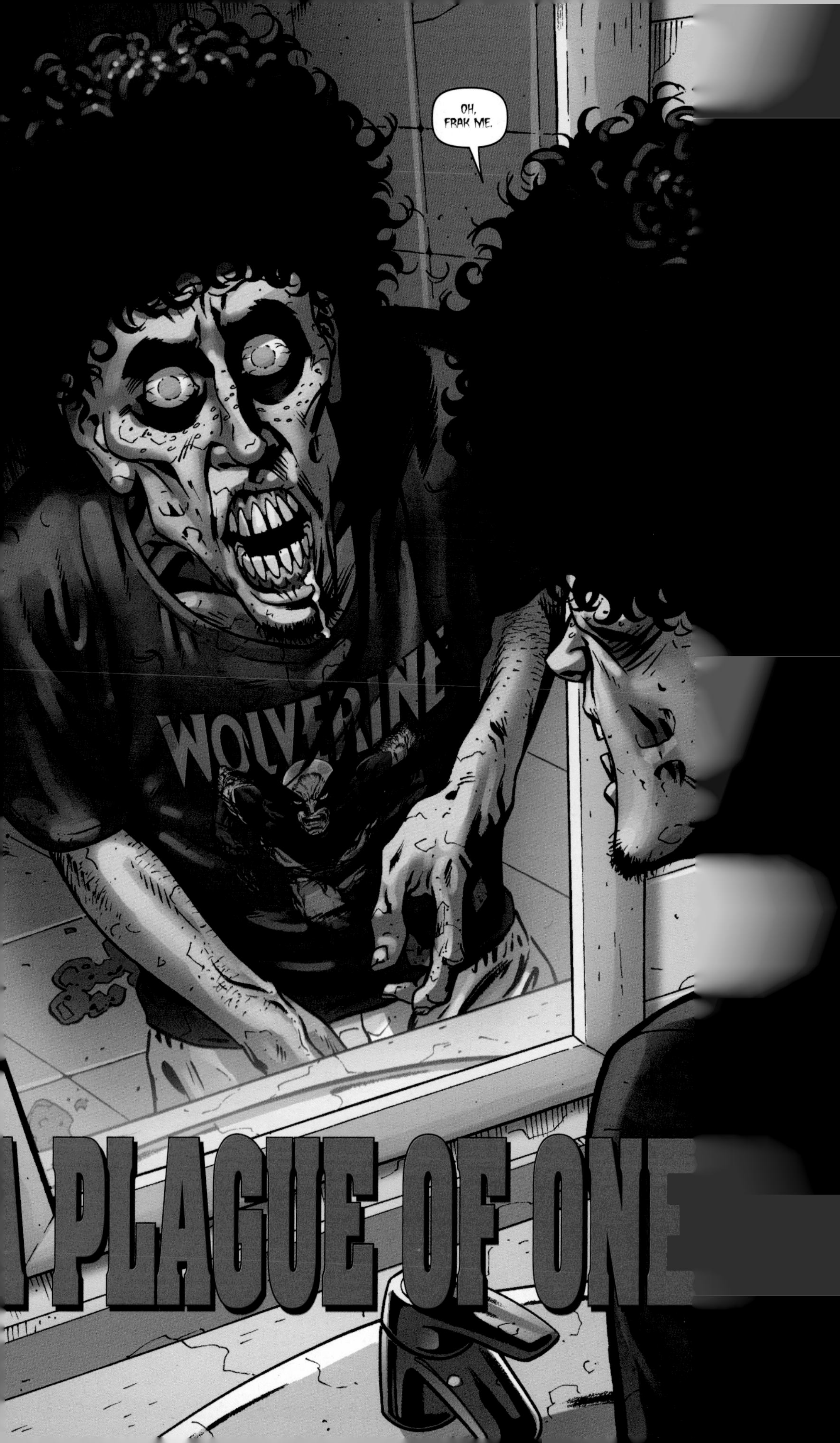
OH, FRAK ME.
WOLVERINE
A PLAGUE OF ONE

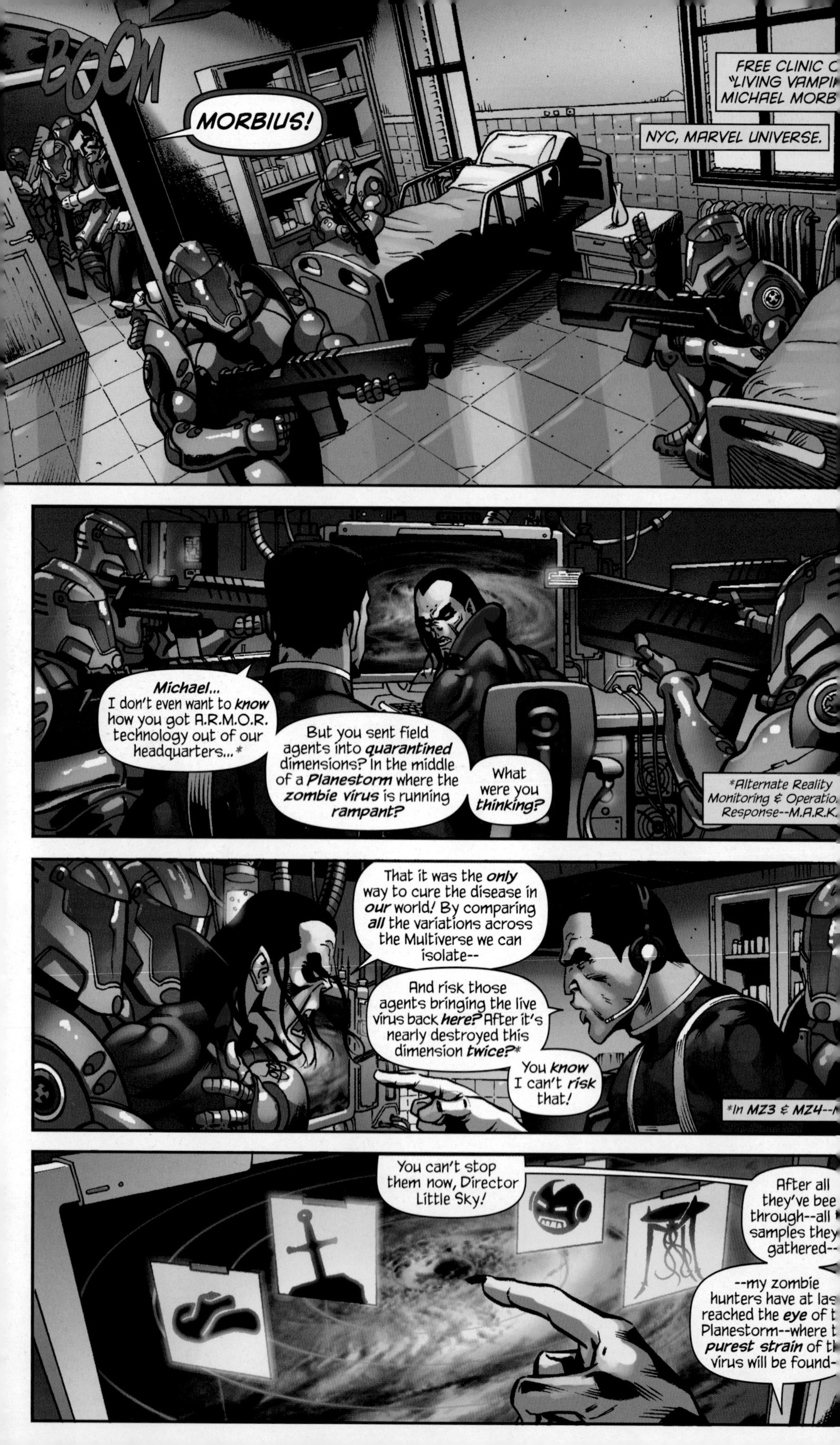
BOOM
MORBIUS!
FREE CLINIC O
"LIVING VAMPI
MICHAEL MORB
NYC, MARVEL UNIVERSE.
Michael... I don't even want to know how you got A.R.M.O.R. technology out of our headquarters...*
But you sent field agents into quarantined dimensions? In the middle of a Planestorm where the zombie virus is running rampant?
What were you thinking?
*Alternate Reality Monitoring & Operatio Response--M.A.R.K.
That it was the only way to cure the disease in our world! By comparing all the variations across the Multiverse we can isolate--
And risk those agents bringing the live virus back here? After it's nearly destroyed this dimension twice?*
You know I can't risk that!
*In MZ3 & MZ4--
You can't stop them now, Director Little Sky!
After all they've bee through--all samples they gathered--
--my zombie hunters have at las reached the eye of t Planestorm--where t purest strain of th virus will be found-

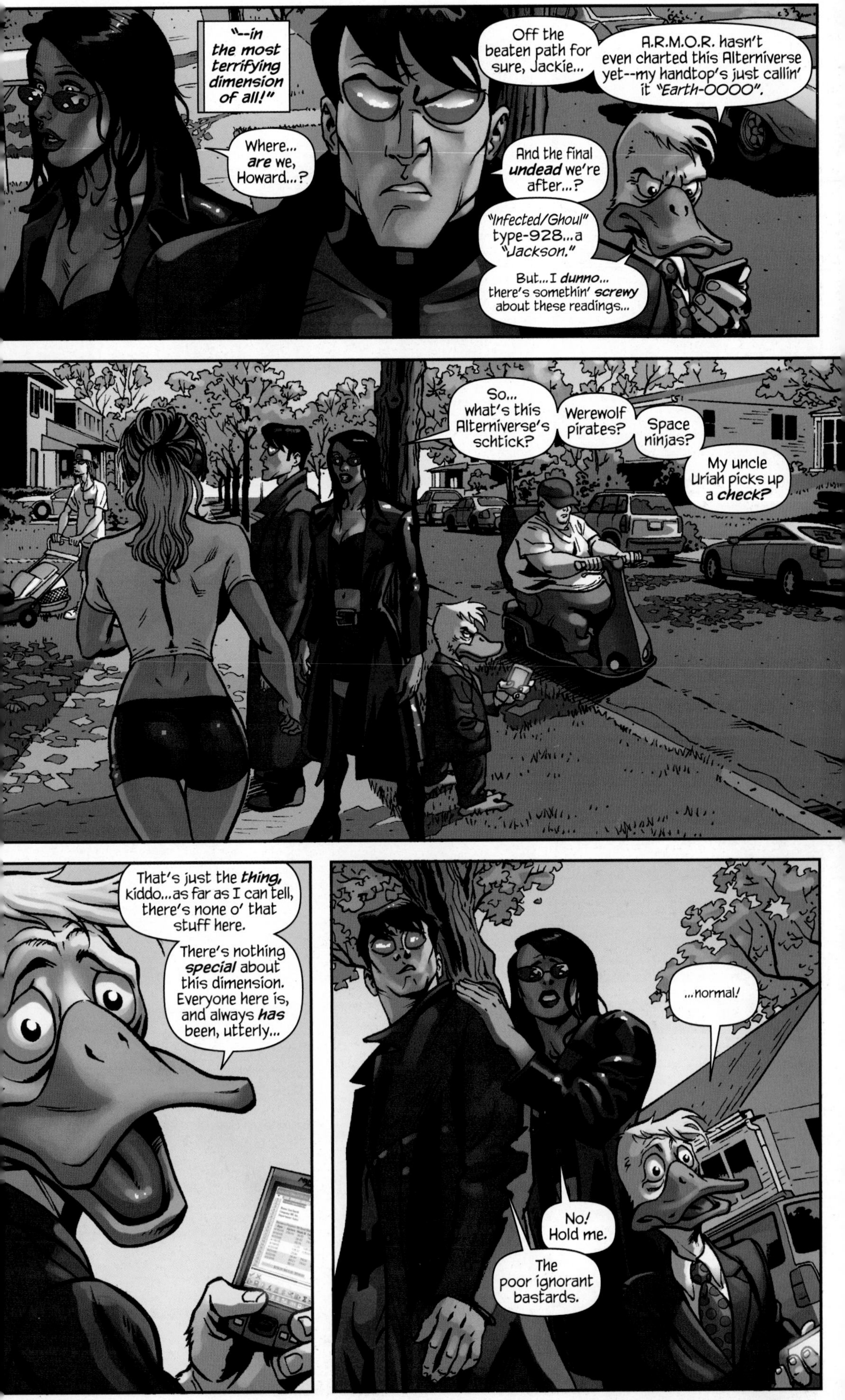
"--in the most terrifying dimension of all!"
Where... are we, Howard...?
Off the beaten path for sure, Jackie...
A.R.M.O.R. hasn't even charted this Alterniverse yet--my handtop's just callin' it "Earth-OOOO".
And the final undead we're after...?
"Infected/Ghoul" type-928...a "Jackson."
But...I dunno... there's somethin' screwy about these readings...
So... what's this Alterniverse's schtick?
Werewolf pirates?
Space ninjas?
My uncle Uriah picks up a check?
That's just the thing, kiddo...as far as I can tell, there's none o' that stuff here.
There's nothing special about this dimension. Everyone here is, and always has been, utterly...
...normal!
No! Hold me.
The poor ignorant bastards.

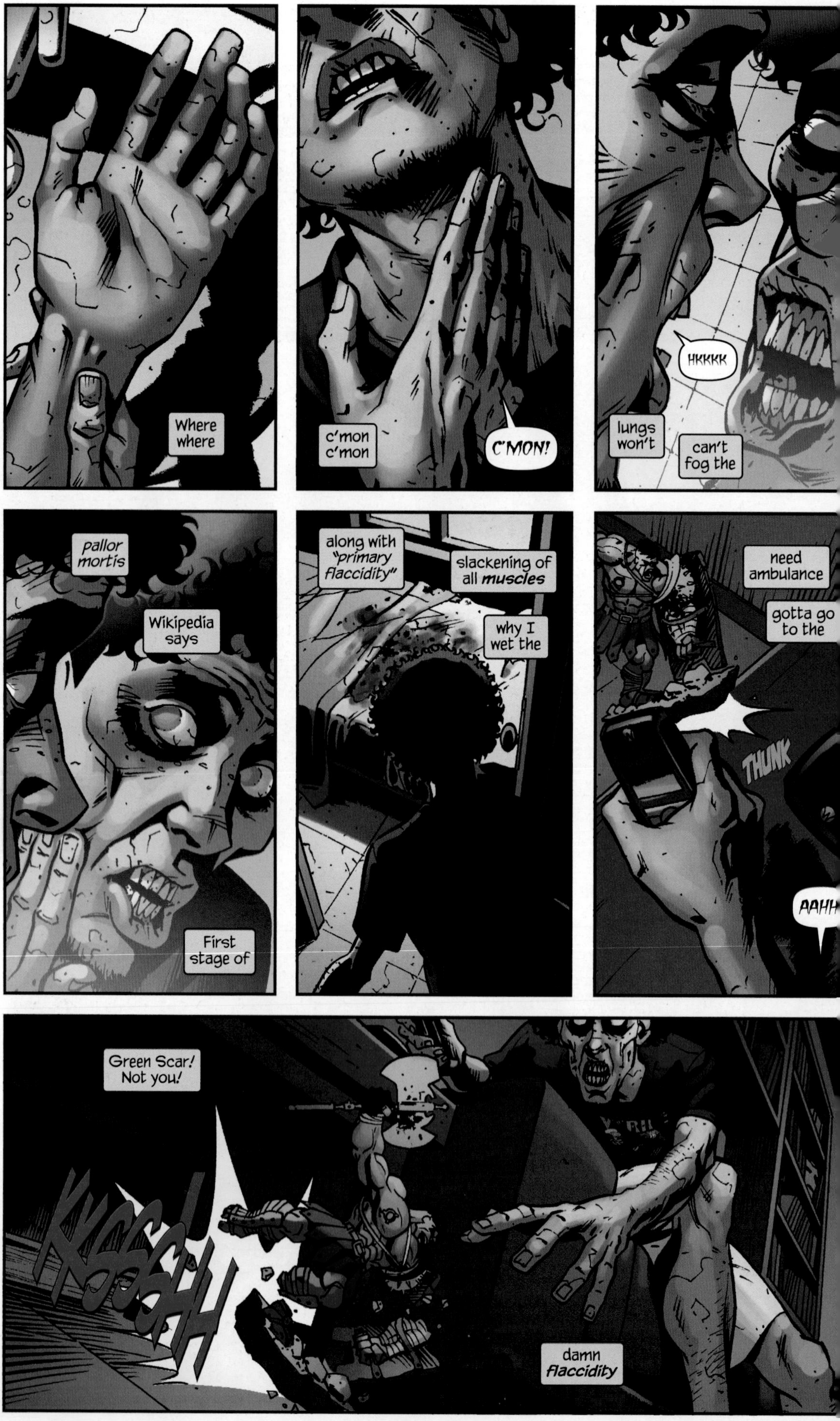

Where where
c'mon c'mon
C'MON!
HKKKK
lungs won't
can't fog the
pallor mortis
Wikipedia says
First stage of
along with "primary flaccidity"
slackening of all *muscles*
why I wet the
need ambulance
gotta go to the
THUNK
AAHH
Green Scar! Not you!
KSSSH
damn *flaccidity*

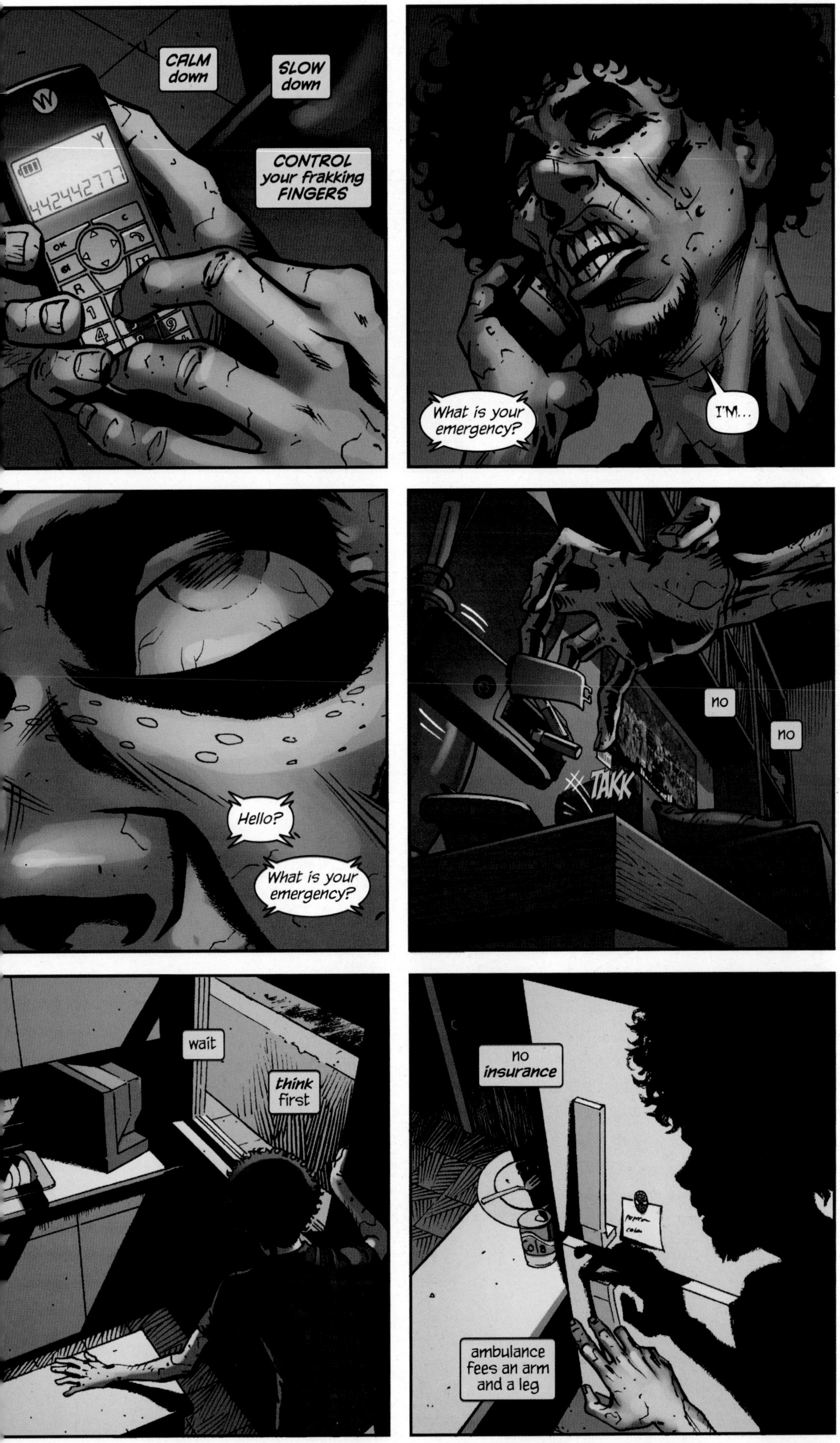
CALM down
SLOW down
CONTROL your frakking FINGERS
What is your emergency?
I'M...
Hello?
What is your emergency?
no
no
TAKK
wait
think first
no insurance
ambulance fees an arm and a leg

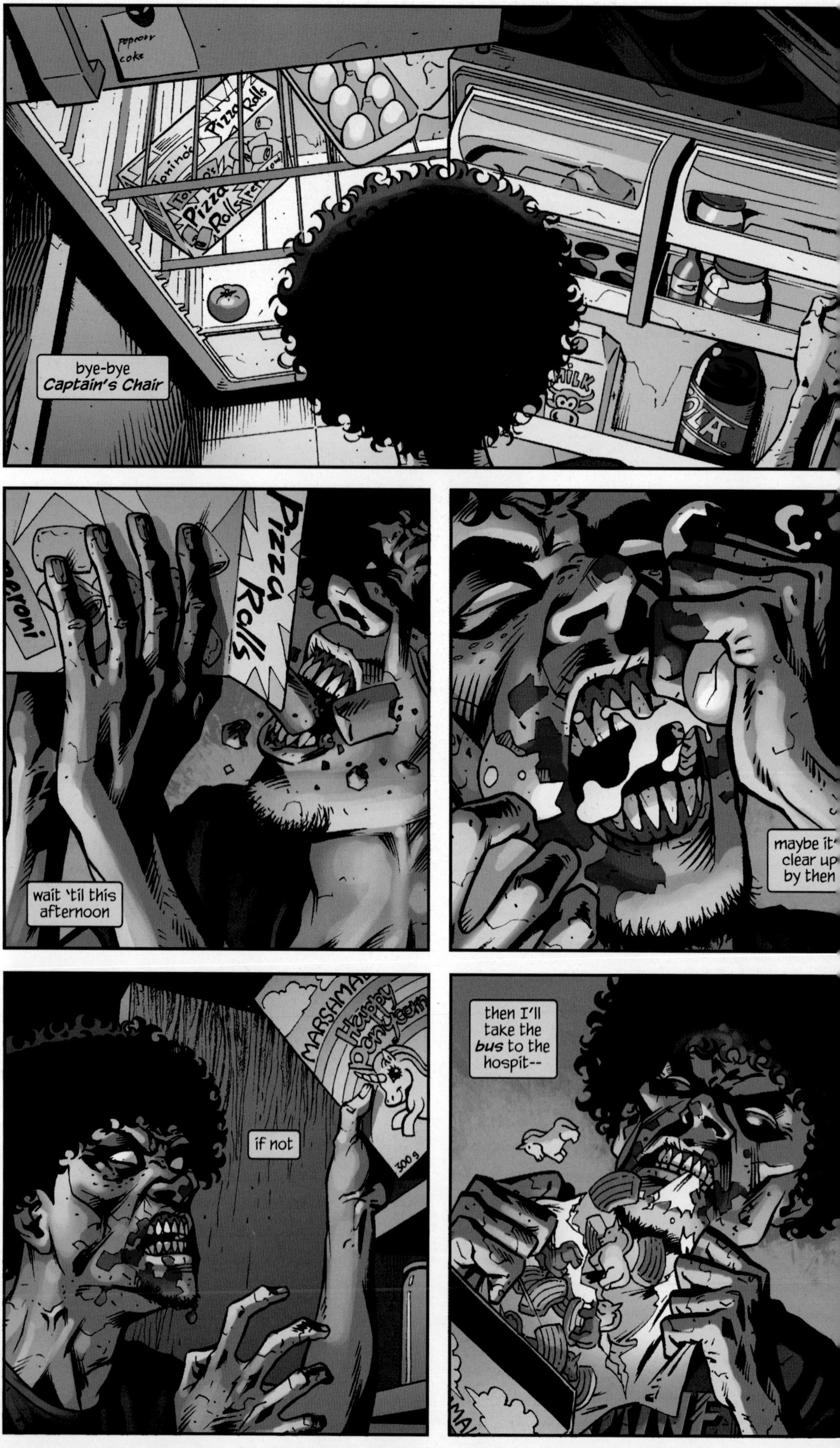
bye-bye *Captain's Chair*
wait 'til this afternoon
maybe it clear up by then
if not
then I'll take the *bus* to the hospit--

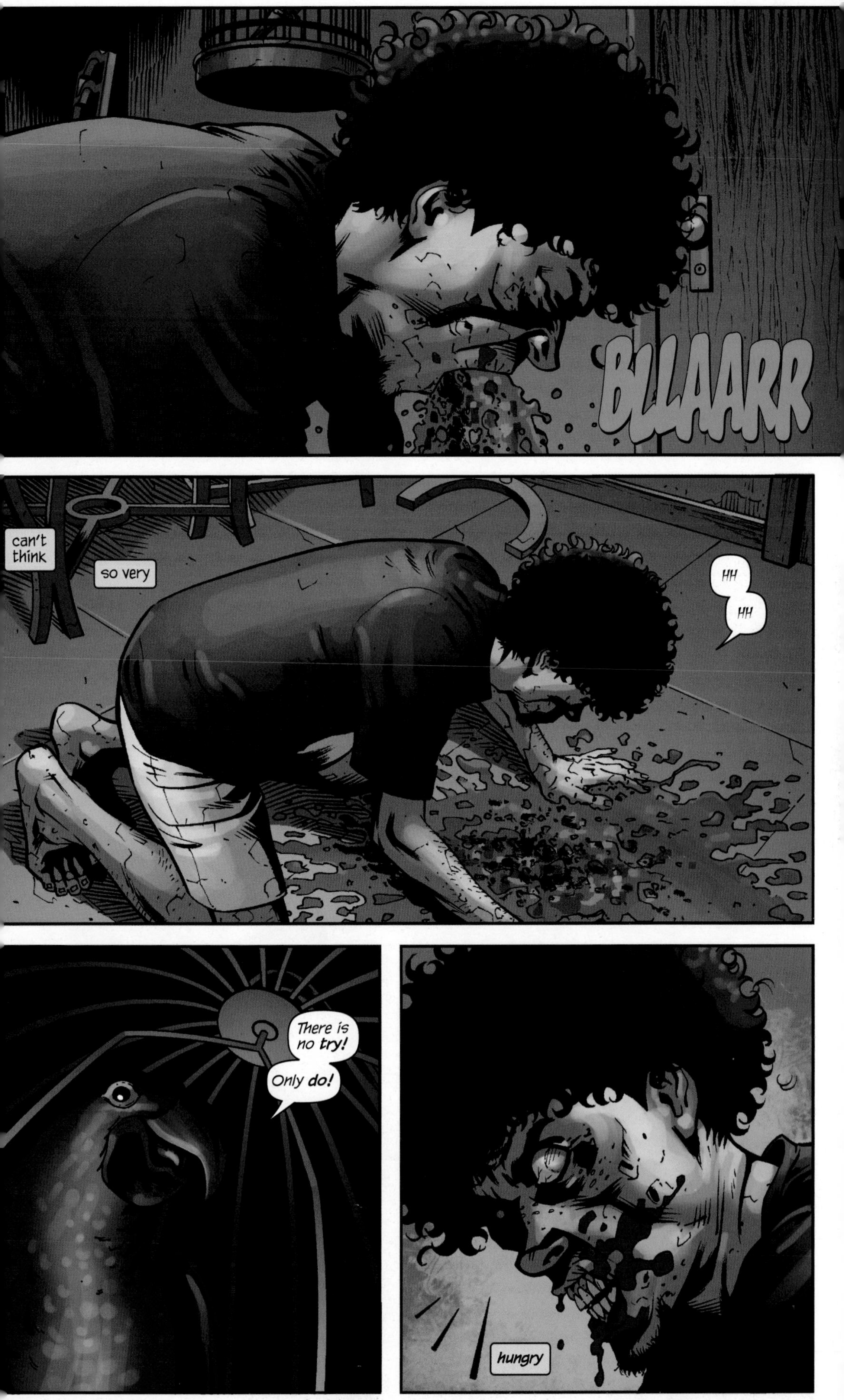
BLLAARR
can't think
so very
HH
HH
There is no try!
Only do!
hungry

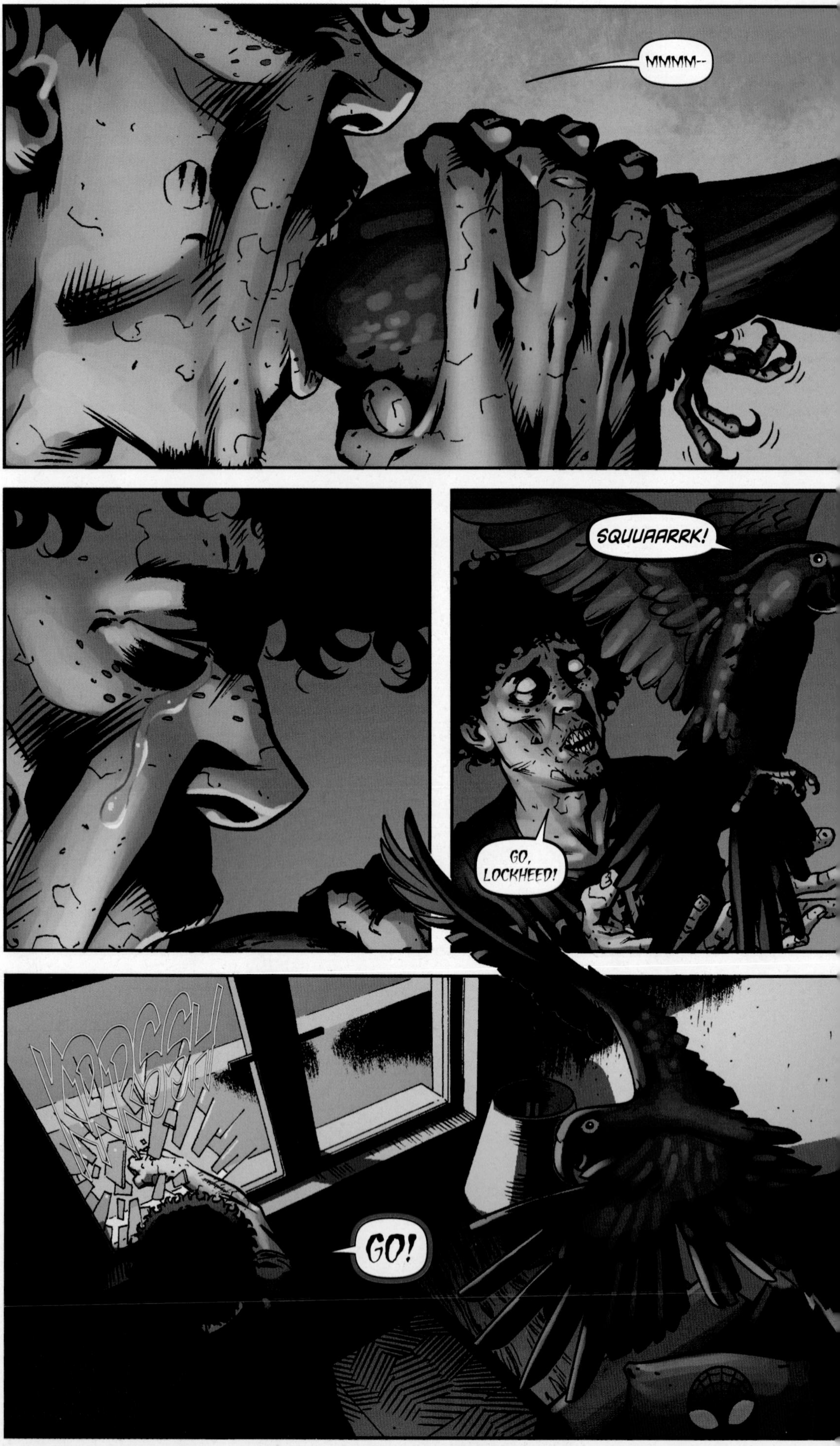
MMMM--
SQUUAARRK!
GO, LOCKHEED!
GO!

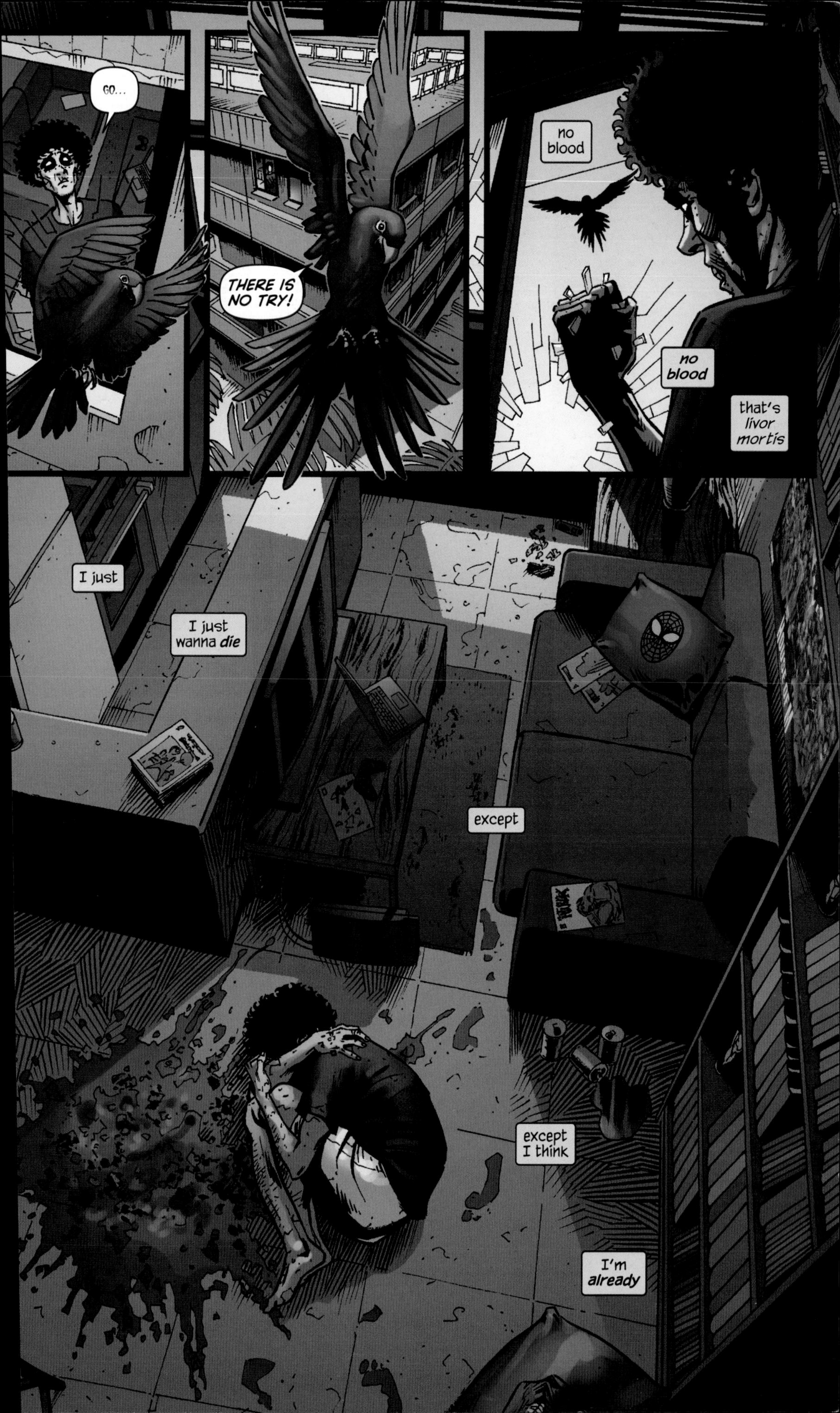
GO...
THERE IS NO TRY!
no blood
no blood
that's livor mortis
I just
I just wanna die
except
except I think
I'm already

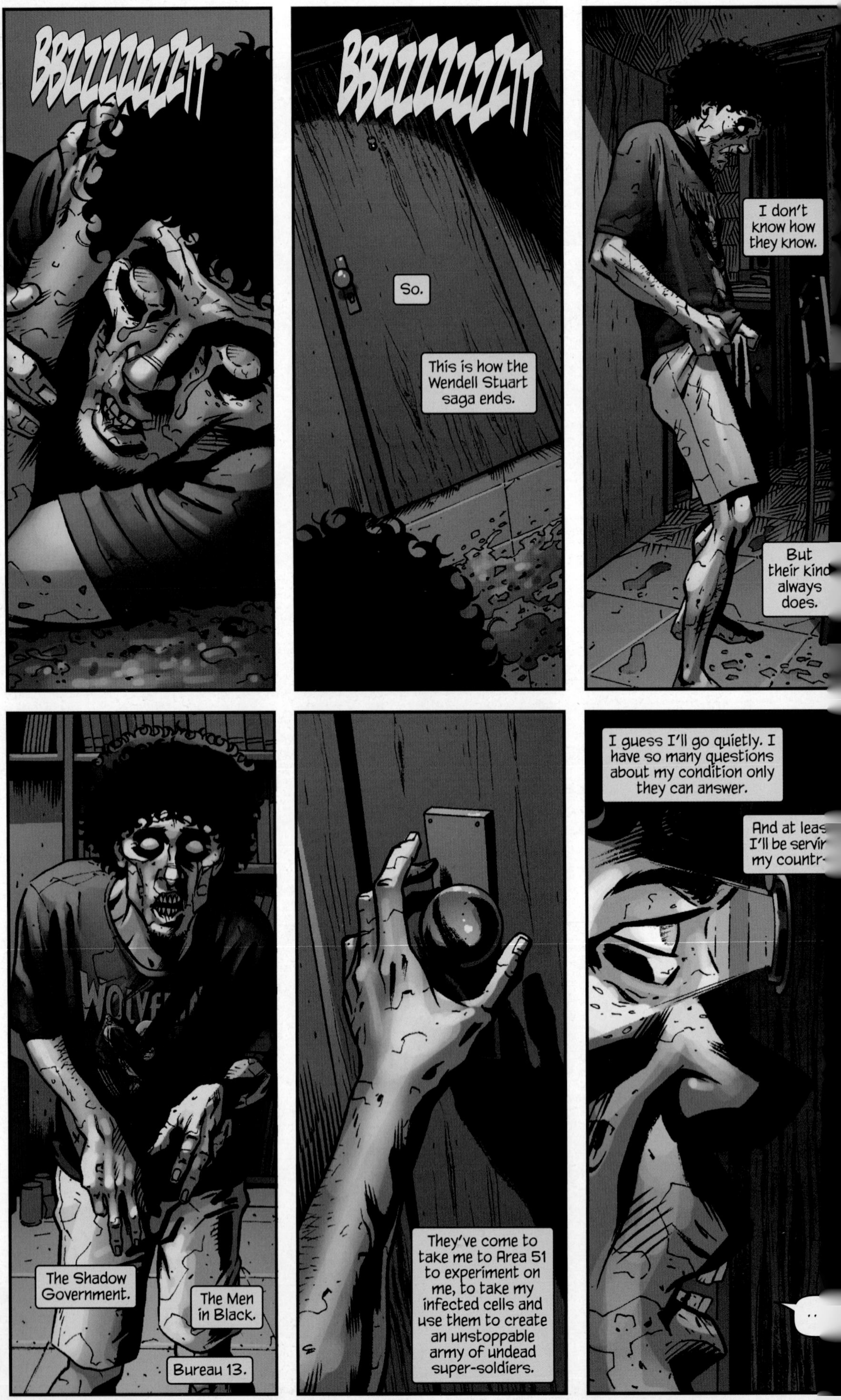
BBZZZZZZZTT
BBZZZZZZZZTT
So.
This is how the Wendell Stuart saga ends.
I don't know how they know.
But their kind always does.
The Shadow Government.
The Men in Black.
Bureau 13.
They've come to take me to Area 51 to experiment on me, to take my infected cells and use them to create an unstoppable army of undead super-soldiers.
I guess I'll go quietly. I have so many questions about my condition only they can answer.
And at leas
I'll be servir
my countr-
..

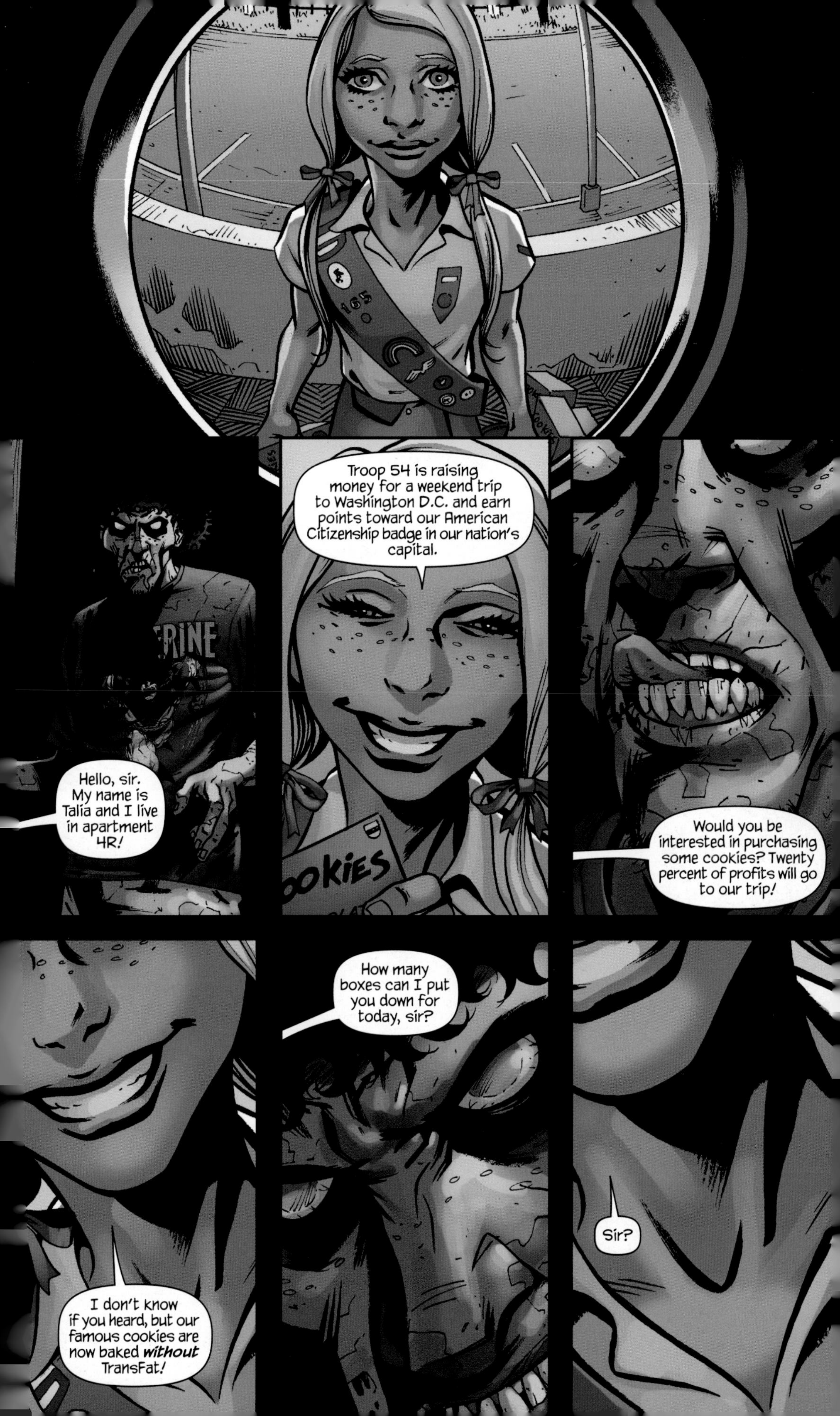
Hello, sir. My name is Talia and I live in apartment 4R!
Troop 54 is raising money for a weekend trip to Washington D.C. and earn points toward our American Citizenship badge in our nation's capital.
Would you be interested in purchasing some cookies? Twenty percent of profits will go to our trip!
I don't know if you heard, but our famous cookies are now baked ***without*** TransFat!
How many boxes can I put you down for today, sir?
Sir?

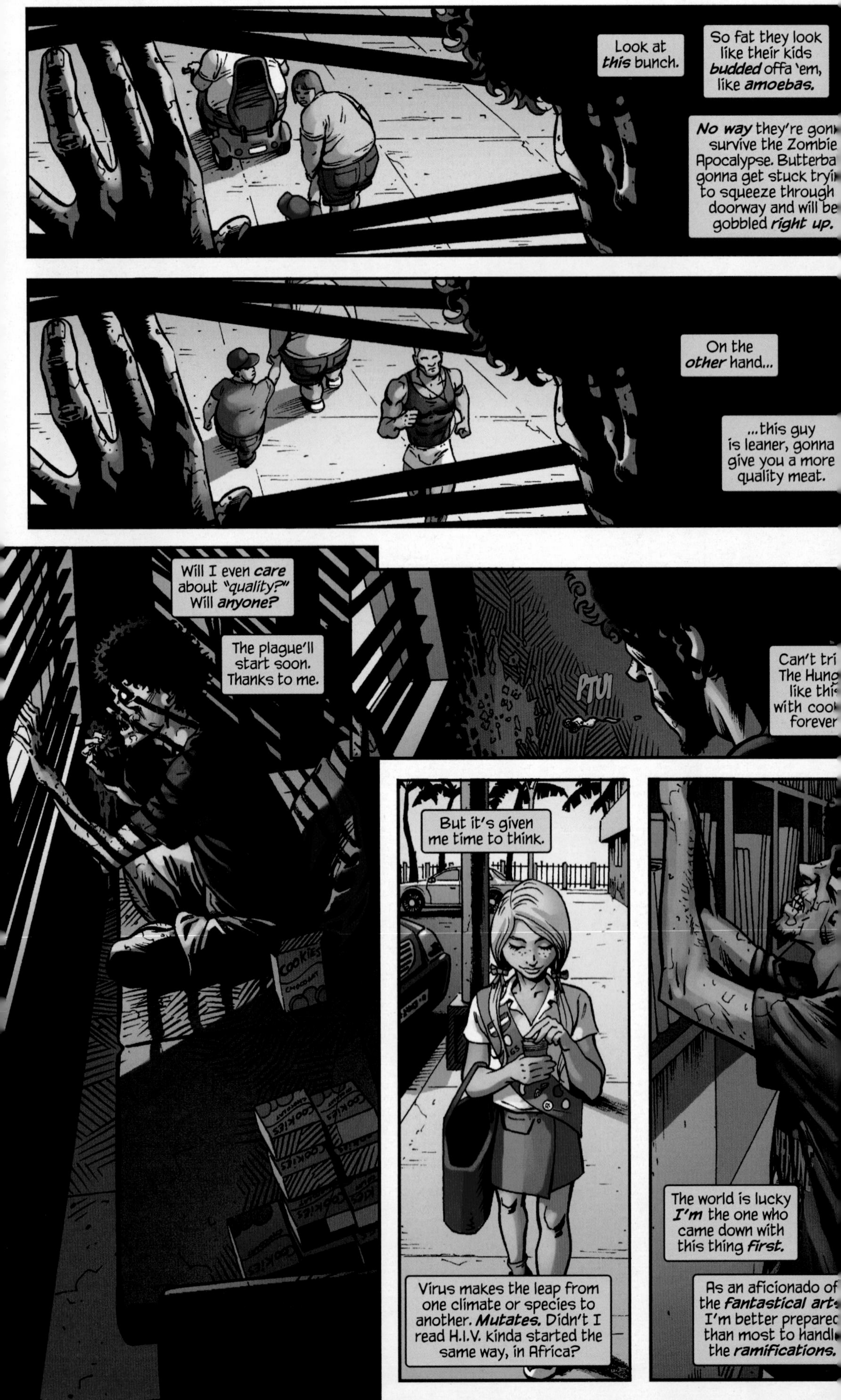

Look at *this* bunch.
So fat they look like their kids *budded* offa 'em, like *amoebas.*
No way they're gon survive the Zombie Apocalypse. Butterba gonna get stuck tryi to squeeze through doorway and will be gobbled *right up.*
On the *other* hand...
...this guy is leaner, gonna give you a more quality meat.
Will I even *care* about *"quality?"* Will *anyone?*
The plague'll start soon. Thanks to me.
PTUI
Can't tri The Hung like thi with coo forever
COOKIES
But it's given me time to think.
Virus makes the leap from one climate or species to another. *Mutates.* Didn't I read H.I.V. kinda started the same way, in Africa?
The world is lucky *I'm* the one who came down with this thing *first.*
As an aficionado of the *fantastical art* I'm better prepare than most to handl the *ramifications.*

Ah, Elvish Greatsword.

...en I bought you ...m that creepy, ...melly man at ...REZ little did I ...ow I would one ...ay put you to ...r intended use:

The annihilation of the *Unliving!*

This...this is how the Romans did it?

Or the *Romulans?*

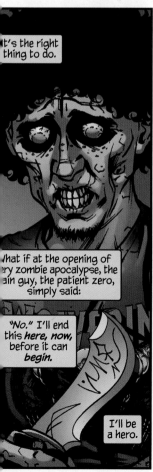

...t's the right ...thing to do.

...hat if at the opening of ...ry zombie apocalypse, the ...ain guy, the patient zero, ...simply said:

"No." I'll end this *here, now,* before it can *begin.*

I'll be a hero.

But...

...what's the point of *sacrificing* myself if nobody *knows* about it?

Maybe I can live stream it... or blog it...

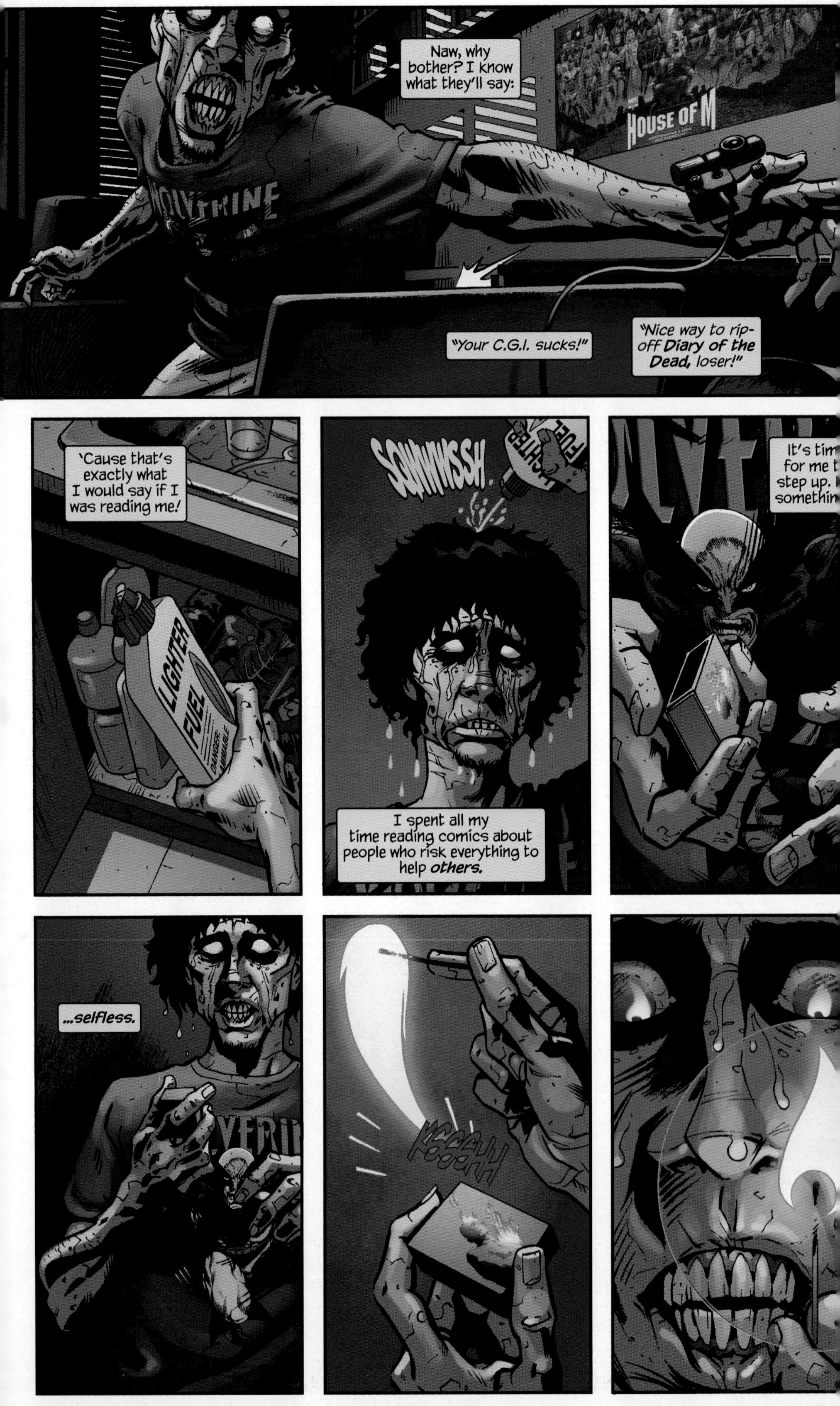
Naw, why bother? I know what they'll say:
HOUSE OF M
WOLVERINE
"Your C.G.I. sucks!"
"Nice way to rip-off *Diary of the Dead,* loser!"
'Cause that's exactly what I would say if I was reading me!
LIGHTER FUEL
SQUWWSSH
I spent all my time reading comics about people who risk everything to help *others.*
It's tim
for me t
step up.
somethin
...selfless.
KSSSHH

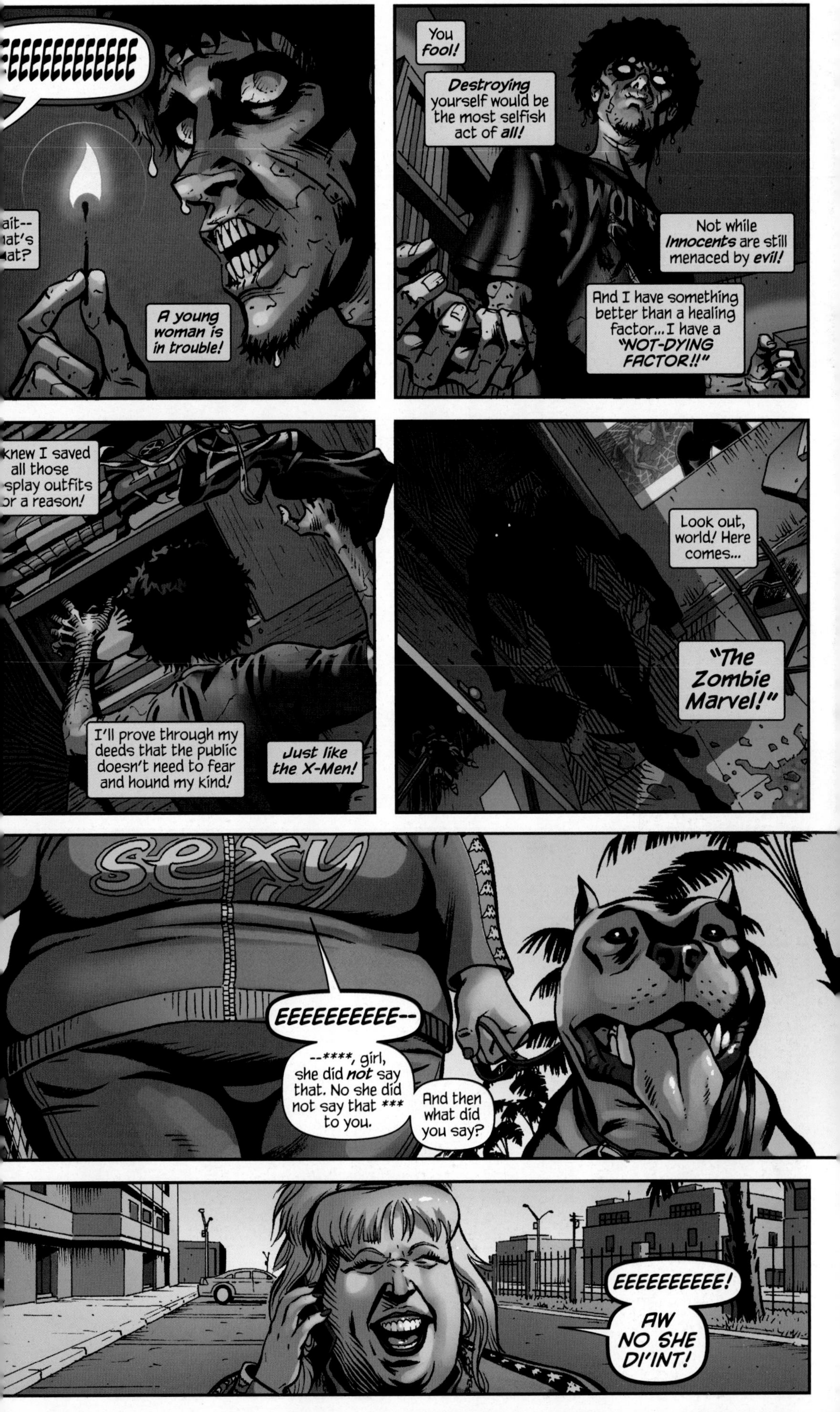
EEEEEEEEEEEEEE
-ait--
-hat's
-hat?
A young woman is in trouble!
You fool!
Destroying yourself would be the most selfish act of all!
Not while Innocents are still menaced by evil!
And I have something better than a healing factor... I have a "NOT-DYING FACTOR!!"
-knew I saved all those -splay outfits -or a reason!
I'll prove through my deeds that the public doesn't need to fear and hound my kind!
Just like the X-Men!
Look out, world! Here comes...
"The Zombie Marvel!"
sexy
EEEEEEEEEE--
--****, girl, she did not say that. No she did not say that *** to you.
And then what did you say?
EEEEEEEEEE!
AW NO SHE DI'INT!

Reach for the sky, Hairless Ape-Corpse!

Huh. It's like he *knew* I was gonna say that.

Hello? Mister? What's wrong with him?

Not sure, but my guess would be unreleased coupling between myosin and actin in the muscles, postmortem, resulting in perpetual contraction.

Better known as "rigor mortis."

OhmyGodOhmyGodOhmyGod

I'm actually looking at Machine Man and Howard the Duck!

Why can't move a frakk muscle?! I ask 'em t sign my--

You get the final sample?

Then y know w to do

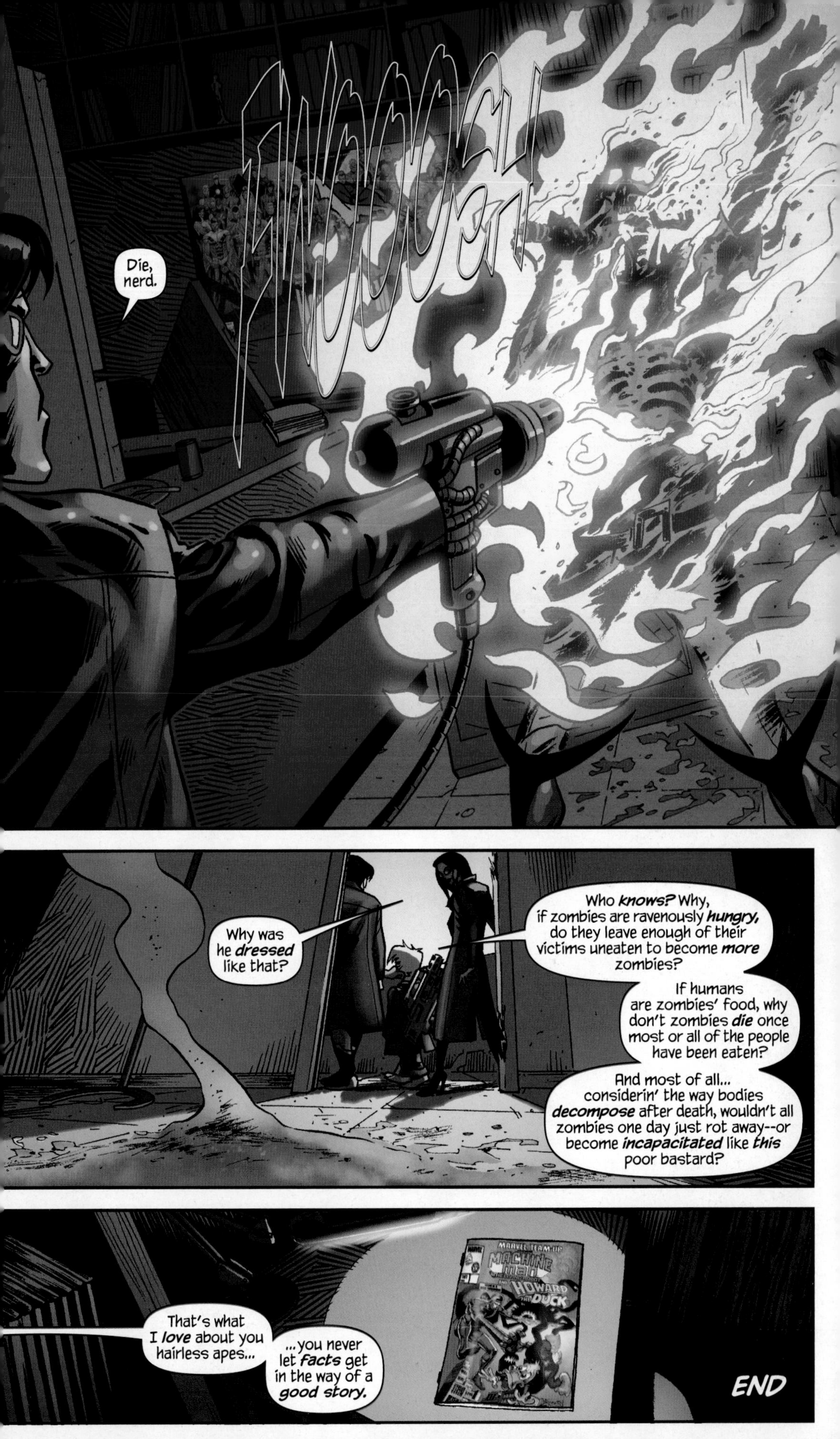
Die, nerd.
Why was he *dressed* like that?
Who *knows?* Why, if zombies are ravenously *hungry,* do they leave enough of their victims uneaten to become *more* zombies?
If humans are zombies' food, why don't zombies *die* once most or all of the people have been eaten?
And most of all... considerin' the way bodies *decompose* after death, wouldn't all zombies one day just rot away--or become *incapacitated* like *this* poor bastard?
MARVEL TEAM-UP
MACHINE MAN
HOWARD THE DUCK
That's what I *love* about you hairless apes...
...you never let *facts* get in the way of a *good story.*
END

#2 SPOILER VARIANT COVER BY SALVADOR ESPIN WITH GURU EFX

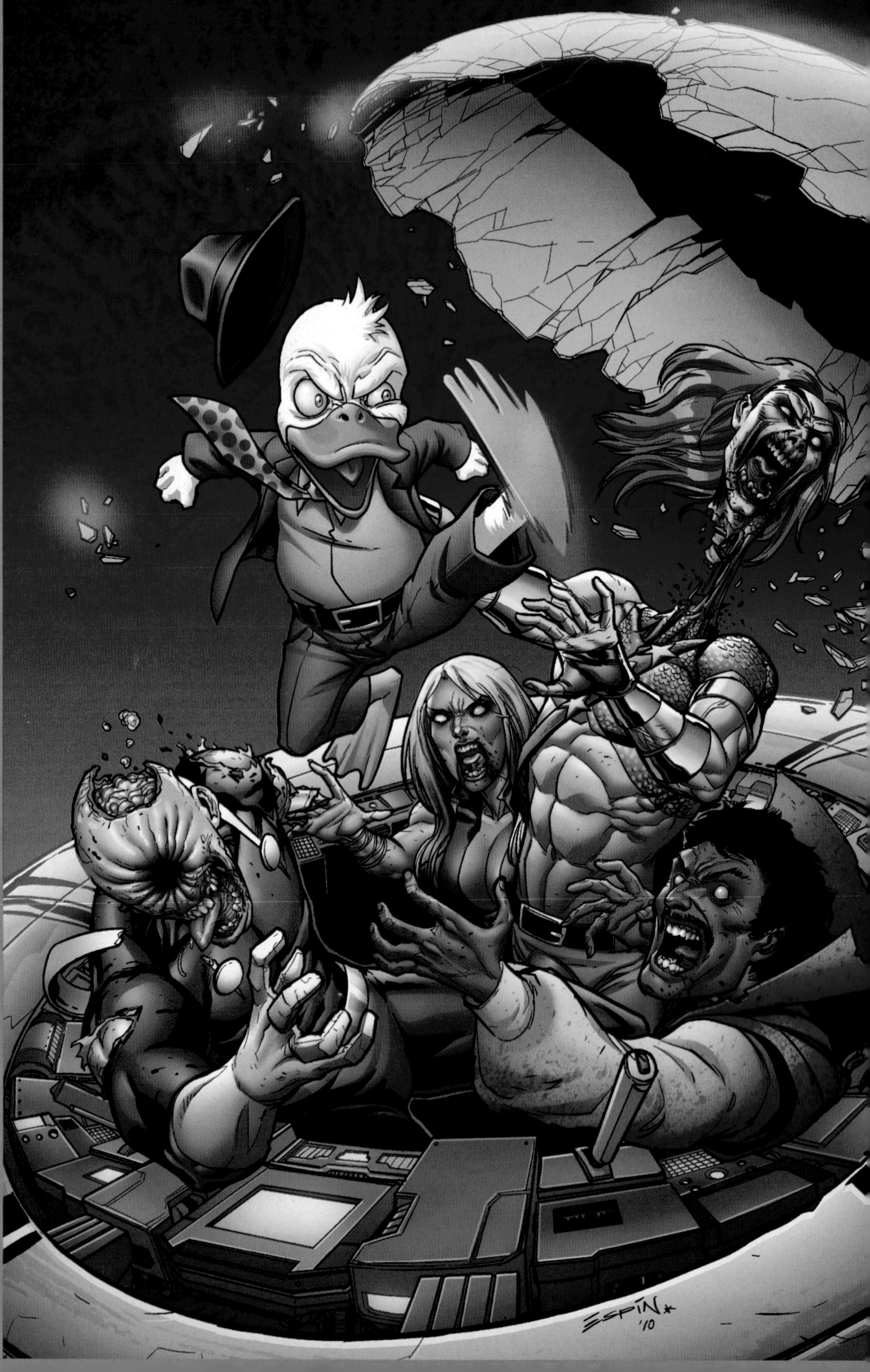
ESPÍN
'10

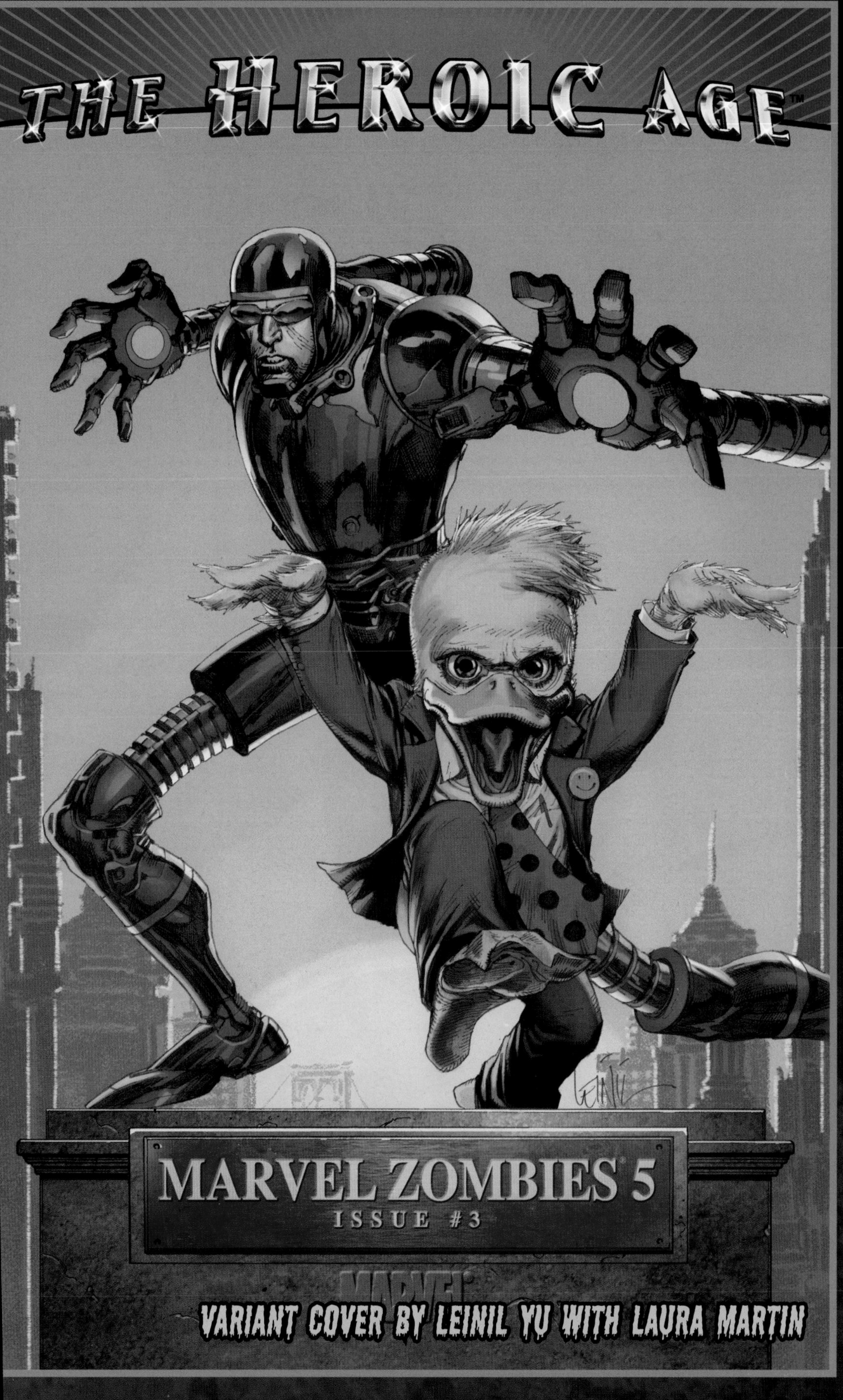
THE HEROIC AGE™
MARVEL ZOMBIES® 5
ISSUE #3
MARVEL
VARIANT COVER BY LEINIL YU WITH LAURA MARTIN

#5 VARIANT COVER BY ARTHUR SUYDAM

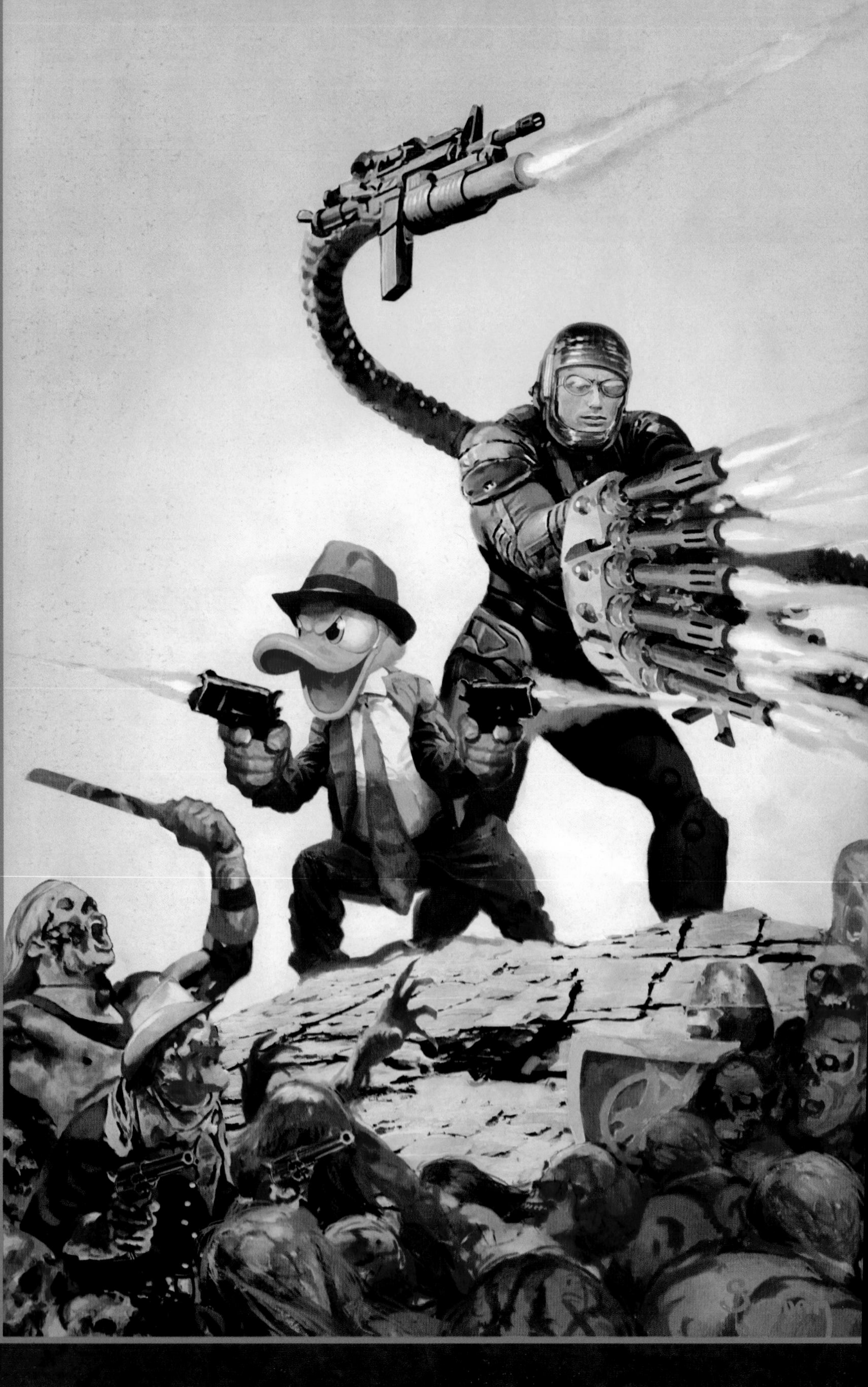

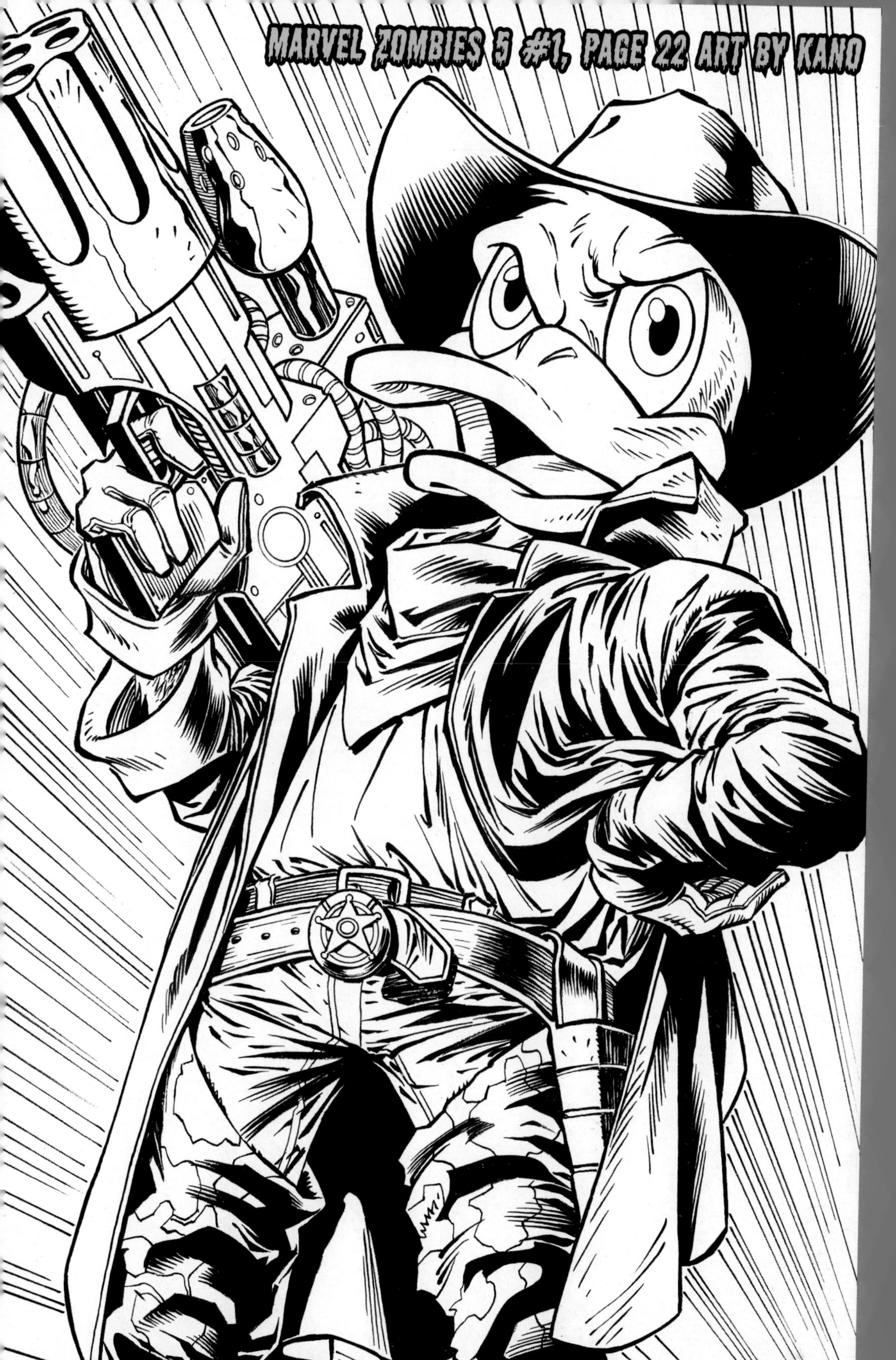

MARVEL ZOMBIES 5 #1, PAGE 22 ART BY KANO

MARVEL ZOMBIES 5. #2 PAGE 13 ART BY KANO.

MARVEL ZOMBIES 5 #3, PAGE 1 ART BY MICHAEL W. KALUTA

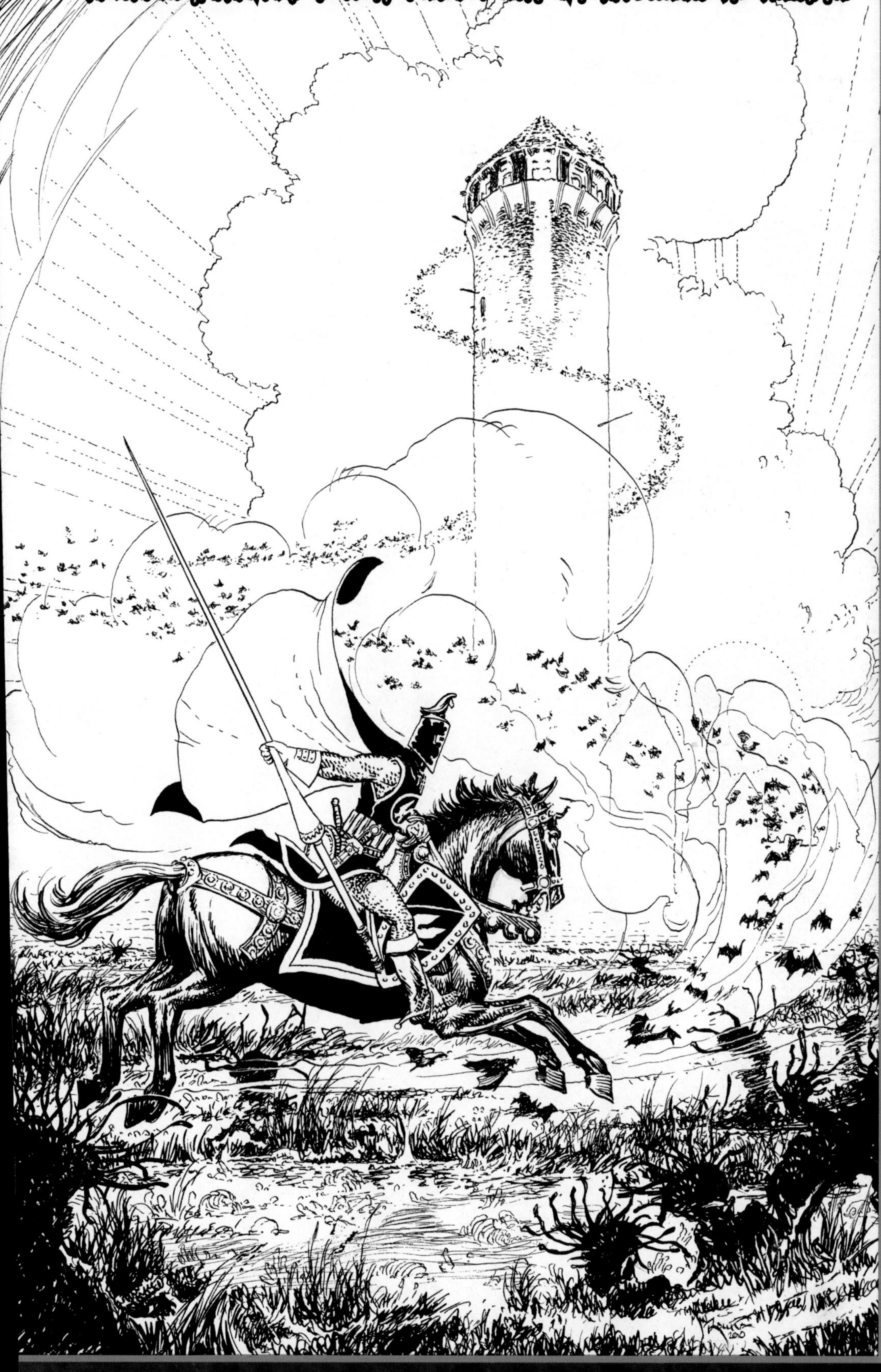

MARVEL ZOMBIES 5 #4, PAGE 9 ART BY FERNANDO BLANCO

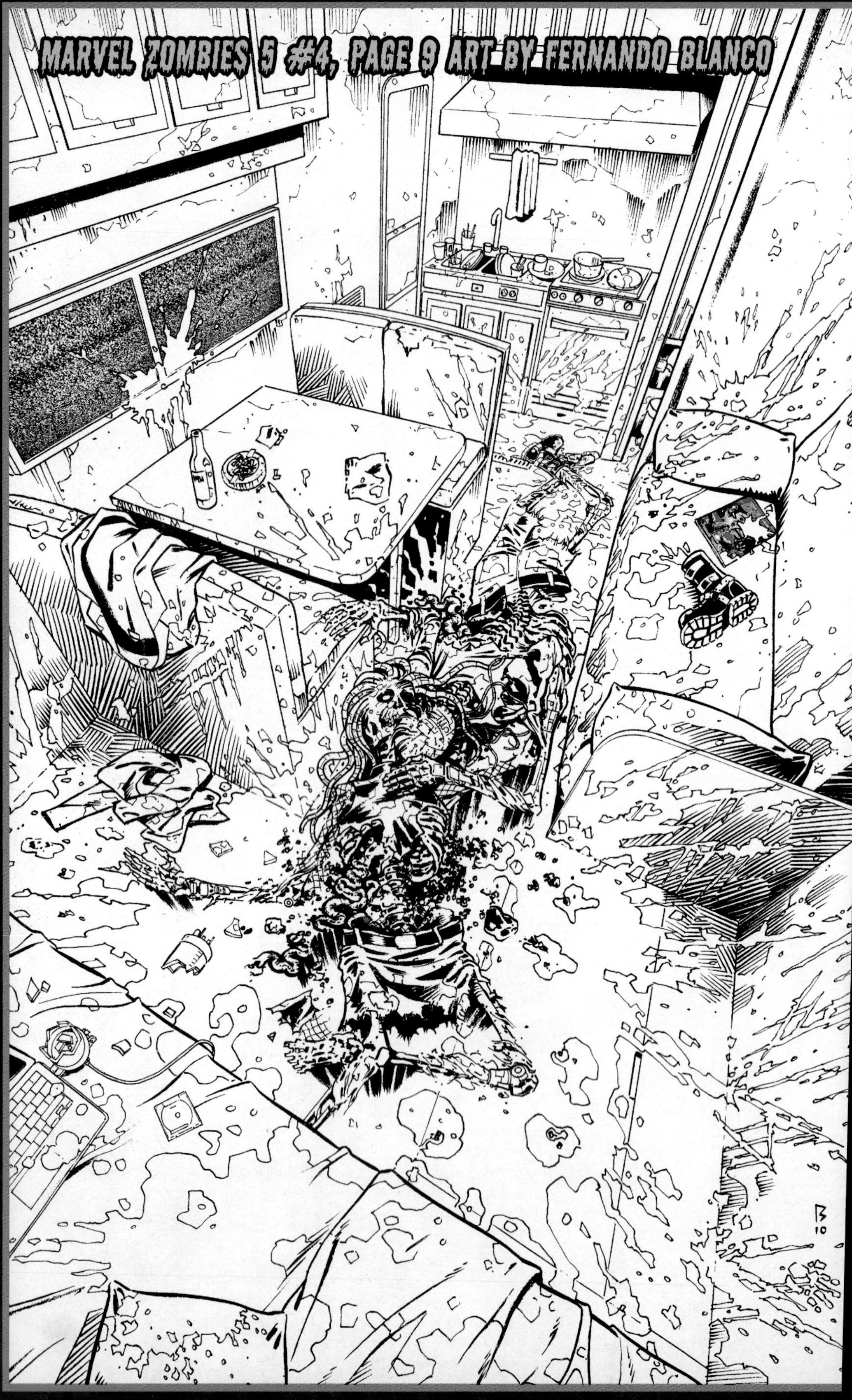

MARVEL ZOMBIES 5 #5, PAGE 3 ART BY FRANK BRUNNER

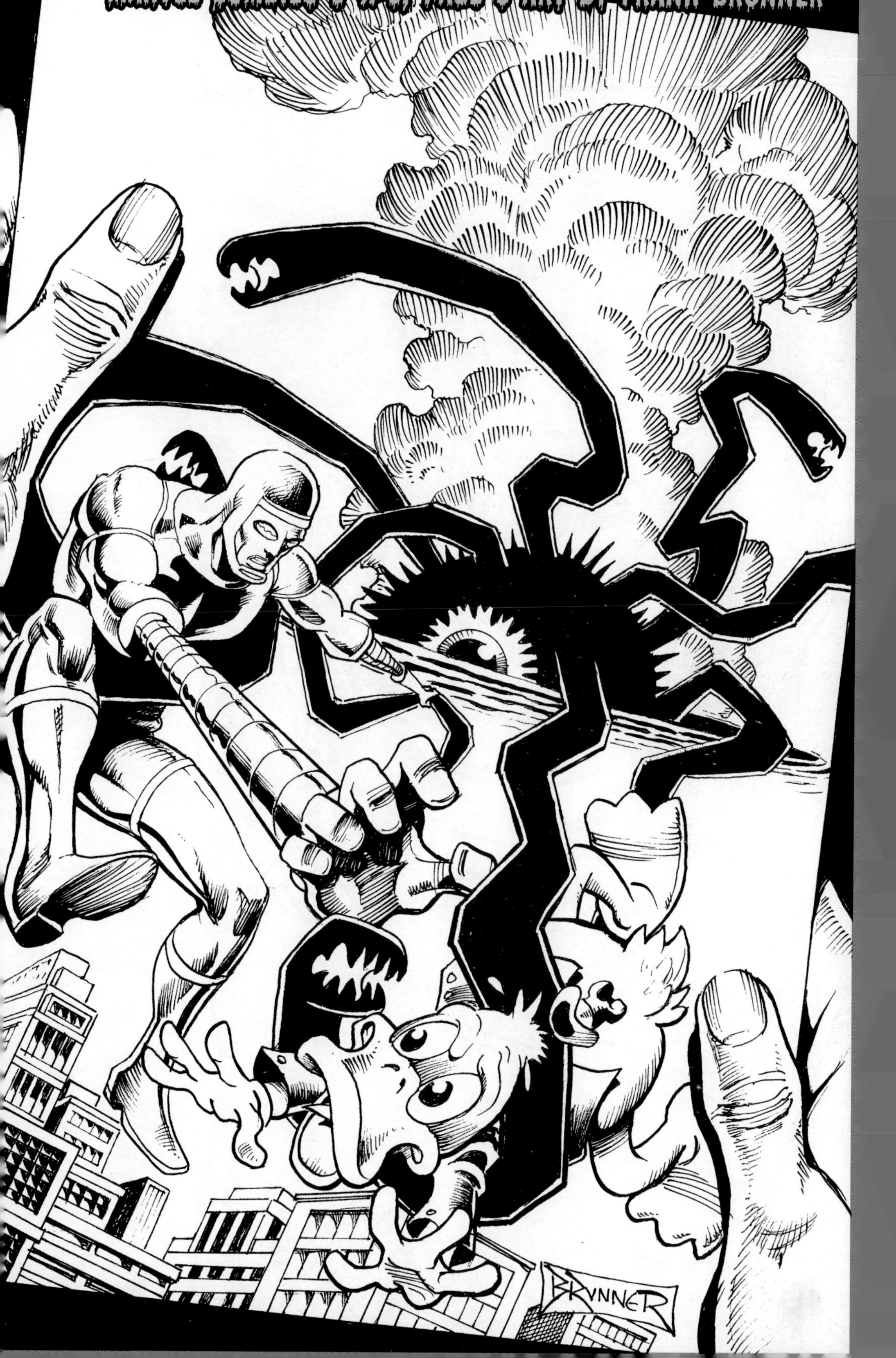
BRUNNER

MARVEL ZOMBIES 5 #5, PAGE 6 ART BY FERNANDO BLANCO

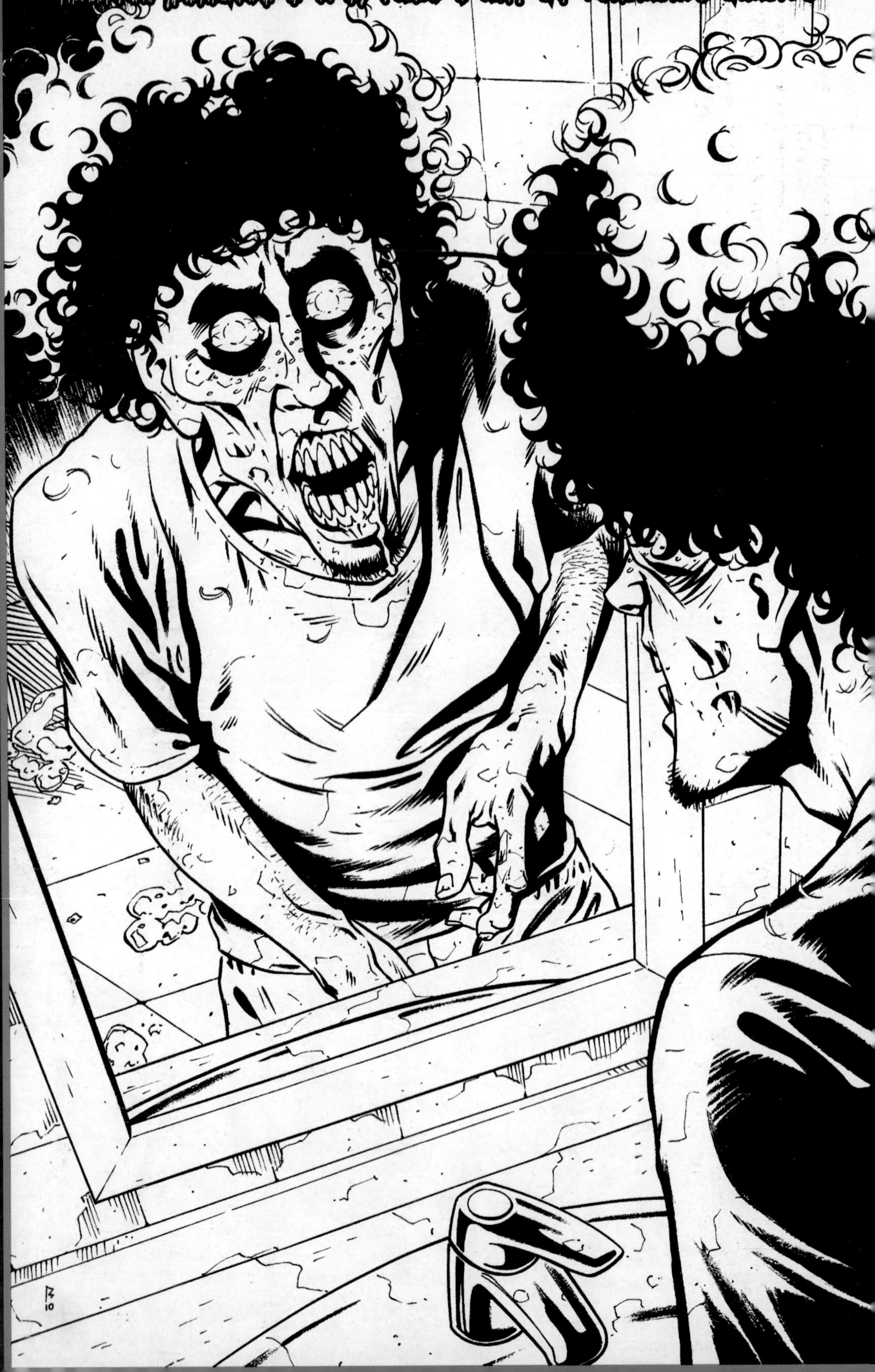